Tennyson's Scepticism

Tennyson's Scepticism

Aidan Day

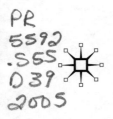

© Aidan Day 2005

First published 2005 by
PALGRAVE MACMILLAN
Houndmills, Basingstoke, Hampshire RG21 6XS and
175 Fifth Avenue, New York, N.Y. 10010
Companies and representatives throughout the world

PALGRAVE MACMILLAN is the global academic imprint of the Palgrave
Macmillan division of St. Martin's Press, LLC and of Palgrave Macmillan Ltd.
Macmillan® is a registered trademark in the United States, United Kingdom
and other countries. Palgrave is a registered trademark in the European
Union and other countries.

ISBN-13: 978–1–4039–9123–2 hardback
ISBN-10: 1–4039–9123–5 hardback

This book is printed on paper suitable for recycling and made from fully
managed and sustained forest sources.

A catalogue record for this book is available from the British Library.

Library of Congress Cataloging-in-Publication Data
Day, Aidan.
  Tennyson's scepticism / Aidan Day.
    p. cm.
  Includes bibliographical references and index.
  ISBN 1–4039–9123–5 (cloth)
  1. Tennyson, Alfred Tennyson, baron, 1809–1892—Philosophy.
  2. Skepticism in literature.   I. Title.
  PR5592.S55D39 2005
  821'.8—dc22   2005043281

10   9   8   7   6   5   4   3   2   1
14   13   12   11   10   09   08   07   06   05

Printed and bound in Great Britain by
Antony Rowe Ltd, Chippenham and Eastbourne

For Ruben

That this is the age of Metaphysics, in the proper, or sceptical Inquisitory sense . . .
we regard as our indubitable misfortune. From many causes, the arena of free
Activity has long been narrowing, that of sceptical Inquiry becoming more and
more universal . . . Belief, Faith has well-nigh vanished . . . the Divinity has
withdrawn from the Earth . . . inquiries of the deepest, painfulest sort must be
engaged with; and the invincible energy of young years waste itself in sceptical,
suicidal cavillings; in passionate 'questionings of Destiny', whereto no answer
will be returned.

Thomas Carlyle, 'Characteristics' (1831)

Contents

Acknowledgements

The late Robindra Kumar Biswas nurtured my interest in Tennyson when I was his student. He was a caring and inspiring teacher whose words still sound in my mind.

For various kinds of more recent help, I am especially grateful to Kath Burlinson. My thanks are also due to Neil Corcoran, Tabish Khair, Inger Hunnerup Dalsgaard, and Per Serritslev Petersen. I am deeply indebted to members of my family for their support.

Parts of Chapters 1, 2 and 5 have appeared, respectively, in 'The Spirit of Fable: Arthur Hallam and Romantic Values in Tennyson's "Timbuctoo"', *Tennyson Research Bulletin* (4, 1983); 'Voices in a Dream: The Language of Scepticism in Tennyson's "The Hesperides" ', *The Victorian Newsletter* (62, 1982); and 'The Archetype that Waits: *The Lover's Tale*, *In Memoriam*, and *Maud*', in *Tennyson: Seven Essays*, ed. Philip Collins (1992).

Notes on the text

Tennyson quotations are from Christopher Ricks, ed., *The Poems of Tennyson*, 3 vols, Longman Annotated English Poets, second edition, 1987; and from Christopher Ricks and Aidan Day, eds, *The Tennyson Archive*, 31 vols, 1987–93.

Introduction

Tennyson was driven throughout his life to find an inclusive explanation of the human condition. He sought what Jean François Lyotard has termed a 'grand narrative' which would satisfy his intellectual, imaginative, spiritual and emotional needs (Lyotard 1986: xxiv). Tennyson's difficulty was that he was heir to the large accounts of meaning in three distinguishable and often incompatible patterns of thought: Christian, Romantic and Enlightenment. Tennyson's most important verse was born out of his attempts to formulate a working sense of meaning out of these frequently contradictory materials. The significance of Romantic and broadly Christian perspectives in Tennyson's poetry is well known. But a metaphysical scepticism that was associated, in part, with rational, scientific perspectives deriving from Enlightenment thought has been seen as something which intrudes upon his work. Scepticism has been viewed as alien to Tennyson's mind and imaginative procedures. It has been understood as something he was unable to assimilate, which he experienced only as an intellectual threat and which is present in his poetry only to the extent that he opposed it from more deeply founded Romantic and religious or quasi-religious positions. Alan Sinfield, for example, takes this view when, in an essay entitled 'Tennyson and the Cultural Politics of Prophesy', he writes that Tennyson conceives of himself as a 'lonely, beleaguered' figure 'committed to spiritual values in an overwhelmingly materialist world' (Sinfield 1996: 36). In the 1996 collection of critical essays in which Sinfield's piece appeared, Rebecca Stott credited Sinfield with having initiated, in the 1980s, what has turned out to be one of the dominant directions in Tennyson criticism of recent years: the politicisation of Tennyson 'scholarship' by 'cultural studies' (Stott 1996: 5). Stott observes that Sinfield's 1986 cultural materialist book, *Alfred Tennyson*, 'altered the course of Tennyson studies' (Stott 1996: 33). In his essay

1

in Stott's collection, Sinfield notes that the effect of what he sees as Tennyson's commitment to spiritual values is apparent in a poem such as 'The Ancient Sage':

> In this late poem (1885), Tennyson does not bother to put much distance between the sage and himself – there is no evident historical or mythic referent. The sage takes as his project the answering of a sceptical materialist, and his key move is a story whose power lies precisely in the fact that it cannot be checked against mundane standards of plausibility:
>
> > And more, my son! For more than once when I
> > Sat all alone, revolving in myself
> > The word that is the symbol of myself,
> > The mortal limit of the Self was loosed,
> > And past into the Nameless, as a cloud
> > Melts into Heaven.
>
> (229–34; Sinfield 1996: 47)

In 'The Ancient Sage', Sinfield observes, Tennyson typically 'declines' a 'rationalist opponent' (Sinfield 1996: 48). Tennyson, Sinfield emphasises, is '*Usually*...on the side of the visionary' (my italics; Sinfield 1996: 35). He finds a correspondence between what he sees as Tennyson's predilection for spiritual vision and the nature of Tennyson's poetic language itself. Tennyson's rich poetic manner is, he says, the corollary of the poet's self-image as seer: 'Magic is what prophets have...The prophet's mystical powers are the direct analogue of Tennyson's verbal magic' (Sinfield 1996: 45). For Sinfield, Tennyson's lavish poetic language conspires to gain the reader's assent to a prophetic, visionary conception of truth which is 'superstitious, reactionary, and dangerous' (Sinfield 1996: 42). This use of a specialised kind of language appears, for example, in 'Œnone' (1832), where Tennyson treats the classical story of Œnone's prefiguring of the Trojan War. Tennyson's Œnone, writes Sinfield,

> wants her utterance to gain substance in the world not through conventional plausibility but through its incantatory magic – in the same way that Troy was built by the music of Apollo. By...the power of the language Œnone is given to speak, Tennyson ratifies the prophetic insight for the reader.
>
> (Sinfield 1996: 36)

The problem is that by this kind of reading, Tennyson could never achieve more than a 'mystical' or 'magical' point of view without abandoning his poetic idiom itself; without forfeiting, that is, the very thing that constituted him a poet. Sinfield's is, curiously, a variant of the old view that Tennyson was good at painting pictures and conjuring sound but deficient in reflective substance. Harold Nicolson's view, for example, of the 'depth' of Tennyson's 'poetic temperament' and 'the shallowness... of his practical intelligence' (Nicolson 1923: 9); or W.H. Auden's extraordinary judgement that while Tennyson may have had 'the finest ear', he was also 'undoubtedly the stupidest' of the English poets (Auden 1944: x). The present study argues that this kind of valuation consistently underestimates and obscures the complexity of Tennyson's poetry and the sort of exploration it can sustain. It argues that even while some of Tennyson's poems, like 'The Ancient Sage', may be taken as evidence that Tennyson held an unproblematised visionary sympathy, there are, in fact, many poems in which Tennyson's sensuous poetic manner is deployed in the interests of rationalist, sceptical critique. It argues that visionary sympathy, while obviously present at points in Tennyson's work, cannot be said to be the *usual* perspective of that work. It sees spiritual scepticism as intrinsic to Tennyson's imagination and as endemic in his poetry. It re-reads particular examples to show that there is a kind of Tennyson poem where his abundant, broadly Romantic poetic idiom is held in a medium of irony, a kind of poem where sceptical impulse challenges spiritual assertion at first hand. At the heart of the 'incantatory magic' of 'Œnone', for example, Tennyson may be seen to be conducting a sceptical exposé of the fiction that there is an adequate spiritual explanation of human suffering in the world.

It is a principle of the present study that it is only through close attention to the verbal detail of Tennyson's poems that the sophistication of his sceptical inquiries can emerge. Rather than making broad, reifying assertions about Tennyson's ideas that do not spring from close attention to the words of his verse, the study adopts such scrutiny as its primary means of understanding the poetry. Many of Tennyson's poems are intellectually extremely intricately conceived, and demand sustained, close interrogation.

The study uses such interrogation to demonstrate, in the first place, the ways in which a sceptical vision controls examples of Tennyson's shorter, earlier works: poems published or first written from the late 1820s to the 1840s. It goes on to show that it is not just Tennyson's simple opposition to, but his internalisation of sceptical perspectives which energises his agonised struggle with the rational secularism of contemporary science in one of the two great poems of his maturity, *In Memoriam* (1850). *In Memoriam* is an example of a work which displays, at key points, a fully internalised scepticism about the possibility of maintaining a spiritual vision, while at the same time refusing, partly out of a sense of social responsibility, to allow the scepticism to control its closing affirmations. If, however, *In Memoriam* shows Tennyson insisting finally on the priority of spiritual inclinations, then *Maud* (1855), the second great work of his maturity, articulates a dramatically contrary position.

The form of the narrative and its conclusion in *Maud* are expressly designed to expose the hollowness of spiritual affirmation. In this design, however, the poem is only opening up possibilities that had been apparent in *In Memoriam*. The American editor and writer J.R. Lowell spoke of *Maud* as 'The antiphonal voice to *In Memoriam*' (Tennyson, Hallam 1897: I.393). This is keenly perceptive and captures the manner in which these two poems demonstrate Tennyson negotiating a common subject from ultimately contrasting positions. Nor is this a matter which concerns just these two poems. One of the principal arguments of this study is that both *In Memoriam* and *Maud* develop preoccupations that had been apparent in *The Lover's Tale*, the long poem which Tennyson first wrote in the late 1820s and early 1830s but did not finally complete and publish until 1879. The early versions of *The Lover's Tale* reveal Tennyson working with an imaginative paradigm, deriving principally from Shelley's work, that resurfaces in both *In Memoriam* and *Maud* and around which he focused his engagement with sceptical insight in both poems. When considered in relation to each other, these two long poems of Tennyson's maturity show him managing, on a large poetic stage, the issue of scepticism that he raised in shorter works from the 1830s and 1840s. Equally, when not only *In Memoriam* but also *The Lover's Tale* are taken into account, *Maud* emerges as the remarkable result of what are, in fact, two earlier poetic essays on the same topic. *Maud* is Tennyson's intellectually most radical work, in which he went to the edge of his conceptual and imaginative frame of reference as he reflected on his own compulsion towards grand order and called in question the credibility of Western narratives of large-scale meaning and purpose in human life. In its rigorous demythologisation of such narratives, the poem stands as one of the great documents of the nineteenth-century sceptical imagination.

In the year that he published 'The Ancient Sage', Tennyson also published the last instalment of *Idylls of the King* (1859–85), a poem which stands, in part, as an allegory of the state of Britain and its Empire in the later nineteenth century. The cultural and political conservatism of the *Idylls*, couched in a medievalism that today appears regressive, nevertheless masks a grave questioning of spiritual authority and it is this questioning which directs Tennyson's doom-laden treatment of the Arthurian story. The gravity of the perspective in *Idylls of the King*, which was started not long after the publication of *Maud*, extends and confirms the pessimism that is apparent in the 1855 poem.

The incompatible intellectual economies that Tennyson worked with could never be resolved into a single, consistent system. Up to a point, his work displays a range of stabilisations, different poems offering contrasting resolutions of the intellectual and spiritual divisions they confront. This study seeks, however, to demonstrate the ways in which metaphysical scepticism is the *touchstone* of Tennyson's intellectual and imaginative life.

1
Discovery: 'Timbuctoo'

Writing to Tennyson in 1833, Francis Garden, one of Tennyson's friends from undergraduate days at Cambridge, spoke of 'the principles of doubt which I have heard you apply to Christianity' (Lang and Shannon 1982–90: I.103). Tennyson had dramatised his religious doubt in an 1830 poem, 'Supposed Confessions of a Second-Rate Sensitive Mind', where the speaker tells of his trauma at having lost the 'common faith' of 'Christians with happy countenances' (33, 20):

> I am void,
> Dark, formless, utterly destroyed.
> Why not believe then? Why not yet
> Anchor thy frailty there, where man
> Hath moored and rested? Ask the sea
> At midnight, when the crisp slope waves
> After the tempest, rib and fret
> The broad-imbasèd beach, why he
> Slumbers not like a mountain tarn?
>
> (121–29)

Tennyson's doubt about Christianity cohered on different levels. He seems never fully to have accepted Christianity as revealed religion. Sir Charles Tennyson observes that in Tennyson's greatest work of spiritual affirmation, *In Memoriam*, the emphasis throughout is 'on the humanity of Christ...Tennyson seems to think of Christ as man rather than God' (Tennyson, Charles 1954: 81). What Tennyson did at points sympathise with in Christianity were features of the Johannine conception of the Word of God, the Logos, the divine reason or intelligence that is diffused throughout the world and which, as it is put in the opening of the Gospel according to St John, existed within the world even before the incarnation of Christ. The idea of an intrinsic spiritual impulse attracted Tennyson and he advanced the concept at several points in his poetry. Section XXXVI of *In Memoriam*, for example, does not foreground the idea of Christ as an aspect of God who entered the physical world from a transcendent spiritual realm. There is no claim that the Gospel story relates a breach in the natural order. Instead, the import of this section is that the Gospel tale was a human creation that was inspired by an immanent spiritual power seeking expression of truth in a form understandable by the mass of humanity. The fable of Christ, with its apparatus of incarnation and resurrection, simply made generally available those mystic truths which lie deep in the human constitution. The expression 'the Word had breath' in the third stanza below originally read, in one of Tennyson's drafts of the poem now at Trinity College, Cambridge, 'the Logos breathed' (Trinity Notebook 13; Ricks and Day 1987–93: XI.17):

> Though truths in manhood darkly join,
>> Deep-seated in our mystic frame,
>> We yield all blessing to the name
> Of Him that made them current coin;

> For Wisdom dealt with mortal powers,
>> Where truth in closest words shall fail,
>> When truth embodied in a tale
> Shall enter in at lowly doors.

> And so the Word had breath, and wrought
>> With human hands the creed of creeds...

(XXXVI.1–10)

If section XXXVI is somewhat indirect in its formulation then Tennyson had made his unwillingness to recognise the Christian revelation explicit in a draft stanza that he withheld from inclusion, perhaps because of its explicitness, from the published version of section LIV. This section is troubled by a sense of the pointless violence of natural life. In the cancelled stanza Tennyson had written:

> For hope at awful distance set
>> Oft whispers of a kindlier plan

> Tho never prophet came to man
> Of such a revelation yet.
>
> (Trinity Notebook 13; Ricks and Day 1987–93: XI.24)

Yet even if Tennyson was not in any strict sense a Christian, it remains the case that his poetry is haunted by a teleological perspective, Christian in origin, that envisions the need for and the promise of an ultimate redemption of human life from what is perceived as a 'fallen' condition; a condition, at least, of division and alienation. The most distinct expression of this kind of perspective lies in the concluding lines of *In Memoriam*, with their vision of 'one far-off divine event, / To which the whole creation moves' (Epilogue 143–44). This formal Christian orientation was juxtaposed and sometimes mixed in Tennyson's mind with another narrative of meaning that also laid primary stress on the interior grounds of spiritual truth. This is the grand narrative of high Romanticism. Tennyson first seriously encountered Romantic writing when he was at Cambridge and the impact of the encounter is apparent in a poem produced at that time, 'Timbuctoo'.

Tennyson's 'Timbuctoo' was the winning entry in an 1829 Cambridge University competition for the best poem in English on the topic of the City of Timbuctoo. Tennyson's poem was, however, only partly written at Cambridge. A substantial portion of it derives from the period of Tennyson's youth, before he went up to Cambridge, in the Lincolnshire hamlet of Somersby. The entire central section of 'Timbuctoo', from lines 62–190, 'was present, with a few trivial variants', in a poem, 'Armageddon', which Tennyson had composed at Somersby (Ricks 1987: I.188). Tennyson himself commented of 'Timbuctoo' that he submitted an 'old poem' with 'a little alteration of the beginning and the end' (Tennyson, Hallam 1897: II.355). But the new beginning and ending were more than simply cosmetic.

'Armageddon' is based on the vision in the Book of Revelation of the final battle between good and evil at the Day of Judgement, a battle which will happen in 'a place called in the Hebrew tongue Armageddon' (Revelation 16.16). The poem's speaker tells us of his own glimpse of this apocalyptic event, though the poem is fragmentary and the vision is never completed. But in his description of the early stages of his vision, the speaker relates how his perceptual faculties grew suddenly and preternaturally acute:

Each failing sense,
As with a momentary flash of light,
Grew thrillingly distinct and keen. I saw
The smallest grain that dappled the dark Earth,
The indistinctest atom in deep air . . .

(II.27–31)

These were among the lines that Tennyson incorporated in 'Timbuctoo' (94–98). But where, in 'Armageddon', they were a prelude to a vision of the last great battle, in 'Timbuctoo' they become a prelude to a vision of the fabled City. There was great western European curiosity about the Saharan City of Timbuctoo in the 1820s. The first European to reach the City and get out alive was a Frenchman, René Caillé, who made his successful journey in 1828. But he did not publish his account of Timbuctoo until 1830, and in 1829 the City, as the subject for a Prize Poem Competition, was of considerable topical interest and speculation. So Tennyson recast his earlier poem about a vision of the battle of Armageddon into one about someone having a vision of the City of Timbuctoo, as yet unknown to Europeans. What is most important about this recasting is that it involves a fundamental alteration in the poem's conception of *how* the vision is achieved.

In 'Armageddon' the vision is granted by the aid of one of God's angels, a 'seraph!' (II.2). It was 'the light' of this seraph's 'great Angel Mind' (II.18–19) which afforded the speaker of the poem his vision of the final battle. At the outset of 'Armageddon' the speaker asserts the impossibility of painting in language the supernatural things seen by him. That would be, he says, 'past the power of man' (I.20):

No fabled Muse
Could breathe into my soul such influence
. . . as to express
Deeds inexpressible by loftiest rhyme.

(I.20–23)

In other words, the seraph of 'Armageddon' fulfils a predictable role within the terms of traditional vision poetry. He is the vehicle and symbol of a grace given to the human from outside the human. He is the external agent, the messenger of God, who allows the speaker of the poem to perceive more-than-natural sights. By contrast, in 'Timbuctoo', although the seraph is retained, he becomes, by virtue of Tennyson's recasting of the poem, the vehicle and symbol of a visionary capacity which is intrinsic to the human mind and which expresses itself in imaginative creations.

It is here that the Romanticism which engulfed Tennyson while he was at Cambridge makes itself felt. Tennyson's exposure to Romantic ideas came in significant part through his membership of the unofficial intellectual Society known as the Apostles. The broad intellectual temper of the Apostles in the late 1820s was conditioned by the thought of the liberal theologian F.D. Maurice, who had been a member of the Society a few years previously. Maurice's influence was well-described by Richard Chenevix Trench, a friend of Tennyson at Cambridge, when in 1828 he referred to the Society as 'Maurice and that gallant band of Platonico-Wordsworthian-Coleridgean-anti-Utilitarians' (Allen 1978: 76).

Maurice came from a religiously dissenting family that had bred him to liberal political views. But his liberalism was of a particular kind. It was held in the medium of a religious, although not sectarian, sensibility. Above all, Maurice was not a materialist. He believed in 'an innate divine principle that may be discovered within oneself' (Allen 1978: 77). This led him to identify with the high Romanticism of Wordsworth and Coleridge. This was the Romanticism that conceived of the human mind as possessing a faculty which, sharing in the nature of the divine, conferred insight into the divine. Wordsworth referred to such a potency of mind when, in 'Lines written a few miles above Tintern Abbey' (1798), he spoke of his experiences of a 'sublime...mood' in which

> the breath of this corporeal frame,
> And even the motion of our human blood
> Almost suspended, we are laid asleep
> In body, and become a living soul:
> While with an eye made quiet by the power
> Of harmony, and the deep power of joy,
> We see into the life of things.

> (38, 44–50)

Wordsworth restates, some lines later, his conviction that the human mind partakes in the animating principle of the universe:

> I have felt
> A presence that disturbs me with the joy
> Of elevated thoughts; a sense sublime

> Of something far more deeply interfused,
> Whose dwelling is the light of setting suns,
> And the round ocean, and the living air,
> And the blue sky, and in the mind of man,
> A motion and a spirit, that impels
> All thinking things, all objects of all thought,
> And rolls through all things.

> (94–103)

In *The Excursion* (1814) Wordsworth explicitly identifies the sublime potential of the mind with the faculty of imagination. Wordsworth's spokesperson in *The Excursion*, the Wanderer, who in the prefatory 'Argument' to Book IV is described as contrasting 'the dignities of the Imagination with the presumptuous littleness of certain modern Philosophers', speaks of the way in which imaginative insights of the mind engage principles of truth in a way that abstract, analytical inquiries do not:

> principles of truth,
> Which the imaginative Will upholds
> In seats of wisdom, not to be approached
> By the inferior Faculty that moulds,
> With her minute and speculative pains,
> Opinion, ever changing!

> (IV.1127–32)

The Romanticism which internalises the agency of transcendental insight, so that the capacity for directly apprehending the more-than-natural becomes a function of the human mind itself, was something that directed Apostolic sympathies at the period of Tennyson's association with the Society. W.E. Houghton placed Tennyson in relation to his Romantic forbears when he made the following observations on Victorian concepts of the writer as 'Vates... Prophet or Poet' (Carlyle 1869–72: XII.95):

The man of letters was generally considered, and often considered himself, no mere artist or craftsman. He was a genius in a period... when young men at Oxford could take *Modern Painters* or *Past and Present*... as nothing short of 'inspired and absolute truth'. That environment... was created by the transformation... of the natural genius of the eighteenth century...into the Romantic Genius of the nineteenth whose imagination was an oracular organ of Truth. This heady doctrine, preached by Wordsworth and Shelley as well as Goethe and Fichte was adopted from those sources by the Cambridge Apostles. Their leading spirit, F.D. Maurice, formulated it in 1828 in terms which bring out the omniscience of the poet's insight:

> The mind of a poet of the highest order is the most perfect mind that can belong to man...He sympathises with all phenomena by his intuition of all principles...
>
> He cannot be untrue, for it is his high calling to interpret those universal truths which exist on earth only in the forms of his creation. One Apostle who listened and believed was Alfred Tennyson.
>
> (Houghton 1973: 152)

Certainly, Tennyson's closest friend at Cambridge, Arthur Hallam, subscribed to the Maurician and Apostolic enthusiasm for Romantic ideas. The principal influences on Hallam's own submission for the 1829 Prize Poem competition are those of Coleridge, Shelley and, particularly, Wordsworth. Hallam quotes the entirety of line 42 of Wordsworth's 'Tintern Abbey' as line 194 of his 'Timbuctoo'. He also observed, in a letter of 14 September 1829 to W.E. Gladstone, that Wordsworth was his 'favourite poet', quoting lines 10–17 of the Fourth Book of Wordsworth's *The Excursion* (Kolb 1981: 317–18). In his 'Timbuctoo' Hallam recalls the 'Prospect' to *The Excursion* where Wordsworth summarised the idea, treated at length across the poem as a whole, that imaginative vision has the capacity to bring about a renovated world:

> Paradise, and groves
> Elysian, Fortunate Fields – like those of old
> Sought in the Atlantic Main – why should they be
> A history only of departed things,
> Or a mere fiction of what never was?
> For the discerning intellect of Man,
> When wedded to this goodly universe
> In love and holy passion, shall find these
> A simple produce of the common day.
> – I, long before the blissful hour arrives,

> Would chant, in lonely peace, the spousal verse
> Of this great consummation...

(47–58)

Hallam's 'Timbuctoo' restates the argument that ancient stories of fabulous Atlantis are evidence of the imagination's capacity to figure the ideal:

> There was a land, which, far from human sight,
> Old Ocean compassed with his numerous waves,
> In the lone West. Tenacious of her right,
> Imagination decked those unknown caves,
> And vacant forests, and clear peaks of ice
> With a transcendent beauty...

(1–6)

But Hallam notes how the post-Columbian reduction of the myth of Atlantis has deprived the world of a focus for the transfiguring power of the imagination. Fables of Atlantis and those intimations of transcendence inherent in such fables are now no longer tenable. Atlantis has been reduced to the New World, the exploitable Americas. Hallam's poem concludes, however, by asserting that the undiscovered City of Timbuctoo can pick up where Atlantis, as it were, left off. Timbuctoo can still function as a focus for and an image of the radiant forms of the imagination. It looks as though a part of the inspiration for Tennyson's reworking of 'Armageddon' into 'Timbuctoo' came from conversations Tennyson had with Hallam, who was reported to have claimed that Tennyson 'borrowed the pervading idea [of the poem] from him' (Gaskell 1883: 139). In the same manner as Hallam, Tennyson preluded his account of Timbuctoo as a city of the imagination with reference to the myth of Atlantis as an instance of the imagination's power to envision the more than earthly:

> Where are ye
> Thrones of the Western wave, fair Islands green?...
> Where are the infinite ways, which, Seraph-trod,
> Wound through your great Elysian solitudes,
> Whose lowest deeps were, as with visible love,
> Fill'd with Divine effulgence...

(40–41, 46–49)

Whatever Hallam's precise role in talking over Romantic perspectives with his friend, the seraph of Tennyson's recast poem clearly emerges as a personification of human expressive and creative capacities, a token of the Romantic mythopoeic or poetic imagination. Where, in 'Armageddon', the speaker had said that no fabled muse could enable him to express what he had seen, in 'Timbuctoo' the seraph is explicitly just such a muse. In the newly composed conclusion to the poem, it is the seraph as the Spirit of Fable which makes possible the vision of the City:

> There is no mightier Spirit than I to sway
> The heart of man: and teach him to attain
> By shadowing forth the Unattainable...
> I play about his heart a thousand ways...

> I am the Spirit,
> The permeating life which courseth through
> All the intricate and labyrinthine veins
> Of the great vine of *Fable*, which, outspread
> With growth of shadowing leaf and clusters rare,
> Reacheth to every corner under Heaven,
> Deep-rooted in the living soil of truth...

> (191–93, 201, 215–21)

And the City fabulated or imagined by this spirit at the heart of man is a type of the infinite and the ideal:

> methought I saw
> A wilderness of spires, and chrystal pile
> Of rampart upon rampart, dome on dome,
> Illimitable range of battlement
> On battlement, and the Imperial height
> Of Canopy o'ercanopied.

> Behind
> In diamond light upsprung the dazzling peaks
> Of Pyramids as far surpassing Earth's
> As Heaven than Earth is fairer.

> (158–66)

The structure of Hallam's 'Timbuctoo' enacts a typically Romantic programme of spiritual decline and recovery. Adopting an unproblematised

Romantic position concerning the redemptive role of the imagination, Hallam identifies in its workings a principle of order which transcends and compensates for the disintegration of human meaning in historical time. Following the Wordsworth of the 'Immortality Ode' (1807), who finds that although the ecstasy may have passed, the 'habitual sway' (95) of nature and his own 'primal sympathy' (185) are not lost, and like the Wanderer of *The Excursion* who, taught by nature's 'humbler power' (IV.1190), finds still a restorative power in the 'imaginative Will' (IV.1128), Hallam anticipates the conclusion of his poem at its outset and sees the 'transcendent beauty' associated with the working of the imagination as

> That which saves
> From the world's blight our primal sympathies,
> Still in man's heart...
>
> (6–8)

Reassured that the envisioned City of Timbuctoo testifies to the abiding power of the human imagination, Hallam ends his poem on a note of confidence. Quoting line 42 of 'Tintern Abbey', he invokes that Wordsworthian mood in which 'laid asleep / In body, and become a living soul: / ... We see into the life of things' ('Tintern Abbey', 45–46, 49):

> Ever may the mood
> 'In which the affections gently lead us on'
> Be as thy sphere of visible life.
>
> (193–95)

The closing moment of Tennyson's 'Timbuctoo', however, is less complacent than Hallam's. Tennyson's poem comes to an end with the Spirit of Fable foreseeing that the city of the imagination – and all its potential for satisfying idealist craving – will lose its power in the world. The Spirit foresees the 'river' which winds through the streets of Timbuctoo 'not enduring / To carry through the world those waves, which bore / The reflex' of the City 'in their depths' (225, 233–35). He envisages the onset of a dissociated world as the imagination is wasted, unable to sustain its idealising and unifying activity:

> the time is well-nigh come
> When I must render up this glorious home

> To keen *Discovery*: soon yon brilliant towers
> Shall darken with the waving of her wand;
> Darken, and shrink and shiver into huts,
> Black specks amid a waste of dreary sand,
> Low-built, mud-walled, Barbarian settlements.
> How changed from this fair City!
>
> (238–45)

Tennyson is reworking a Romantic paradigm here. The word 'Discovery', the bringing to light of that which was previously unknown, was a potent early nineteenth-century term signifying the demythologising energies of the modern world. Tennyson has the light of 'Discovery' shedding darkness on the projections of the imagination. The energies of 'Discovery' are the energies of what Lyotard refers to as 'the Enlightenment narrative' (Lyotard 1986: xxiii), the grand narrative of Western modernity with its ideal of universal reason and its secular vision of the potential for improvement of the human race. As is well known, the spirit of philo-sophical and especially scientific inquiry or discovery was an inalienable part of the rationalism of the Enlightenment. At the same time as endorsing abstract inquiry in philosophy and in the natural sciences, the Enlightenment was sceptical about revealed religion, including Christianity. A part of the Enlightenment project was to dispel, in the light of reason, the darkness of traditional Christian belief. It viewed that belief and its reliance on the critically untested authority of the past, the idea of divine mysteries having been revealed in specific scriptures at a particular time to an elect few, as a superstition which depended on inspiring fear, even as it obstructed free thought. The grand narrative of the Enlightenment sought to displace that of Christianity just as it was sceptical about all traditional religious, fabulous and mythological systems and modes of thought. One of the principal mediators of Enlightenment perspectives to the nineteenth century was the founder of Utilitarianism, Jeremy Bentham (1748–1832). John Stuart Mill observed in 1838 that 'to Bentham more than to any other source might be traced the questioning spirit' of the early nineteenth century, 'the disposition to demand the *why* of everything':

> Bentham has been in this age and country the great questioner of things established. It is by the influence of the modes of thought with which his writings inoculated a considerable number of thinking men that the yoke of authority has been broken, and innumerable

opinions, formerly received on tradition as incontestable, are put upon their defense and required to give an account of themselves... Bentham... is the great *subversive*, or, in the language of continental philosophers, the great *critical*, thinker of his age and country.

(Cowling 1968: 16–17)

Mill praises Bentham's pursuit of the practical implications of rationalist Enlightenment speculation. Characterising the eighteenth century as an age of philosophic scepticism, he proposes that Bentham carried the light of reason into the realm of the everyday:

An age of formalism in the Church and corruption in the State, when the most valuable part of the meaning of traditional doctrines had faded from the minds even of those who retained from habit a mechanical belief in them, was the time to raise up all kinds of skeptical philosophy. Accordingly, France had Voltaire and his school of negative thinkers, and England (or rather Scotland) had the profoundest negative thinker on record, David Hume...

If Bentham had merely continued the work of Hume, he would scarcely have been heard of in philosophy... We must not look for subtlety or the power of recondite analysis among his intellectual characteristics. In the former quality, few great thinkers have ever been so deficient; and to find the latter, in any considerable measure, in a mind acknowledging any kindred with his, we must have recourse to the late Mr [James] Mill – a man who united the great qualities of the metaphysicians of the eighteenth century with others of a different complexion, admirably qualifying him to complete and correct their work. Bentham had not these peculiar gifts, but he possessed others, not inferior, which were not possessed by any of his precursors, which have made him a source of light to a generation which has far outgrown their influence...

To speak of him first as a merely negative philosopher – as one who refutes illogical arguments, exposes sophistry, detects contradiction and absurdity – even in that capacity there was a wide field left vacant for him by Hume and which he has occupied to an unprecedented extent, the field of practical abuses. This was Bentham's peculiar province; to this he was called by the whole bent of his disposition, to carry the warfare against absurdity into things practical.

(Cowling 1968: 18–19)

Attending Cambridge in the late 1820s, Tennyson himself could not have avoided exposure to Bentham's version of the critical Enlightenment temper. This was more than just a matter of the *anti*-Utilitarian sympathies of a minority group like the Cambridge Apostles. In November 1828, shortly after he had arrived in Cambridge, a year after Tennyson, Arthur Hallam commented, in a letter to W.E. Gladstone, upon the biases of the Cambridge Union: 'what I have seen I dislike. The ascendant politics are Utilitarian, seasoned with a plentiful seasoning of heterogeneous metaphysics' (Kolb 1981: 244). Whatever the ascendancy of Utilitarianism, Hallam's dislike is symptomatic of the reaction of a substantial number of thinking people in the nineteenth century to the critical perspectives of the Enlightenment. The problem with those perspectives was that what they often succeeded in doing was to unsettle faith in traditional verities without answering to a felt need for spiritual and moral wholeness. The energies of modernity which were released across a broad spectrum of disciplines and fields during the Enlightenment drove the crisis of intellect and faith that characterised the Victorian period. At the threshold of that period, in 1833, Edward Bulwer Lytton wrote of his age as one in which 'old opinions, feelings – ancestral customs and institutions [were] crumbling away' (Lytton 1874: 281). But the Victorian crisis was not simply a matter of the loss of past certainties. It was that new ones did not appear to be on the horizon. Not until late in the century were thinkers able to embrace with enthusiasm a relativistic perspective on meaning. For a large part of the period people were traumatised by the feeling that, in the new condition of culture, the principle of synthesis itself appeared to have been superseded. In 1855 Matthew Arnold described his despairing sense of his own situation as a 'Wandering between two worlds, one dead, / The other powerless to be born' ('Stanzas from the Grande Chartreuse', 85–86). Comparably, in 1842, Tennyson had the speaker of 'The Epic' caricature a parson who was experiencing the vertigo of the modern:

> I, tired out . . .
> Fell in a doze; and half-awake I heard
> The parson taking wide and wider sweeps . . .
> Now hawking at Geology and schism;
> Until I woke, and found him settled down
> Upon the general decay of faith
> Right through the world, 'at home was little left,
> And none abroad: there was no anchor, none,
> To hold by'.

> (9, 13–14, 16–21)

But what is important in the case of Tennyson is that these lines *are* a caricature. It is as if a part of Tennyson, at least, was receptive to precisely the things that the parson reacts against.

The clearest poetic precedent for Tennyson's contrast, in 'Timbuctoo', between the reconciling power of the imagination, on one hand, and those rationalist powers of modernity signified by the word 'Discovery', on the other, may be found in the words of Wordsworth's Wanderer in the fourth book of *The Excursion*. Wordsworth's Wanderer explores the reductive force of rational and scientific knowledge both in terms of the private experience of the individual (the loss of the 'visionary powers of eye and soul / In youth', IV.111–12) and in terms of humankind's loss of an aboriginal innocence; the loss of the world of the Chaldean Shepherds, for example, when 'The imaginative faculty was lord / Of observations natural' (IV.707–708). The Wanderer protests against the sceptical inquiries of the modernising intellect, comparing rationalistic habits of thought with the mythopoeic conceptions of the ancients and, by implication, of those who in the present time assert the vital importance of the creative imagination:

> 'Now, shall our great Discoverers', he exclaimed,
> Raising his voice triumphantly, 'obtain
> From sense and reason less than these obtained ...
> Enquire of ancient Wisdom; go, demand
> Of mighty Nature, if 'twas ever meant
> That we should pry far off yet be unraised;
> That we should pore, and dwindle as we pore,
> Viewing all objects unremittingly
> In disconnection dead and spiritless'.

> (IV.941–43, 957–62)

Saree Makdisi has observed that Romanticism may to a significant extent be 'understood as a diverse and heterogeneous series of engagements with modernisation' (Makdisi 1998: 6). One kind of engagement – and Wordsworth's attack on 'our great Discoverers' in Book IV of *The Excursion* is part of such engagement – involved an outright resistance to the ideology and processes of modernisation. Makdisi takes Wordsworth's 'notion of the spot of time (as articulated in Book XII of *The Prelude*)' as a means of understanding the resistance to the world of modernisation – through the offering of an alternative space and time – which may be found in Byron's Orient, Scott's Highlands and Wordsworth's Nature. 'Seen as spots of time', such alternatives can be understood . . . as self-enclosed and self-referential enclaves of the anti-modern, each defined by its own unique structures of feeling and its own distinct temporality. Each is conceived as a hitherto untransformed enclave that, when discovered and colonized by the outside world, is seen to experience a fall . . .

For the spot of time is always threatened by assimilation, by incorporation into that reorganization of spatial and temporal practices and institutions called modernization (new forms of production and exchange, new ways of thinking time, new histories of the world, new territorialities, new ways of regulating flows of energy and desire). The spot of time is . . . threatened by the very acts of discovery . . . that reveal it to the outside world. The hidden bower in Wordsworth's poem 'Nutting' is an ideal example: its existence is discovered, registered, and appealed to, precisely at the moment when it faces sudden and irreversible annihilation as a result of that discovery.

(Makdisi 1998: 12)

Tennyson's presentation of Timbuctoo as a city of the imagination about to be desolated by 'keen Discovery' is a comparable figure. The spirit of Fable in Tennyson's poem is in no doubt that the 'brilliant towers' of Timbuctoo will very shortly 'darken' and 'shrink'. In this poem, the future of the imaginative life appears doomed. This contrasts with Houghton's statement that Tennyson was one Apostle who listened to and believed in F.D. Maurice's doctrine of the Romantic genius whose imagination was an oracular organ of Truth. But Houghton's statement is too one-sided. Rather than showing an uncomplicated adoption of Romantic perspectives, Tennyson's earlier poetry displays an urgent struggle with key aspects of the Romantic inheritance. Tennyson could certainly write poems of willed Romantic affirmation, such as 'The Poet's Mind' (1830) and 'The Poet' (1830). There is a defensiveness in 'The Poet's Mind', but it is counterbalanced by the poem's assertion of the imagination's living and viable claim to have access to more profound truths than are available to the logic-chopping rationalist:

I

Vex not thou the poet's mind
With thy shallow wit . . .

II

Dark-browed sophist, come not anear;
All the place is holy ground . . .

> In the heart of the garden the merry bird chants.
> It would fall to the ground if you came in.
>   In the middle leaps a fountain...
> It springs on a level of bowery lawn,
> And the mountain draws it from Heaven above...
> And yet, though its voice be so clear and full,
> You never would hear it; your ears are so dull...
> It would shrink to the earth if you came in.

> (1–2, 8–9, 22–24, 31–32, 34–35, 37)

In 'The Poet' Tennyson went further than this and claimed an universal authority for the insights of the imagination:

> The poet in a golden clime was born...
> He saw through life and death, through good and ill...
> The marvel of the everlasting will,
>   An open scroll
> Before him lay...

> (1, 5, 7–9)

The poet in this poem assimilates the category of 'Freedom', in whose 'raiment's hem was traced in flame / WISDOM' (37, 45–46). And when Freedom spoke, we are told, she spoke not with a 'sword' but with 'one poor poet's scroll, and with *his* word / She shook the world' (53, 55–56).

Much of Tennyson's earlier poetry moves between the poles defined by the conclusion to 'Timbuctoo', with its picture of the imminent victory of modern rationalism, on the one hand, and the assertion – rather than the imaginatively persuasive demonstration – of the individual imagination's self-sufficiency and global authority in 'The Poet's Mind' and 'The Poet', on the other. Tennyson's poetic mode in his earlier poetry is clearly derived substantially from Romantic models. At its best it exemplifies a Romantic sensuousness of poetic language and a Romantic disposition towards metaphoricity and mythopoeia. Keats's grounding of 'knowledge and poetic inspiration in color, sound, texture' has always been recognised as one of the most important influences on the manner in which Tennyson anchors his own early poetic world to, as Margaret Lourie puts it, 'concrete sense-impressions described in meticulous detail' (Lourie 1979: 4). But Lourie further observes that Tennyson was equally influenced by Shelley and that the debt runs 'the gamut from superficial verbal echoes to underlying psychic predispositions' (Lourie 1979: 7).

A Keatsian richness of language together with a Shelleyan psychological structure influence the inward voyage to imaginative resource in Tennyson's 1830 'Recollections of the Arabian Nights'. This poem celebrates a sense of unqualified fulfilment as its speaker finally *sees* the object of his imaginative journey inwards:

> Six columns, three on either side,
> Pure silver, underpropt a rich
> Throne of the massive ore, from which
> Down-drooped, in many a floating fold,
> Engarlanded and diapered
> With inwrought flowers, a cloth of gold.
> Thereupon, his deep eye laughter-stirred
> With merriment of kingly pride,
> > Sole star of all that place and time,
> > I saw him – in his golden prime,
> > THE GOOD HAROUN ALRASCHID.

> > > > (144–54)

Such an uncomplicated celebration of a moment of imaginative access is, however, the exception rather than the rule in early Tennyson. The speaker of 'The Palace of Art' (1832), for example, retreats from the world into her palace and into herself in order to indulge the imagination. The palace is a cornucopia of aesthetic representations: tapestries displaying a variety of legendary scenes from the Indo-European cultural traditions; portraits of great writers and philosophers; and so on. But the poem is interested in exposing the narcissistic dimension of the cult of the self-authorising imagination. In its very self-sufficiency that imagination relativises all positions that lie outside itself. In relativising it reduces and in reducing it seeks to dominate:

> I take possession of man's mind and deed
> > I care not what the sects may brawl.
> I sit as God holding no form or creed,
> > But contemplating all

> > > > (209–12)

The interior voyage in this poem comes to define and to be defined in terms of what Isobel Armstrong describes as 'power out of control' (Armstrong 1993: 80). This was an aspect of the Romantic inheritance that alienated Tennyson. It was as if the egoism of the self-authorising imagination might, paradoxically, cut if off from precisely the universal authority that is accorded the poet's mind in 'The Poet'. Where the inner recesses of the mind in 'The Poet's Mind' are 'holy ground' (9), and where the poet's word in 'The Poet' can shake the world, the solipsistic speaker of 'The Palace of Art' touches danger in her magnificent integrity: 'in dark corners of her palace stood/Uncertain shapes.../...white-eyed phantasms weeping tears of blood' (237–39).

One of the major strands in Tennyson's varied relationship with Romanticism involves the question of the spirit of rational inquiry that, at the end of 'Timbuctoo', is set to reduce the mythic City back to what Tennyson, with the reflex Eurocentrism of his time, describes as its actual 'barbaric' form. The ending of 'Timbuctoo' posits a straightforward contrast between the city of the imagination and the rational forces of demythologisation. The poem appears to regret reason's threat to the life of the imagination. But such a simple contrast will not work for reading a whole dimension of Tennyson's poetry. Because what is interesting about that dimension is the great extent to which Tennyson's imagination may, in fact, be seen to have assimilated and incorporated the critical, rational spirit. A sceptical vision may be found at crucial points throughout his verse, even when the metaphoric and sensuous mode of such verse may appear to contradict such a critical model. However much Tennyson was affected by Romantic ideology, the narrative of rationalism and scepticism lodged itself with equal force in his mind. Just how forcefully is shown by works such as 'The Hesperides', 'The Lotos-Eaters', 'Tithonus' and 'Œnone'.

2
Wasted Lands: 'The Hesperides', 'The Lotos-Eaters', 'Tithonus'

I

'The Hesperides', which appeared in Tennyson's 1832 *Poems* but was not reprinted in his lifetime, reworks classical stories about the Hesperidean Sisters. The poem appears gnomic. But its intensely focussed mythologizing holds a pressing metaphysical argument.

In Greek mythology the Sisters, together with the ever-vigilant Dragon Ladon, guarded the golden apples which Earth had given to Herè on her marriage to Zeus. In several traditions the Sisters possessed the power of sweet song and lived in the far West where the sun sets. Classical legends relate that in his eleventh labour, Hercules killed the dragon and carried away the apples. The prologue to 'The Hesperides' has the Carthaginian explorer, Hanno, who sailed down the west coast of Africa in the fifth century BC, hearing the singing of the Sisters coming from a mysterious land mass whose 'slope/...ran bloombright into the Atlantic blue' (8–9).

In a classic interpretation of 'The Hesperides', G. Robert Stange spoke of Tennyson's Sisters' desire to protect the apples from outside interference as an 'allegory of personal and inward experience' (Stange 1960: 100). It allegorises, in other words, Tennyson's sense of the need to preserve the integrity of artistic vision, the integrity of the creative life of the mind, against the distracting demands of society at large.

Stange notes that the poem's epigraph from Milton's *Comus* – 'Hesperus and his daughters three,/That sing about the golden tree' (982–83) – reminds us that

> this nineteenth-century vision is to be compared with Milton's description ... of the paradisaical home of the Attendant Spirit. Milton's Garden of the Hesperides ... has been best described ... as

a symbol of life itself ... In Tennyson's version the religious implications of *Comus* are lacking. The chief resemblance of his poem to
Milton's is in the parallel conception of the gardens as a ... source
of creativity – in Milton's case of the higher life, and in Tennyson's of
the life of art.

(Stange 1960: 101)

The idea that 'The Hesperides' deals with personal and inward, specifically imaginative, experience is important. But there is no reason to
accept the view that the ethical, metaphysical and religious range of
significance in Milton's use of the Hesperidean Garden is lacking in
Tennyson. Tennyson may very well have included this epigraph from
Comus exactly because he wanted to draw attention to the larger
implications of his presentation of the Garden. It is not that Tennyson
is arguing a religious position identical to that in Milton; the exact
opposite, in fact. Through his treatment of the Garden, Tennyson
articulates doubt concerning the existence of a providential order in
the universe. This questioning of broadly Christian terms of reference
coexists in the poem with an allegory about the inner life of the imagination. But the metaphysical scepticism in the poem means that its
assertions about that life can be seen to be fundamentally different
from the way in which Stange conceived them. The interiority of 'The
Hesperides', its exploration of what Stange terms 'the roots of being
from which the poet's visions arise' (Stange 1960: 107), invokes the
Romantic stress on the interior sources of poetic insight and the way
in which, in high Romantic views of mind and reality, statements
concerning the inner life of the individual imagination imply at once,
if not a religious, at least some kind of metaphysical concern. What is
important is that the poem's metaphysical scepticism includes a critique
of that optimism concerning the relation between the finite realm and
the infinite which lies at the centre of high Romantic conceptions of
the imagination.

In the 'Song' of the Sisters, which forms the main body of 'The
Hesperides', we are told that the root of the Hesperidean 'fruittree' is
'charmèd' (17) and that its blossom 'Evermore ... is born anew' (31).
The laws of natural process and temporal succession are suspended.
In this image of renewal, which involves a conflation of the several
stages of the seasonal cycle, decay and death have no reality as states
distinguishable from birth. An unnatural and ahistorical perspective
is established in which the Garden is seen as existing in the perpetual
luxury of springtime. This is an equivalent of the condition of life

found in the Hesperidean Gardens of Milton's Attendant Spirit in *Comus*, those 'happy climes' situated in the 'broad fields of the sky' (976, 978), where

> The Graces, and the rosy-bosomed Hours,
> Thither all their bounties bring,
> That there eternal summer dwells . . .
>
> (985–87)

The idea of the Hesperidean Garden as a realm exempt from the logic of life in time is realised throughout 'The Hesperides' in Tennyson's use of present and present continuous tenses to describe all forms of activity in the Garden. It is also rendered through an emphasis on an inclusive and unbroken ritual circularity: the Sisters never cease their singing and they watch 'Every way' both 'night and day' (40, 41). Father Hesper must 'twinkle not' his 'stedfast sight' (45) and must forever 'Number, tell them over and number / How many the mystic fruittree holds' (49–50). This unremitting attentiveness appears either to dictate or to be dictated by the quiescence, even the torpor, of other life in the Garden which appears to be the necessary condition of the song. The Sisters sing:

> Standing about the charmèd root.
> Round about all is mute,
> As the snowfield on the mountain-peaks,
> As the sandfield at the mountain-foot.
> Crocodiles in briny creeks
> Sleep and stir not: all is mute.
>
> (17–22)

The vigilance and the stupefaction which together characterise the Garden are not, paradoxically, contradictory or mutually exclusive states. We notice, for example, that the redcombed dragon's 'ancient heart is drunk with overwatchings night and day' (54). Similarly, the Sisters mysteriously insist that 'Hesper, the dragon, and sisters three, / Daughters three' (107–108) are a single reality composed of five elements: 'Five links, a golden chain, are we' (106). But in the interdependence of Father Hesper, the redcombed dragon with his ancient heart, and the Sisters themselves, connotations of extreme age, of experience and tired time, on one hand, are fused with connotations of youth, innocence and vigour on the other. The poem offers ńo clues as to how these contradictions may be reconciled: the Sisters' incantation seems expressly designed to maintain a level of being which escapes formulation in rational terms. The fruit-tree is 'mystic', there is a 'bliss of secret smiles' (78), and 'Honour comes with mystery; / Hoarded wisdom brings delight' (47–48).

Notwithstanding their role as the voice of the Garden, the Sisters' own wisdom appears not to partake of the discursive and critical examinations of ordinary self-consciousness. In referring to the redcombed dragon they define a condition of consciousness that is unreflective with regard to its own motivation and is without autonomous, individuated will:

> If he waken, we waken,
> Rapidly levelling eager eyes.
> If he sleep, we sleep,
> Dropping the eyelid over the eyes.

> (59–62)

The 'treasure / Of the wisdom of the west' (26–27) that is defined by this condition is equated in the 'Song' with the truth of the whole, the truth of 'All things' (79). This truth, like the dragon which helps and must be helped to preserve it, is 'older than the world' (58) and is identified with properties of eternity: the Sisters declare that if their chant comes to an end: 'We shall lose eternal pleasure, / Worth eternal want of rest' (24–25).

The 'ancient secret' (72) which the Sisters are so concerned to preserve acquires a more specific connotation through the analogues to Tennyson's Hesperidean fruit-tree which, with its 'golden apple' (14) and sap of 'Liquid gold' (37), is the embodiment of the wisdom of the Garden. The tree's association with a perpetual renewal of life invokes an important aspect of classical versions of the myth of the Garden of the Hesperides: the idea that the Hesperidean tree confers immortality (Rose 1928: 216). It is a point picked up in *Paradise Lost* when Milton recalls classical descriptions of the golden Hesperidean fruit as he reports that the 'tree of life' (IV.218) in Eden stood 'High eminent, blooming ambrosial fruit / Of vegetable gold' (IV.219–20). The 'golden tree' of the Attendant Spirit's Hesperidean Gardens in *Comus*, to which we are referred in Tennyson's epigraph, is itself connected with the idea of eternal life through its identification with a realm of spiritual purification. In the Attendant Spirit's 'gardens fair / Of Hesperus' (980–81) we learn that the

> young Adonis oft reposes,
> Waxing well of his deep wound
> In slumber soft, and on the ground
> Sadly sits the Assyrian queen . . .

(998–1001)

In the somewhat baroque cosmology of Milton's Masque, classical and Christian elements are, of course, compounded in a highly individual poetic conception of the spiritual hierarchy of the universe. Milton's picture of Adonis healing in the Hesperidean Gardens represents a higher mode of regeneration than that principle of merely natural regeneration represented by his poetic precursor, Edmund Spenser, in his portrayal of the Garden of Adonis in *The Faerie Queene* (III.vi). As John Carey has noted, in an explanation of the Platonic dimension of the cosmology of *Comus*, whereas Spenser's Garden of Adonis is on earth, Milton's Venus and Adonis lie in a transitional state 'in the Elysian fields of the moon' where they await the 'separation of soul and mind, when mind will finally return to its source, the sun', a sun which is 'to be distinguished from that of mere earthly fruitfulness' (Carey 1971: 227). At the very opening of *Comus*, the Attendant Spirit makes explicit the spiritual orientation of his realm of repose. His abode, he declares, is where 'those immortal shapes / Of bright aerial spirits live ensphered' above the 'dim spot' of earth (2–3, 5) where men

> Strive to keep up a frail, and feverish being
> Unmindful of the crown that virtue gives
> After this mortal change, to her true servants
> Amongst the enthron'd gods on sainted seats.
> Yet some there be that by due steps aspire
> To lay their just hands on that golden key
> That opens the palace of eternity . . .

(8–14)

In the light of these kinds of mythical and literary antecedents, and Tennyson's own presentation of the special attributes of the Garden, Tennyson's Hesperidean realm emerges as a metaphor for a higher principle of life, for an ultimate reality where logical opposites are reconciled and where the pains of earthly existence are not felt.

Tennyson's presentation of the Hesperidean Garden in 'The Hesperides' does not rehearse the fine distinctions employed by Renaissance writers in their representation of paradisaical gardens. There is, for example, no question of our being invited to view his Garden of the Hesperides as a false paradise in the manner of Spenser's description of the Bower of Bliss in *The Faerie Queene* (II.xii); or as a symbol of purely natural regeneration, as in Spenser's portrayal of the Garden of Adonis. Tennyson's reference to *Comus*, where the Hesperidean Gardens are associated with a spiritual principle of life does, however, establish a broad context of meaning for the Garden in 'The Hesperides'. Tennyson allows by this reference the highest possible significance for his Garden as an image of the absolute. But the elaborate Platonic-Christian cosmology within which Milton places the Hesperidean Gardens in *Comus* is not carried over into Tennyson's work. Tennyson resolves the several possible levels of traditional classical-Christian cosmology to two basic terms: the supramundane reality of the Garden in the West stands in stark opposition to the quotidian world represented by the East.

In contrast to the intact and unitary condition represented by the West, the East of the 'Song' is a state characterised by deviation and discontinuity. The Sisters compare, for example, the subliminal integrity of their western 'seawind' with the more disturbed 'landwind' belonging to the East:

> Every flower and every fruit the redolent breath
> Of this warm seawind ripeneth,
> Arching the billow in his sleep;
> But the landwind wandereth,
> Broken by the highland-steep...
>
> (83–87)

The nature of the dissociation intrinsic to the East becomes clearer when we recall the observation of the Sisters that if the golden apple be taken by 'one from the East' (42) the 'world will be overwise' (64); so wise, indeed, that the 'old wound of the world' will 'be healèd' (69). There are obvious connotations of the Fall in this reference to the 'old wound of the world'. In *Paradise Lost* Milton speaks of the hurt felt in the frame of creation at the moment when Eve first tasted the apple: 'Earth felt the wound, and nature from her seat / Sighing through all her works gave signs of woe' (*Paradise Lost* IX.782–83). In 'The Hesperides' an identification of the West with an otherworldly state of unity and harmony, and of the East with the fallen, imperfect and incomplete 'world' (104) of human experience, resides in the opposition that the Sisters make

between the stable eternity of their Garden and the realm of historical
and natural process:

> Father, twinkle not thy stedfast sight;
> Kingdoms lapse, and climates change, and races die;
> Honour comes with the mystery...

(45–47)

The problematic aspect of the relation between these finite and infinite
worlds, between the world of time and change on one hand and the
sphere of the Garden on the other, is that the Sisters are committed to
maintaining an absolute separation between the two. Tennyson's
line about one from the East who *threatens* (from the point of view of
the Sisters) to take the golden apple is clearly to be linked with classical
stories about the slaying of the guardian-dragon of the Hesperidean tree
and the theft of the fruit by Hercules. The unwillingness of Tennyson's
Sisters to let the apple be taken is entirely consistent with this story.
But the situation involving the defence of the Garden is complicated
by the further possibilities of meaning introduced through Tennyson's
allusion to the Biblical theme of the Fall. There is a straightforward
parallel, in the instinct of the Sisters to protect the apple, to both the
Greek myth of Hercules and the 'Hebrew-Christian Eden myth', where
man was prevented from eating the fruit of the tree of life 'after he defied
God and ate the fruit of the tree of knowledge of good and evil' (Fricke
1970: 100). Tennyson's Miltonic epigraph, however, in referring us to
Comus, does not refer us simply to this part of the 'Hebrew-Christian
Eden myth'. In Christian thought, although man may be supposed to have
forfeited at the Fall the right to physical immortality, the tree of life is
made available to him again, in the sense that the possibility of spiritual
regeneration is made available to him, through the endeavour and
sacrifice of Christ. This larger idea of the tree of life supports Milton's
presentation of the Hesperidean Gardens in *Comus*. As J.B. Leishman has
written, 'Milton's world, unlike Plato's, is a Christian world, a redeemed
world' (Leishman 1969: 222). Within the cosmology of *Comus* the
Hesperidean Gardens are above earth but are associated with a plane of
spiritual purification lower than that represented by Cupid and Psyche,
who exist 'far above in spangled sheen' (1002). There is a higher spiritual
reality than all the 'sphery chime' (1020), however, and despite all
the Platonic elements in *Comus*, in the Attendant Spirit's concluding
words the idea of Divine Grace is confirmed as an essential feature of

the poem. Here the Spirit reassures us that if human virtue alone is insufficient to climb higher than the celestial spheres, there nevertheless remains a higher dispensation at the service of man:

> Mortals that would follow me,
> Love Virtue, she alone is free,
> She can teach ye how to climb
> Higher than the sphery chime;
> Or if Virtue feeble were,
> Heaven itself would stoop to her.

(1017–22)

This passage is usefully glossed in *The Poetical Works of John Milton*, edited in six volumes by Henry John Todd in 1801. Tennyson's own copy of this edition is still extant in the Tennyson Research Centre at Lincoln (Campbell 1971–73: Item 1601). In the fifth volume (pp. 410–11) Todd prefixes his own note on a manuscript variant in line 1022 of *Comus* (Trinity College, Cambridge: MS. R.3.4) with a quotation from 'the Rev. Mr. Egerton' who observes that in the last six lines of the poem Milton contemplates

'that stupendous Mystery, whereby *He*, the lofty theme of *Paradise Regained*, stooping from above all height, "bowed the Heavens, and came down" on Earth, to atone as Man for the Sins of Men, to strengthen feeble Virtue by the influence of his Grace...' [Todd then continues:] The last line had been written thus by Milton: 'Heaven itself would *bow* to her'. He altered *bow* to *stoop*, because the latter word expresses greater condescension. So, in his *Ode on the Passion*, he applies, to the Son of God when he took our nature upon him, the phrase '*stooping* his regal head'.

In *Comus* the ultimate power presiding over the Attendant Spirit's ethereal Hesperidean Gardens is sympathetic to the 'sin-worn mould' (1.17) of earthly existence. In Tennyson's poem this is flatly contradicted. The powers of Tennyson's Garden are bent, not merely on denying access to the tree of life in the sense that the 'Hebrew-Christian' God originally denied man access to the tree of life in Eden, but on refusing all possibility for the redemption of what is already described as the 'old' wound of the world.

There are important conclusions to be drawn from Tennyson's presentation of 'one from the East' who *promises* (from the point of view of the world) to heal the old wound of Earth. The image of a potential redeemer in Tennyson's line goes beyond the possibilities of meaning inherited directly from classical accounts of the eleventh labour of Hercules. Tennyson is apparently drawing on a traditional Christian interpretation of the figure of Hercules as type of Christ (Milton himself makes such a comparison in *Paradise Regained*, IV.563–71). While, however, there is an obvious suggestion of a Redeemer figure in Tennyson's line, it is not there as part of a larger Christian idea governing the poem as a whole. The Garden, with its fruit-tree, dragon, Father Hesper, and the Hesperidean maidens, serves as a compound image of an absolute which does not sanction – and which is intractably alien to the purpose of – the one from the East.

Although the East, understood as the 'fallen' world of everyday experience, must logically be derived from the West, viewed as the eternal principle of 'All things', there is in 'The Hesperides' no presentation of the fall as the historical event of Christian doctrine, enacted under the view of a God whose providential purpose has been revealed to human beings. Key elements of Christian doctrine are suggested only to have their meaning and validity cancelled by the larger metaphysical frame of reference established through Tennyson's characterisation of the Hesperidean Garden. If there is a Christian motif involved in the idea of one who is to come from the East, it is a motif which, by the metaphorical terms of the poem as a whole, can never be completed. The picture of the absolute stability of the Garden and the image of a potential Redeemer are held in tension, the attributes of the one perpetually denying the possibilities of the other. 'The Hesperides' presents us with a radical split between the interests of man and the operation of an essentially blind, impersonal absolute. There is no uniquely personal Deity in the Garden responsible to the world of activity and strife. In the detached and clinical manner in which the Sisters note the existence of a realm of flux and instability we can detect a kind of constitutional inability to sympathise with the painful problems of that world. However the world of history may be related to them, in their ritual activity they are bound to an automatic principle of guarding their secret and maintaining the mystery. They are bound absolutely by the laws of their own Being which they cannot alter because they are without independent, individuated will. 'The Hesperides' is an early formulation of that vision of an indifferent and impersonal force driving the universe which Tennyson was to define in the light of contemporary geological and biological science in *In Memoriam*.

Tennyson can hardly be seen to be endorsing the Sisters' refusal to let the old wound of the world be healed, or to allow the 'ancient secret', the key to joy, to be revealed. The Sisters observe that 'The world is wasted with fire and sword, / But the apple of gold hangs over the sea' (11. 104–105). The dramatic irony of these lines tells us of the Sisters' inhumanity: while the world may be suffering, all is well from their point of view so long as the apple of gold hangs secure and unaccountable over the sea. The Sisters may not be able to help themselves in their inveterate and callous disregard of the world, but the poem registers feelings of moral revulsion at the kind of absolute they represent.

The discontinuity between the secret joy of the Garden and the troubled world of human experience carries considerable implications for the poem viewed as a statement about the grounds of poetic vision. Tennyson's 'Timbuctoo' defines Timbuctoo as a city of the imagination that now fulfils the role once assumed by myths of island paradises in the Western ocean. Like Hallam, following Wordsworth, Tennyson makes an identification in 'Timbuctoo' of the Western Isles of the Blest with the sphere of the imagination. This identification in 'Timbuctoo' directs us to the Romantic possibilities of meaning in Tennyson's symbolic geography of West and East in 'The Hesperides'. In 'Timbuctoo' the 'Thrones of the Western wave' are associated with an image of the organic life of the 'vine of *Fable*' which provides a refuge for man (at least until the closing lines of the poem) amid its 'complicated glooms, / And cool impleachèd twilights' (223–24). There is a correlation between these motifs and the imagery of western sea, of darkness, and of vegetative generation in 'The Hesperides'. Certainly, the central figure of 'The Hesperides', by which the growth of the fruit is conditional upon the Sisters' mesmerised singing while, in the same breath, they draw their energy from the root and the tree, is characteristic of high Romantic metaphors of mind which emphasise the primacy of unconscious genius and organic growth in the creative life of the artist. The qualities of timelessness and trance which distinguish the Garden also invite comparison with the Romantic interest in these states as conditions associated with the functioning of the creative imagination. These are the states associated, for example, with the sleep and music-haunted bower of Adonis in Keats' *Endymion* (1818), where the 'feathered lyrist' (II.432) who watches over the sleeping Adonis welcomes Endymion as he descends far 'past the scanty bar / To mortal steps' (II.124–25):

> Though from upper day
> Thou art a wanderer, and thy presence here
> Might seem unholy, be of happy cheer!
> For 'tis the nicest touch of human honour

When some ethereal and high-favouring donor
Presents immortal bowers to mortal sense...
    here is manna picked from Syrian trees,
In starlight, by the three Hesperides...

(II.433–38, 452–53)

But where, for Keats, at least at this stage of his career, before he had entered upon the dubieties of the *Odes*, there is the possibility of a meaningful transcription by the poet of more-than-normal experience, the emphasis in Tennyson's 'The Hesperides' is that that area of experience lying beyond the rational, imaged in the life of the Hesperidean Garden, is entirely unusable in earthly terms. The 'wisdom' whispering in a corner (28), which the Sisters insist must not be opened up to the scrutiny of the world, is presented under a different light from that celebrated in Tennyson's 'The Poet'. There the poet 'saw through life and death' (5), the 'marvel of the everlasting will, / An open scroll, / Before him lay' (7–9), and with such 'WISDOM' (46) he 'shook the world' (56). In 'The Poet' the infinite mysteries are translated into legible characters and the poet's wisdom is justified as a meaningful transcendental vision which engages and can enlighten the world. But while Tennyson's Garden of the Hesperides is not strictly one of dumb enchantment, there are essentially no intelligible sounds in Hanno's dream voices (we hear only ritual utterances – the gnomic impenetrability of the truth of the absolute is suggested through the indecipherable code of the number symbolism in which the Sisters deal: 'Five and three / ... make an awful mystery', 28–29). As the Sisters maintain their secret of 'All things', Hanno is provided with no language by which to relate the truths of the Garden to his conscious life or to interpret the mystery to the world. Likewise, the Sisters' song of hate ('Hesper hateth Phosphor, evening hateth morn', 82) is to be contrasted with that 'song of undying love' which is heard in the interior garden in 'The Poet's Mind'. What the energies of Tennyson's Hesperidean Garden tell us about the everlasting will, as manifest in the human mind and personality, is that it is an enemy to those self-consciously formulated values by which human beings strive to mould a sensitive and a moral universe. Identification with the root and spring of imaginative life is not presented in 'The Hesperides' as something which, while involving a modification of ordinary consciousness and will, nevertheless constitutes an expansion and fulfilment of identity. For we see only an obliteration and negation of recognisable human meaning in the mindless, amoral drive of the Sisters' incantation. Draining the sea of time and space off the top of the mind is not in this poem a necessarily energising process. Hanno cannot return to the world as Endymion from the bower of Adonis, regenerated with manna plucked by the three Hesperides, and enlightened by a loving interpreter who gives him proper knowledge of the immortal things around him.

The high Romantic confidence in an interior interchange, through the faculty of imagination, between the mundane and the sublime no longer holds, any more than such interchange can be envisaged in outward metaphysical or religious terms. The revulsion against the absolute which Tennyson articulates in the 'The Hesperides' appears again in 'The Lotos-Eaters' – first published in 1832 and extensively revised when it was republished in *Poems*, 1842.

II

Founded upon a detail of Homeric story (*Odyssey*, IX.82–104), in which some of Odysseus' sailors, having eaten of the Lotus-fruit, became unwilling to carry on with the effort of the epic voyage, 'The Lotos-Eaters' is most readily placed within the tradition of English poetry dealing with the human impulse to retreat from the stresses of ordinary existence into sensuous lethargy and indolent forgetfulness. Spenser, as Christopher Ricks notes, 'was the major influence on the style and tone' of the poem: 'in particular', Spenser's descriptions in *The Faerie Queene* of the Cave of Morpheus (I.i.41), the blandishments of Despair (I.ix.40), the Idle Lake 'and its enervating island' (II.vi.10), and the Bower of Bliss (II.xii.32; Ricks 1987: I.468). But Tennyson does not present his poetry of *accidie* within the same context of Christian spiritual and moral values as Spenser. Nor does he present it within the Homeric context of the heroic ideal, which Odysseus' sailors fail to fulfil in their unwillingness to return to ship. At first sight, it seems that Tennyson does not present his mariners' escapist impulse clearly within any governing frame of reference. John Bayley contrasted Spenser's treatment of the Cave of Despair with Tennyson's Lotos-Eaters when he wrote that 'whereas Spenser knows what he thinks about [his material], and fits the description into the pattern of traditional ethics to which he adheres, Tennyson merely exploits the imaginative situation as a thing in itself: he is not conditioned to relate his imagination to a settled scheme of thought and belief' (Bayley 1957: 64). Contrasting Tennyson with Homer, Christopher Ricks has observed that instead of showing, as in Homer, the mariners restored from Lotos-land, Tennyson's poem 'preserves a potent silence' (Ricks 1989: 86). The silence raises several questions. On the one hand, there is the opening of the poem's narrative prologue: ' "Courage!" he said, and pointed toward the land.' Yet that *he* 'does not return in the poem' and Ricks questions whether the 'note of command' at the very outset of the poem is authoritative enough to command the work as a whole (Ricks 1989: 86). At the same time, we are entitled to ask whether the 'he' is 'simply dropped? He is assuredly not among those who eat the lotos; perhaps he broods over those who brood' (Ricks 1989: 86). While the poem 'does not ever return to its narrative from the "Choric Song" ',

> this is not at all the same as saying that the mariners are not to return from the land of the Lotos-eaters (did Odysseus never complete his journey?). Our wishes – the poem tacitly reminds us – are not necessarily sovereign.
>
> (Ricks 1989: 86)

Yet it is not only through the 'he' in the opening line that a controlling frame of reference is established in the poem. The narrative voice of the poem is distinguishable from the figure referred to by the third person. And that voice exercises an authority over the entire poem which is greater than the 'he' simply because it speaks in the past tense. The voice is unidentified and unlocated but it has a temporal placing which postdates and is distanced from the experience it recounts. It offers an organising perspective which is outside and larger than the present tense of the 'Choric Song'. But what is particularly interesting is that the narrative prologue spoken by this voice is in a Spenserian stanza that is as laggard as the song reportedly sung by the mariners themselves. In this way the narrative renders with a disturbing and disturbed intimacy of understanding the condition of the isle and of the mind intoxicated by the lotos-fruit. The owner of this voice has experienced the lotos-drugged condition at first hand. The disturbance is evident in lines from the prologue which describe the approach of the natives of the isle:

> A land where all things always seemed the same!
> And round about the keel with faces pale,
> Dark faces pale against that rosy flame,
> The mild-eyed melancholy Lotos-eaters came.
>
> Branches they bore of that enchanted stem,
> Laden with flower and fruit, whereof they gave
> To each, but whoso did receive of them,
> And taste, to him the gushing of the wave

Far far away did seem to mourn and rave
On alien shores; and if his fellow spake,
His voice was thin, as voices from the grave...

(24–34)

The suggestion of paradoxical threat in the description of 'Dark faces pale' modulates into an account of an offer which at first sight might well have been thought (and by some of the mariners obviously *was* thought) to hold out possibilities of enriching growth, of fulfilment and culmination ('enchanted... flower... fruit'). But whatever the mariners may have wished to believe, the narrative voice is quite clear that all was not as it may have seemed. Rather than *and*, the voice says '*but* whoso did receive of them...' and so, alerted by this qualifying preposition, we are prepared for what the voice knows to have been an experience more properly characterised in terms of loss, madness, alienation, impoverishment, and death ('mourn... rave... alien... thin... grave'). Whatever acquaintance the narrative voice may have had with the lotos-eating life, and however much it may demonstrate that acquaintance in the prologue, it is clear that lotos-intoxication does not constitute its present condition. The voice places the lotos-eating life as the experience of others, or as *remembered* experience, and what we witness of laziness in the prologue seems to be only the capacity of the mind to empathise with, or potently to recall a condition that is not, or is no longer, its own. This kind of capacity coexists with the critical faculty that exposes the false offer of the Lotos-eaters from the perspective of a present that is not the lotos-eating past. The use of the past tense denotes a consciousness engaged in historical process rather than the continuous present of a world where 'all things always' *are* 'the same'. Whatever share in the lotos-eating experience might be claimed by the voice for itself, it speaks from the point of view of standing outside and from the position of having a standard by which to measure that experience. The double perspective of the narrative prologue, at once both inside and outside the drugged condition, means that at the end of the 'Choric song' the poem has no need to return literally to its narrative, for the principle of return or of separation from Lotos-land is captured through the temporal arrangements and the evaluative perspectives of the prologue. An evaluative distance from the experience of lotos-eating is conveyed by other devices in the poem: the dramatic ironies of the 'Choric song' itself, for example, where the mariners refer to Lotos-land as 'barren' (145) and 'hollow' (154).

But why construct an ironic perspective on the lotos-eating experience without drawing explicit and detailed attention to a body of values by which the escapist impulse may be judged? If there is not exactly the silence noted by Ricks, there is yet a curious silence in the poem. The critical point here is that Tennyson was writing in an age when 'continental areas of common values were breaking up' (Carr 1960: 43). There is something discrepant in a straightforward comparison of Tennyson with either Spenser or Homer because it is precisely the absence of any settled scheme of thought and belief that constitutes the conceptual framework of the poem. Tennyson reworks the classical story in a way which records the atmosphere of a time when, as J.A. Froude spoke of the eighteen-forties, 'the intellectual lightships had broken from their moorings . . . the lights all drifting, the compasses all awry' (Froude 1897: I.311); a time, as Tennyson's nineteenth-century voyagers put it, of 'confusion worse than death' (128) to 'hearts worn out by many wars / And eyes grown dim with gazing on the pilot-stars' (131–32).

The idea that Tennyson's Lotos-land lies beyond traditional spiritual and moral charts does not allow easy justification of the mariners' desire to escape. What does happen under this idea is that an authority – an authority granted neither to Spenser's nor to Homer's recalcitrants – is imparted to Tennyson's mariners' questionings of the meaning of human pain:

> Why are we weighed upon with heaviness,
> And utterly consumed with sharp distress,
> While all things else have rest from weariness?
> All things have rest: why should we toil alone,
> We only toil, who are the first of things . . .

> (57–61)

Such dissenting questions acquire a special kind of legitimacy when there is no system of explanation to forestall the questions. Tennyson's mariners are not morally delinquent in the same way as Spenser's Phaedria when she tries to tempt men away from responsibility through an unfavourable comparison of the 'carefull paines' of mankind with the careless life of nature (*Faerie Queene*, II.vi.15). Tennyson's mariners are displaced and disoriented in that they do not have an external system of meaning and values from which they *can* deviate. In the revised conclusion to 'The Lotos-Eaters', published in 1842, Tennyson chose to develop that element of legitimate protest which runs through many of the mariners' utterances.

The gods to whom the mariners refer in the 1842 conclusion are based on Lucretius' account of Epicureanism:

> Let us swear an oath, and keep it with an equal mind,
> In the hollow Lotos-land to live and lie reclined
> On the hills like Gods together, careless of mankind.
> For they lie beside their nectar, and the bolts are hurled
> Far below them in the valleys, and the clouds are lightly curled
> Round their golden houses, girdled with the gleaming world:
> Where they smile in secret, looking over wasted lands,
> Blight and famine, plague and earthquake, roaring deeps
>   and fiery sands,
>
> Clanging fights, and flaming towns, and sinking ships,
>   and praying hands.
>
>   (153–61)

The most apt commentator on the stridency of these lines has been F.E.L. Priestley. They are, he writes,

> not lines expressive of lassitude, they are marked by strong indignation over man's lot, a measured, stately, and angry denunciation of the gods who find man's tragedy meaningless or amusing. When, at the end of the chorus, the lines lose their energy and relax...the lassitude is not that of the drugged pleasure-seeker, but of the exhausted and toil-worn sufferer.
>
>   (Priestley 1973: 58)

The mariners' protest carries a moral authority deriving from the fact that the metaphysic they are working within offers no moral rule which might be transgressed. At the same time, however, there is no hedonistic justification of their desire to be hedonistic; their desire, as it were, to be able to transgress. The mariners want to be like the gods whom they at once morally condemn. They themselves, in other words, rather than any external authority provide the moral terms by which their desire for irresponsibility may be judged. The irony by which this evaluative distance is achieved chimes with the ironic perspective on the false promise of Lotos-eating conveyed by the narrative voice in the poem's prologue. It is an irony that does not amount to an assertion of the existence of a divinely founded moral order in the universe. In 'The

Lotos-Eaters', as in 'The Hesperides', the dignity of morality holds in the human sphere and not at some higher level.

The metaphysic of 'The Lotos-Eaters' has many points in common with that in 'The Hesperides'. There is a parallel between Lotos-land as an Island of the Blest seen under the aspect of a sunset that 'lingered low adown/In the red West' (19–20) and Tennyson's symbolic geography of West and East in 'The Hesperides'. By this symbolism of the West, Lotos-land connotes an order which is set apart from the world of historical and natural process. The point is reinforced by the way in which the word 'charmèd', a key term in Tennyson's description of his Hesperidean Garden, reappears to help define what turn out to be the unnatural and ahistorical potentialities of the Lotos-isle: 'The charmèd sunset lingered low adown...'. The exemption from the logic of life in time which is the distinctive feature of the Hesperidean Garden also finds a parallel in the manner that Lotos-land is presented as a place where 'all things always seemed the same!' (24):

> above the valley stood the moon...
> From the inner land: far off, three mountain-tops,
> Three silent pinnacles of agèd snow,
> Stood sunset-flushed: and, dewed with showery drops,
> Up-clomb the shadowy pine above the woven copse.
>
> (7, 15–18)

Here, elements of night and day and antithetical connotations of darkness and light, cold and heat, age and youth, and stasis (snow as immobile water) and movement (the melting transitions from 'snow' to 'flushed' to 'drops'), are juxtaposed to produce the effect of an abnormal simultaneity of occurrence. The need to suggest a realm beyond ordinary terms of reference provoked Tennyson to some of his most superb, graphic evocations of a narcotic sense of near-suspended animation:

> like a downward smoke, the slender stream
> Along the cliff to fall and pause and fall did seem...
>
> (8–9)

The somnambulism of Tennyson's Hesperidean Sisters is recalled when we are told that those who ate the lotos-fruit seemed 'deep-asleep...yet all awake' (35). The imagery of gold is common to both the account of the Hesperidean tree and the account in 'The Lotos-Eaters' of the 'golden houses' (158) of the gods, whose mode of being the mariners equate with the lotos-eating life. And if the Hesperidean Sisters – as part of a Garden which images the absolute – impassively note a world 'wasted with fire and sword' whilst affirming the 'bliss of secret smiles', the gods who are the presiding spirits of place in Tennyson's Lotos-isle are careless of the world of mankind and 'smile in secret, looking over wasted lands' (159).

Bereft of any sense of ultimate meaning, Tennyson's mariners try to convince themselves that carelessness is an adequate response to a careless universe. And yet, whatever their stated desire for escape, they never move beyond desire and they never cease to care. They fantasise bliss. They imagine delights which the act of imagining puts out of reach. They want to forget and the wanting prevents the forgetting. Perhaps the gap between the mariners' consciousness and that of the narrative voice is not, after all, so great.

More than this, however, Tennyson establishes not only that the mariners never forget, he also suggests, through his representation of the Epicurean gods as governing spirits of the island, that the mariners are constitutionally unable to forget the 'sharp distress' (58) of mankind and achieve peace. If, in 'The Hesperides', humanity has no access to the joy of the Garden, we find in 'The Lotos-Eaters' a further contradiction inherent in the mariners' comparison of life in Lotos-land to the life of the Epicurean gods. This comparison may help to define the metaphysical limits of their universe. It may tell us, symbolically, that an uncaring principle rules all and that what the mariners think they want is a comparable, trouble-free, peaceful carelessness. But while, at one level of the poem, the mariners are literally successful in landing on their western isle beyond the sea of history, at another level, through the mariners' identification of the island with what is by definition the humanly unattainable condition of the gods, we find Lotos-land connoting an order of being from which humanity is in reality forever excluded. It is a foregone conclusion that the mariners will not stay in Lotos-land.

The predicament of humanity as defined in 'The Lotos-Eaters' is different from the predicament of Cymochles when faced with Phaedria's temptation in *The Faerie Queene*. There, human beings have the problem of deciding between the higher and the lower as meaningful alternatives. The question of choice is real and so too is the principle of dilemma as a structural principle for the poem in which the episode is set. But the predicament of the mariners in 'The Lotos-Eaters' is that they have no real choice. As human beings they have no sense of calm and no sense of belonging. They do not belong simply to nature ('all things else have rest from weariness', 59) and there is no heaven available to accommodate them. In a world where clear distinctions between higher and lower have collapsed, 'The Lotos-Eaters' is not structured around a dilemma. Its central note is one of protest at the lack of alternatives. The human situation in the poem is cast as the potentially tragic one of permanent exile and homelessness.

A tragic displacement of the human is again the subject of a poem which Tennyson first compared in 1833, but which he did not finally publish until 1860, 'Tithonus'.

III

In classical myth (told in the Homeric *Hymn to Aphrodite*, for example, or in Horace's *Odes*: I.xxviii and II.xvi), Tithonus was a man who fell in love with and was loved by Aurora, goddess and personification of the dawn. He had asked her to grant him immortality, which she did, neither of them pausing to think that a gift of eternal life ought to be very carefully formulated. Tithonus did not get eternal youth, just life, so that he was caught in the unimaginable nightmare of growing older and older for ever. Tennyson's Tithonus speaks from this condition and craves the capacity to die:

> Me only cruel immortality
> Consumes: I wither slowly in thine arms,
> Here at the quiet limit of the world,
> A white-haired shadow roaming like a dream
> The ever-silent spaces of the East,
> Far-folded mists, and gleaming halls of morn . . .
> Release me, and restore me to the ground;
> Thou seëst all things, thou wilt see my grave:
> Thou wilt renew thy beauty morn by morn;
> I earth in earth forget these empty courts,
> And thee returning on thy silver wheels.

> (5–10, 72–76)

Tennyson fashions, out of the fable of Tithonus' impossible state, an image of the human condition which parallels that in 'The Lotos-Eaters'. The lotos-eating mariners envy what they see as the ease of purely natural life:

> Lo! in the middle of the wood,
> The folded leaf is wooed from out the bud

With winds upon the branch, and there
Grows green and broad, and takes no care ...
The full-juiced apple, waxing over-mellow,
Drops in a silent autumn night.
All its allotted length of days,
The flower ripens in its place,
Ripens and fades, and falls, and hath no toil,
Fast-rooted in the fruitful soil.

(70–73, 77–83)

Being human, however, the mariners cannot lose themselves in the unselfconscious rhythms of natural life. Standing at odds with nature, they know themselves 'consumed with sharp distress' (58). At the same time they are not divine. They are alienated, exiled between realms. So, too, with Tithonus. In his immortality he is more-than-natural. In his endless ageing he is less than supernatural. The poem takes the paradoxical nature of his state as a type of the human condition itself. Tennyson's Tithonus is outcast in the universe, like the humanity he represents.

Tennyson's description in lines 50–63 of the divine appeal that Aurora held for Tithonus images the human taste for forbidden knowledge, the key to higher things. Tennyson captures, through the figure of Tithonus' desire for Aurora, the erotics of the human drive towards a sublimity of intellect which is represented in the lines through the reference to Apollo:

Ay me! ay me! with what another heart ...
I used to watch ...
The lucid outline forming round thee; saw
The dim curls kindle into sunny rings;
Changed with thy mystic change, and felt my blood
Glow with the glow that slowly crimsoned all
Thy presence and thy portals, while I lay,
Mouth, forehead, eyelids, growing dewy-warm
With kisses balmier than half-opening buds
Of April, and could hear the lips that kissed
Whispering I knew not what of wild and sweet,
Like that strange song I heard Apollo sing,
While Ilion like a mist rose into towers.

(50–63)

Through the particular story that he uses, the story of Aurora's endless vanishing, Tennyson allegorises an aspiration where the object of the aspiration can never finally be possessed, where the human is doomed to desire and never to achieve fulfilment:

> Once more the old mysterious glimmer steals
> From thy pure brows, and from thy shoulders pure,
> And bosom beating with a heart renewed.
> Thy cheek begins to redden through the gloom,
> Thy sweet eyes brighten slowly close to mine,
> Ere yet they blind the stars, and the wild teams
> Which love thee, yearning for thy yoke, arise,
> And shake the darkness from their loosened manes,
> And beat the twilight into flakes of fire.
>
> Lo! ever thus thou growest beautiful
> In silence, then before thine answer given
> Departest, and thy tears are on my cheek.
>
> (34–45)

No more than in 'The Hesperides' or 'The Lotos-Eaters' does Tennyson envisage a meaningful relation between the human and the divine. The divorce of interest between the human and the more-than-human is irresolvable. No machinery of redemption is imagined. The sceptical vision in these poems shows human beings dispossessed of a home either in nature or in some higher realm. In the very opening lines of the poem, Tithonus himself, desperate to escape the alienation of his nature, imagines a happier human condition. But it is actually not a human condition at all. It is a fiction of a humanity assimilated to an idealised state of nature, much as the lotos-eating mariners imagine themselves absorbed within a natural, unselfconscious paradise:

> The woods decay, the woods decay and fall,
> The vapours weep their burthen to the ground,
> Man comes and tills the field and lies beneath,
> And after many a summer dies the swan.
>
> (1–4)

No human just comes, 'tills the field', and quiescently dies. Human beings are born and at last die but the space between is filled with varying but significant degrees of labour, yearning, frustration and anguish. More than simply animal they cannot transcend their mortality. Tennyson's symbolic figure of Tithonus can neither die nor be elevated to the heavens. In the classical story, Aurora, unable to rescind her gift, at last releases him by turning him into a cicada. It is not exactly a human death. But at least he ceases being endlessly human, endlessly estranged.

As with his use of the classical fable of the Hesperidean Garden, Tennyson's treatment of the legend of Tithonus, to figure existential and metaphysical predicament, may be seen as involving at the same time a critique of Romantic assertions about the infinite reach of the poetic imagination. Elaine Jordan has finely observed that Tennyson's poem 'undoes Shelley's notion of an ideal, quasi-divine, endorsement for poetic language' (Jordan 1988: 73). Shelley's spirit of the sympathetic imagination, his spirit of poetry, his Witch of Atlas in the 1824 poem of that name, was 'said to be able to take a human being and mingle it with her own identity' (Jordan 1988: 73):

> She, all those human figures breathing there,
> Beheld as living spirits – to her eyes
> The naked beauty of the soul lay bare...
> And then she had a charm of strange device,
> Which, murmured on mute lips with tender tone,
> Could make that spirit mingle with her own.
>
> Alas! Aurora, what wouldst thou have given
> For such a charm when Tithon became gray?
>
> (569–71, 574–78)

Shelley's Witch of Atlas, as the spirit of poetry, is, appropriately enough, the daughter of Apollo. It is appropriate because Apollo was, among other things, the god of song, of lyric verse and music. And in Tennyson's poem Tithonus recalls that in the old days Aurora's voice had appealed to him in the same manner as the song he had heard Apollo sing as the god brought the City of Troy into being. Aurora entranced Tithonus with a magic as of poetry. Tithonus' aspiration towards a more-than-human nature describes at once a Romantic aspiration towards the more-than-earthly insight of the poetic imagination. But that aspiration is denied as Tithonus discovers the gulf between himself and the goddess. The point about the poem's self-reflexiveness is that it implicitly signals that its own fantastic beauty has no ultimate or higher authority. It signals that the beauty of the poem circles, like its speaker, in a void, with no significance beyond itself. This is perhaps the reason for the almost studied *excess* of beauty in this poem. It is as if poetic effect has no place to go but to fall back upon itself in an ultimately decadent loop. Tennyson's poem expresses both Tennyson's anxiety about there being no meaningful connection between the transcendent and the human and an anti-Romantic frustration that his own poetic imagination, in all its wonder, cannot redeem that anxiety.

Tennyson's concern with the problematical nature of the relation between the finite and the infinite receives a different kind of definition in 'Œnone', another 1832 poem which was republished, substantially revised, in 1842.

3
The Abominable: 'Œnone'

Critical interest in 'Œnone' has proven less intense than Tennyson's own preoccupation with the poem. He worked and reworked 'Œnone' with an almost obsessive, certainly an extremely intricate, attention to detail. The manuscript variants of the work are legion. It is an important poem, central to the issue of Tennyson's early engagement with metaphysical issues.

The poem takes the classical legend of the Judgement of Paris as its subject. This story relates how all the gods, except Eris, goddess of Strife or Discord, were once invited to the marriage of Peleus and Thetis. Angry at her exclusion, Eris cast a golden apple, inscribed with the words 'For the most fair', amongst the guests. The goddesses Herè, Aphroditè, and Pallas Athena each claimed the apple for herself and Zeus ordered that the Trojan shepherd Paris, actually the second son of the King of Troy, should decide the dispute. Herè, wife of Zeus, offered Paris power in the world. Pallas, in the tradition followed by Tennyson, offered him wisdom. Aphroditè offered him the most beautiful of women for his wife. Paris awarded the golden apple to Aphroditè and the decision provoked in Herè and Pallas deep hostility towards all things Trojan. Under Aphroditè's protection Paris sailed to Greece and seized Helen, the wife of Menelaus and the most beautiful woman in the world. The abduction provoked the Trojan War. The War came to fulfil the dream of Paris' mother, Hecuba, before his birth, that she would bring forth a firebrand, the flames of which would consume the City of Troy. Tennyson's poem is spoken, on a midday shortly after the Judgement has happened, by Œnone, the wife whom Paris abandoned after his decision in favour of Aphroditè.

Tennyson has been seen to be using this classical legend in order to draw a very conventional moral about the war between Sense and Conscience. By this kind of reading the poem endorses a broadly Christian idea of the moral life: the idea that human beings, while tainted with sin, retain a freedom of will to control natural appetite and to act in the direction of a divinely sanctioned purity through obeying the dictates of conscience. The moral of 'Œnone' would be that Paris is at fault in choosing the sensuality of Aphroditè because, in so doing, he acts not according to the promptings of higher law but only according to lower impulse. Certainly, moral polarities are established in the poem in the form of the gifts offered to Paris by the three goddesses. Herè is committed to operating solely within the term of nature ('Power fitted to the season', 121). Douglas Bush noted in 1937 'the parallel between the substance and language of Herè's offer to Paris and *Paradise Regained*, III.255 ff' (Bush 1969: 204). The passage echoed by Tennyson is that in which Satan tempts Christ with a prospect of temporal power, an offer which Christ rejects as 'ostentation vain of fleshly arm' (387). Aphroditè, obviously, is associated with all that tempts to abandonment in the life of the senses. Pallas, however, insists that it is only through the exercise of ' "Self-reverence, self-knowledge, self-control" ' (142) that true power, the power to live in accordance with ethical rule, is achieved. Asserting that the will is a pure moral force which can remain uncompromised in the world, she rests on the belief that the human will is free to bring itself into the ' "perfect freedom" ' (164) of harmony with absolute law. But these moral polarities are not introduced uncritically into 'Œnone'. To approach the critical spirit in which they are held, I want first to refer to one of Tennyson's most important classical sources for 'Œnone', the *Heroides* of Ovid.

In the sixteenth epistle of the *Heroides* Paris declares to Helen the unquenchable fire of his love. He invokes the dream of his mother Hecuba in order to stress the inevitability of this love:

> I am in love . . . Thus have the fates decreed . . . Listen to words told faithfully and true. I was still in my mother's bosom . . . It seemed to her in the vision of a dream that she put forth from her full womb a mighty flaming torch. In terror she rose up, and told the dread vision of opaque night to ancient Priam; he told it to his seers. One of the seers sang that Ilion would burn with the fire of Paris – that was the torch of my heart, as now has come to pass!
>
> (*Heroides*, XVI.40b, 41a, 42–43a, 45–50)

The irony here and throughout this epistle is that, despite Paris' preoccupation with fire, he fails to grasp the more disturbing implication of

Hecuba's dream: that the fire of his love, or his lust, will ignite the fires of war that will ultimately consume Troy. In Œnone's own address to Paris, she describes his inconstancy – again in terms which foreshadow the burning of Troy – as the lightness of dried leaves or the 'tip of the spear of grain, burned light and crisp by ever-shining suns' (*Heroides*, V.111b–112). But it remains very clear that Ovid's Œnone 'remains chaste' (*Heroides*, V.133), that she does not succumb, like Paris, to a dangerous passion. In Ovid, fire as a conventional metaphor for the heats of love is used with specific reference to Paris, and through Paris is built a strict and limited application of the image to the literal fires of Troy.

Tennyson's poem does not, of course, forget the basic story of the fateful passion of Paris and the conflagration of Troy –

> the wild Cassandra . . . says
> A fire dances before her, and a sound
> Rings ever in her ears of armèd men.

> (259–61)

– but in 'Œnone' the principal and distinctive function of the imagery of fire is to define neither the situation of Paris nor that of Troy but, rather, Œnone's experience of herself after the Judgement:

> fiery thoughts
> Do shape themselves within me . . .

> (242–43)

Not only does Tennyson's Œnone burn after the Judgement but, at certain points, the poem presents the landscape in which she is set as being withered and consumed along with her. Stopford Brooke wrote in 1894 that 'we can no more divide Œnone from the Nature in which she is placed than we can separate the soul from the body of a friend' (Brooke 1894: 117). Landscape functions in a general sense in 'Œnone' as an index of Œnone's state of mind and feeling. Complementing this generalised figurative dimension of the landscape, there are also a number of distinct image-motifs. These appear largely, not entirely, within the landscape descriptions. The specifically symbolic elements in the verse enable Tennyson to intimate not only Œnone's state of mind and feeling but also her spiritual and moral condition.

The distinguishing physical characteristic of Œnone's world on the dawn of the Judgement day is a pristine coldness – specifically that of frozen snow:

> I waited underneath the dawning hills . . .
> Far up the solitary morning smote
> The streaks of virgin snow.

(46, 54–55)

The snow in this landscape is part of a symbolic strand in the poem which defines spiritual innocence and purity, ethical rectitude, through an imagery of cold. Of the three goddesses who arrive to be judged, it is, of course, Pallas who is associated with coldness:

> Pallas where she stood
> Somewhat apart, her clear and bared limbs
> O'erthwarted with the brazen-headed spear
> Upon her pearly shoulder leaning cold,
> The while, above, her full and earnest eye
> Over her snow-cold breast and angry cheek . . .

(135–40)

Throughout 'Œnone' the cold and snow identified with Œnone's virginal morning world and with the august and upright Pallas are set against an imagery of heat and fire. This imagery is related to a particular phase of the time scheme observed in the poem. It is when the sun has reached its zenith on the day of the Judgement – in the 'deep midnoon' (90) when the goddesses arrive – that the element of fire first appears in the landscape:

> Naked they came to that smooth-swarded bower,
> And at their feet the crocus brake like fire . . .

(93–94)

The moral connotations of the motif of heat and fire are apparent in the way that Aphroditè is presented, in contrast with the fixity of Pallas' 'snow-cold breast', in terms of fervid watery flow:

> Idalian Aphroditè beautiful,
> Fresh as the foam, new-bathed in Paphian wells,

> With rosy slender fingers backward drew
> From her warm brows and bosom her deep hair
> Ambrosial, golden round her lucid throat
> And shoulder: from the violets her light foot
> Shone rosy-white, and o'er her rounded form
> Between the shadows of the vine-bunches
> Floated the glowing sunlights, as she moved.

(170–78)

In the way that an imagery of fire and heat defines both sensual charge and the fires of war that Cassandra prophesies will consume Troy, Tennyson rehearses the image pattern of Ovid's *Heroides*. But, as I have suggested, the distinctive function of Tennyson's imagery of heat and fire is to define Œnone's experience of herself after the Judgement. While we know that Paris succumbs to Aphroditè's warm sensuality, we notice at the same time that on the afternoon of her song Œnone herself, losing control, becomes an intense, vibrantly anguished extreme of Aphroditè as elements of heat and water combine in the description of her desire for Paris:

> Most loving is she?
> Ah me, my mountain shepherd, that my arms
> Were wound about thee, and my hot lips prest
> Close, close to thine in that quick-falling dew
> Of fruitful kisses, thick as Autumn rains
> Flash in the pools of whirling Simois.

(197–202)

It is a deeply erotic passage, which defines the way in which Œnone is racked by energies of envy, jealousy and sexual desire. Tennyson's Œnone may not find another lover, but neither can she be said to remain emotionally and spiritually continent. Œnone's desperate abandonment here contrasts with the virginal frigidity of her dawn world on the day of the Judgement and with the sympathy she expresses for the ideals of self-knowledge and self-control when, in the course of the Judgement itself, she appeals to Paris to award the fruit to Pallas.

If Tennyson's poem is committed to exploring the failure of self-control in relation to Œnone, then a part of this attempt is its curious lack of clarity in its presentation of Paris' behaviour. That representation raises more questions than it answers about the moral issues at stake in the poem. Rather than being able to identify in Paris's actions the cause and explanation of Œnone's predicament after the Judgement, there is an important sense in which we are forced by Tennyson's handling of the story to look directly at Œnone's experience for insights into both her own and Paris's condition. This point turns, in the first place, on the fact that Tennyson's Judgement of Paris conceived as moral drama serves at once as an emblem of the Fall itself.

The contrast marked out in the poem between Œnone before and after the Judgement is that between a state of innocence and one of experience. The overall contrast is given detailed expression in the poem in Tennyson's transformation of a small item in Ovid. After the Judgement, Tennyson's Œnone complains that the pines of her valley were cut down. 'The germ' of this complaint, Paul Turner has observed, comes from the *Heroides* (V.41–42), where Œnone tells how her 'firs were felled, the timbers hewn'. In Ovid, Turner notes, 'Œnone's only objection to the felling of the pines is that it provides transport for Paris and Helen', while Tennyson gives her 'a more poetical attitude to trees' (Turner 1962: 66–67). But the matter is more interesting than that. In Tennyson's passage Œnone laments the loss as the passing of an early, unchartered world and of the integrity of being associated with that world:

> They came, they cut away my tallest pines,
> My tall dark pines, that plumed the craggy ledge
> High over the blue gorge, and all between
> The snowy peak and snow-white cataract
> Fostered the callow eaglet – from beneath
> Whose thick mysterious boughs in the dark morn
> The panther's roar came muffled, while I sat
> Low in the valley. Never, never more
> Shall lone Œnone see the morning mist
> Sweep through them; never see them overlaid
> With narrow moon-lit slips of silver cloud,
> Between the loud stream and the trembling stars.

(204–15)

Œnone's account of the environment which remains, and it is a notable example of Tennyson's talent for projecting psychic disturbance onto a desolated landscape, suggests a state of violated innocence, a condition of spiritual dislocation:

> I wish that somewhere in the ruined folds,
> Among the fragments tumbled from the glens,
> Or the dry thickets...
>
> (217–19)

The lapsarian connotations of Œnone's experience in Tennyson's version of the Judgement of Paris are highlighted during the course of the Judgement scene itself, when Œnone describes Paris's response to Herè's offer:

> She ceased, and Paris held the costly fruit
> Out at arm's length...
>
> (133–34)

The fruit is made out of 'pure Hesperian gold' (65), therefore costly; but there is also a reminiscence in the description of Christian metaphors concerning the price or wages of sin, the spiritual cost to man of eating the Forbidden Fruit. Tennyson draws on a traditional identification of the Apple of Strife with the fatal fruit of Eden. He further emphasises the importance of his Judgement of Paris as a type of Fall, and also directs us to the lapsarian connotations of the imagery of fire in his poem, precisely at that point in the narrative when the goddesses arrive to be judged:

> It was the deep midnoon...
> Naked they came to that smooth-swarded bower,
> And at their feet the crocus brake like fire,
> Violet, amaracus, and asphodel,
> Lotos and lilies: and a wind arose...
>
> (90, 93–96)

Christopher Ricks compares these lines with *Paradise Lost*, IV, lines 700–702, which deal with the *pre*-lapsarian bower of Adam and Eve:

> underfoot the violet,
> Crocus, and hyacinth with rich inlay
> Broidered the ground...

Ricks also notes that a draft version (in a manuscript fragment of 'Œnone' now in the Henry E. Huntington Library, California) of Tennyson's lines 94–95 above 'included further allusions to Milton' (Ricks 1987: I.426):

> That darkened all with violets underneath
> Thro' which like fire the sudden crocus came,
> Amaracus, immortal asphodel, ...

> (HM 19501; Ricks and Day 1987–93: XXVII.159)

But there is an even closer allusion in Tennyson to Adam and Eve's *post*-lapsarian condition in a bower in *Paradise Lost*, IX. 1036–41:

> ... Eve, whose eye darted contagious fire.
> Her hand he seized, and to a shady bank,
> Thick overhead with verdant roof embowered
> He led her nothing loth; flowers were the couch,
> Pansies, and violets, and asphodel,
> And hyacinth, earth's freshest softest lap.

It is the breaking out of a metaphorical fire amid a paradisal nature that is important and which distinguishes the account of this bower in Book IX from the original bower of Adam and Eve in Book IV. In *Paradise Lost* fire is something associated specifically with the change that takes place in the nature of human experience as a result of the Fall. Before the Fall, man was 'Guiltless of fire' (IX.392) in both a literal and a figurative sense. As in the passage from Book IX, fire is a symbol of the lower drives, the precursor of all those unruly forces which shake the human mind after the Fall: 'high passions, anger, hate, / Mistrust, suspicion, discord' (IX.1123–24). Fire does have a more positive aspect in *Paradise Lost* and is associated with the technology employed by post-lapsarian humanity in order to cope with a hostile natural environment so different from the benign pastoral world of Eden. But since the establishing of civilisation is itself necessitated only as a consequence of the Fall, fire, as an image of man's constructive abilities, inevitably retains a demonic and destructive aspect. When Adam is granted a vision of future human history before his expulsion from the Garden, he sees it afflicted with the pains of war and with the 'sulphurous fire' of besieged cities (XI.658). The lapsarian connotations of Tennyson's Judgement of Paris are underlined by the way the element of fire that breaks out in Œnone's bower echoes the fire that suddenly darts in Book Nine of *Paradise Lost*. And just as fire comes to define fallen human experience in *Paradise Lost*, so in Tennyson's poem fire goes on to define Œnone's spiritual decline, the transformation of her ideal pastoral world, and beyond that the destruction of Troy: 'the wild Cassandra... says / A fire dances before her, and a sound / Rings ever in her ears of armèd men' (259–61).

If there are Miltonic possibilities in the metaphorical fire which appears in the 'bower' at the 'deep midnoon' (92, 90) of Tennyson's Judgement day, then there are also parallels between the time of day specified by Tennyson for the Judgement and Milton's specification in *Paradise Lost* of the time of temptation on the day of the Fall:

> Mean while the hour of noon drew on, and waked
> An eager appetite...

> (IX.739–40)

Similarly, just as the stable world of Eden begins to suffer 'change' in *Paradise Lost* (X.213; XI.193) after the eating of the Forbidden Fruit, the herald of those many changes which will affect the state of humanity and creation as a consequence of the Fall, so Œnone complains of the 'change' (223) from her experience of the world before the Judgement.

Œnone's complaint brings us to the root complexity of Tennyson's poem. She wishes that she could find Eris, goddess of strife or discord:

> I wish that somewhere in the ruined folds,
> Among the fragments tumbled from the glens,
> Or the dry thickets, I could meet with her
> The Abominable, that uninvited came
> Into the fair Peleian banquet-hall,
> And cast the golden fruit upon the board,
> And bred this change; that I might speak my mind,
> And tell her to her face how much I hate
> Her presence, hated both of Gods and men.

> (217–25)

In Milton, neither Adam nor Eve would have sanction to make such a protest. They are both plainly responsible for disobeying the Divine command against eating the Forbidden Fruit. For Œnone, however, while she has experienced a change in both inner and outer worlds, she cannot locate a cause of that change in some act of her own will. If there were nothing more than a straightforward problem of an altered human relationship and a straightforward moral drama in the poem then we should expect Œnone to trace the origin of her discomfort simply and directly to Paris. That she does not do this returns us to the special aspects of Tennyson's treatment of the story of the Judgement of Paris. In the first place, as I have noted, there is a sense in which qualitative distinctions between Paris' and Œnone's behaviours are erased as we see Œnone, on the afternoon of her song, capitulating to Aphroditè's mode of being. By the absolute moral standards of Pallas, it is clear that Œnone, as she loses self-control, fails in a manner comparable to Paris and that there is a dimension of her experience after the Judgement for which he cannot be held simply responsible. Second, the question of the nature and origin of Œnone's pain is affected by Tennyson's representation of the processes by which Paris makes his own Judgement. It is a representation that raises questions about his moral responsibility. Tennyson's treatment of the events of the Judgement scene raises a doubt as to how far Paris may really be held accountable for his actions. Through his treatment of the Judgement scene Tennyson effectively removes Paris from consideration as the primary cause of Œnone's suffering.

The reader of 'Œnone' is not given the details of any decision-making process on Paris's part. While there is a fair amount of information in Œnone's recounting of the scene, there is a notable lack of clarity at critical points of the drama. Paris, we hear, was so taken with Herè's offer that he 'held the costly fruit / Out at arm's length, so much the thought of power / Flattered his spirit' (133–35). The gesture of proffering the fruit in this manner seems to represent a positive response to Herè. The reader might be forgiven for thinking that it represents a decision to award the fruit to her. It is not so. Œnone's speech moves directly into an account of Pallas's words: 'but Pallas where she stood . . . / . . . made reply' (135, 41). The reader is left entirely in the dark concerning the resolution of Paris's action of holding out the fruit. If it was not a ruling in favour of Herè then we are not shown the route by which Paris decides against his initial thought to hold the fruit out to her. He might, of course, simply be waiting to hear all three offers before coming to a decision. His action of stretching out his arm might be insignificant in itself. But such a reading, as I shall show, is not entirely satisfactory. After the end of Pallas's speech, we are told that Paris 'pondered' (165). But here Œnone intrudes with a plea to Paris to grant the fruit to Pallas. In her report of the events Œnone raises the possibility that Paris deliberately refused to heed her call ('he heard me not, / Or, hearing, would not hear me', 166–67). This would be first and foremost a decision to disregard Œnone rather than a direct refusal of Pallas. After Œnone's appeal, Aphroditè immediately moves into the picture. And, as in the case of Herè, events progress in the absence of any definite and explicit refusal to grant the fruit to Pallas. Once again, Paris may just be waiting to hear all three offers before reaching a conclusion. But then there is the matter of Œnone's acute apprehension regarding Aphroditè. Œnone relates that she shut her sight 'for fear' when Aphroditè 'spoke and laughed' (184). The reader might take this reaction as meaning that Paris has already definitely denied the fruit to Herè and Pallas. Because, if the issue is still genuinely open, it is not clear why Œnone should have such forebodings about Aphroditè. She may know her man only too well, of course. But even if this were the case, there remains a telling obscurity in the scene's representation of decision-making process. And even if we suppose either that Paris has already made up his mind, or that he is deferring judgement, there are further complications in the granting of the fruit to Aphroditè. Œnone says:

> I shut my sight for fear:
> But when I looked, Paris had raised his arm,
> And I beheld great Herè's angry eyes,
> As she withdrew . . .

(185–87)

Here, Paris no more than raises his arm and the drama is suddenly over. If we are to take this gesture as evidence of a decision in favour of Aphroditè, we might ask why Paris's positively outstretched arm to Herè should not have signalled just such a decision. There may have been a stage of deliberation accompanying the presentation of the fruit to Aphroditè which distinguishes this gesture from the earlier one. But, again, no details of it are presented. At no point in the Judgement scene are we presented with unmistakable and unambiguous decision and action. We have, in effect, a drama of judgement presented so indirectly as to force us at all times to assume or infer choice. The indistinctness of the fundamental processes of the Judgement scene gives rise to a sense of unreality about Paris's involvement with and responsibility for the developing pattern of the action (he maintains complete silence throughout the scene). It gives the impression that his supposed freedom of choice may be something of a fiction.

A central idea of the original legend is, after all, that Paris's career is a fated one, a theme which is evident in the story of Hecuba's dream before his birth. The idea is very clear in the *Epitome* of Appollodorus, where we find the notion that the Trojan war had long been planned by Zeus and that the events leading up to it, including the Judgement of Paris, all had a predetermined character. It appears that the idea of fate was not far from Tennyson's mind in his conception of 'Œnone'. In the 1832 version of the poem, Paris, showing the golden apple to Œnone before the Judgement, seems to have an inkling of the way things will turn out:

> Behold this fruit, whose gleaming rind ingrav'n
> 'For the most fair,' in aftertime may breed
> Deep evilwilledness of heaven and sere
> Heartburning toward hallowed Ilion;
> And all the colour of my afterlife
> Will be the shadow of today...

> (70–75)

Alterations to this passage written by the poet in a copy of the 1832 *Poems* now in the Tennyson Research Centre, Lincoln, show an attempt to strengthen the implication that a dark issue to the Judgement is in some sense a foregone conclusion. Making minor changes in lines 71 and 72 of the 1832 text, Tennyson inserted a line between lines 73 and 74 and substituted 'That' for 'And' at the beginning of line 74, so that the speech reads:

> Behold this fruit, whose gleaming rind ingrav'n
> 'For the most fair,' in years to come may breed
> Deep sense of injury from heaven and sere
> Heartburning toward hallowed Ilion;
> And in my mind I certainly foreknow
> That all the colour of my afterlife
> Will be the shadow of today...

> (Lincoln 1832 Revised Copy B; Ricks and Day
> 1987–93: XXIII.199)

In his later revisions of Paris's speech Tennyson omitted any direct reference to the dark fatefulness of Paris's career. Perhaps he thought it rather clumsily subversive of the overt drama of moral choice. But in a draft revision of the opening lines of the speech in a manuscript notebook at Trinity College, Cambridge, Tennyson drew attention to the inherent complexities in Paris's position as arbiter through reminding us of the manner in which he is – by virtue of the gods' own inability to decide – the heir of primordial strife in heaven. Tennyson emphasises, in other words, that the very grounds of Paris's new found freedom are infected with discord and confusion and that the apparent gift of a power to choose constitutes in itself a kind of curse:

> Behold this fruit, whose gleaming rind engrav'n
> 'For the most fair' among the happy Gods
> Breeds question & perplexeth Heaven with feud
> And unto me, selected arbiter
> To judge betwixt them, Here comes to-day...

> (Trinity Notebook 26; Ricks and Day 1987–93: XIII.51)

By the time he came to publish the revised version of 'Œnone' in 1842, Tennyson had resolved upon the following, more subtle indication of the fated tendency of Paris's life:

> Behold this fruit, whose gleaming rind ingraven
> 'For the most fair,' would seem to award it thine,
> As lovelier than whatever Oread haunt
> The knolls of Ida, loveliest in all grace
> Of movement...

> (70–74)

Paris expresses in these lines, more clearly than at any point in the Judgement scene, a preference regarding the person to whom he would award the fruit. But he cannot make the award to Œnone because he is caught up in a drama not of his own making. He must act out his part in a divine plan. By putting these words into Paris's mouth Tennyson quietly draws attention to the fact that, while Paris may have been given a role which appears to open up a realm of ethical choice, there are conditions attached to the dispensation which limit the nature and scope of his freedom.

Tennyson's handling of the Judgement scene allows for a level of meaning in the poem at which both Œnone and Paris may be seen to be caught up in a developing pattern of action for which they are not entirely responsible. It is wholly consistent with the larger meanings attached to the story of the Judgement of Paris in Tennyson's version that Œnone should direct the thrust of her protest not at her erstwhile lover but at Eris. The predicament Tennyson constructs for Œnone is one in which she enters a world of dispossession and pain but is without an adequate explanation of the origins of that condition. We are invited to look at Œnone's experience after the Judgement as imaging specifically the problems of a fallen world. Yet behind the presentation of this world there is no supporting Christian fable: no conception of evil as stemming from a personal rebellion against a personal rule, no God of absolute goodness and love, and no scheme of redemption. Behind the story of the Judgement of Paris lie only the capricious divinities of Greek mythology. As I noted earlier, the basic story of the Judgement of Paris recounts that all was well at the marriage-feast of Thetis and Peleus until Eris, seeking revenge for not having been invited to the ceremony, cast among the attendant gods the golden apple. Dispute broke out in heaven as to whom it should be awarded and since, for his own reasons, Zeus declined to arbitrate, it was agreed to delegate the decision to Paris. Stopford Brooke observed of Tennyson's Œnone: 'Her common sorrow is lifted almost into the proportions of Greek tragedy by its cause and its results. It is caused by a quarrel in Olympus, and the mountain-nymph is sacrificed without a thought to the vanity of the careless gods' (Brooke 1894: 119). 'Œnone' may not be Greek tragedy, but it dramatises a nineteenth-century sense of the tragic difficulty of living in a world unprotected by a Christian vision of divine justice and mercy.

The gods in 'Œnone' are important, of course, insofar as they reflect, in their fundamental anthropomorphism, qualities within the human condition itself; or insofar as the forces with which they are associated represent forces in nature. This is evident not only in the presentation of Pallas, Herè and Aphroditè, but also in the treatment of Eris.

The particular human significance of the first three goddesses emerges in the manner that they are associated with an imagery of water – the contrasting affiliations of the two most important figures, Pallas and Aphroditè, being with cold and with warm water respectively. This links them with the primary association that is made in the poem between Œnone and water. Tennyson's Œnone affirms that she is 'the daughter of a River-God' (37) and that her mother is 'many-fountained Ida' (22). Throughout the poem, water and the modifications of water constitute a symbolic motif through which Œnone's identity and changing experience are explored. Her spiritual development is symbolically registered as a movement, in the first place, from landscapes characterised by cold and frozen water to those characterised by warmth and flowing water. The final stage of her development is figured by desiccated landscapes. The 'dry thickets' (219) after the Judgement stand in simple contrast to the landscape on the morning before the Judgement when 'the mountain lawn was dewy-dark, / And dewy dark aloft the mountain pine' and when 'Far-off the torrent called me from the cleft' (47–48, 53). In their accommodation to the terms of the motif of water the goddesses complement the use of landscape in the symbolic representation of tendencies of Œnone's own being. And if, at a dramatic level, the god-desses define the overt terms of the moral drama as it relates to Paris, then through the imagery of water they involve Œnone in that drama. As I have suggested, the peculiar assumption of Tennyson's poem is that the problems of the Judgement scene are problems of Œnone's experi-ence of herself. The demonstration at a symbolic level of Œnone's engagement with the issues and tensions of that scene is reinforced by the manner in which she does, to a degree, actively participate in the drama. There is the instance of her intrusion in support of Pallas, but more than this there is the prevailing tone of her account of Aphroditè in lines 170–78 (quoted pp. 50–51). In this passage, Œnone's nervous apprehension concerning the charms of Aphroditè combines with and perhaps springs from the fact that she is herself clearly deeply affected by the sensual beauty of the goddess. The entranced, admiring rhythms of her descrip-tion may tell us little about Paris's reaction to Aphroditè, but they quite directly betray Œnone's own. If we are looking for evidence of a tension between the claims of Pallas and those of Aphroditè within Œnone herself, evidence of a shift in her disposition away from the frigid purity of the dawn and with Pallas before her afternoon display of the exagger-ated features of an Aphroditè, then it is here that we find it, although there is no question of her response being presented as something which involves a freely willed decision to change allegiance.

With regard to the treatment of Eris in lines 217–25 (quoted p. 55), we find that at the same time as the literal, dramatic terms of the story are preserved, Eris's distinct identity as a personification of Strife is dissolved so that she may appear simply a fact of human experience, a reality inherent in the order of things. It is not because Eris has literally entered Œnone's world and then literally disappeared again that Œnone cannot find her to accuse her to her face. Nor is it merely that she is unavailable because she began a chain of events which led to Œnone's sorrow in some place quite removed from Ida. As Œnone says, Eris is immediately at hand in her world, but only in the sense that she is a 'presence' (225) diffused temporally and spatially throughout that world. The point of Œnone's complaint, a point perhaps emphasised by the fact that Œnone never actually addresses her by name, is that Eris is inscrutable in personal terms. Discord may be a pressing reality of Œnone's experience after the Judgement but she is destined to be frustrated in her attempt to identify any individual first cause of the phenomenon. As an ineluctable presence the most that discord is allowed in Œnone's song is the status of a capital-ised abstraction: 'The Abominable' (220). It is as such a presence that Eris is 'hated both of Gods and men' (225). A detail of the classical story, the exclusion of Eris from the list of wedding guests, acquires a special signifi-cance in the context of Œnone's metaphysical complaint. Œnone's use of the word 'uninvited' (220) to describe Eris at once contains the literal meaning of the classical story and points to the absence of any willing invitation to evil on the part either of men or of gods as men.

If the portrayal of the events of the Judgement scene leaves us uncertain as to the precise nature of the process by which both Œnone and Paris 'fall', then there is some indication, in the presentation of the midnoon landscape, that the energies which characterise their experience after the Judgement are derived by an organic process of evolution out of their pre-Judgement world.

The spiritual focus of Œnone's dawn world is indicated, as I have men-tioned, through its association with water and especially with frozen water: 'the solitary morning smote / The streaks of virgin snow' (54–55). Here, the symbolic connotations of spiritual and moral purity combine with suggestions of a natural form of stability and firmness of definition, although our attention is called to the threat presented to the cold fixity of that state by the rising of the sun. In Œnone's later account of her beloved dawn world (204–15) water and snow appear again: 'all between / The snowy peak and snow-white cataract / Fostered the callow eaglet' (206–208). In the same passage we also note Œnone's fond regard for the 'narrow moon-lit slips of silver cloud' (214). At the noon of the Judgement day one of these clouds appears again, no longer moon-lit but held in the glare of the ascendant sun:

> It was deep midnoon: one silvery cloud
> Had lost his way between the piney sides
> Of this long glen. Then to the bower they came,
> Naked they came to that smooth-swarded bower,
> And at their feet the crocus brake like fire.
> Violet, amaracus, and asphodel,
> Lotos and lilies: and a wind arose
> And overhead the wandering ivy and vine,
> This way and that, in many a wild festoon
> Ran riot . . .

(90–99)

Martin Dodsworth has observed that 'The cloud and Œnone are both lost at this moment of the story. The cloud is out of its element in the fire of the sun, as Œnone is out of hers when Paris draws the fiery goddesses to him' (Dodsworth 1969: 32). It is true that the cloud is intimately associated through the element of water with Œnone. Yet the important point about this cloud mislaid under the midday sun is that it is not an isolated symbol of Œnone but that it belongs to a dawn landscape. It is Œnone's cold and watery dawn landscape which is out of place here in the midnoon. There are, in fact, two landscapes, or conditions of landscape, in this scene. One is astray and out of place at midnoon and looks back through the silvery cloud to the early part of the Judgement day. The other is one where the sun finds an answering fire in the crocus and where the ivy and vine are directed out of their wandering into a riot. The fundamental contrast in this passage is not between the wateriness of the cloud and of Œnone, on one hand, and the fire of the goddesses, on the other, but between two landscapes, both symbolic of Œnone's psychological and spiritual being. Martin Dodsworth reads the firelike appearance of the crocus as the fieriness of the goddesses. But the arrival of the goddesses is not presented simply as a destructive influx of energy: the active verb 'brake' establishes the impression, rather, of a release of energy. The violent appearance of the crocus is linked with the other manifestation of energy in the scene: the wind which produces the riot of nature. The manner in which this wind *arises* again points not to a simple invasion but to an eruption of potencies latent within Œnone's pastoral world. That we do not merely have an alien power disrupting the perfect equanimity of an unsuspecting world, but a development intrinsic to that world is evident in the manner in which the cloud, the ivy, and the vine are lost and wandering, pressing for somewhere to go, *before* the goddesses arrive. There is a delicate restlessness about the little cloud poised and waiting above the valley which indicates that the stillness of the scene before the arrival of the goddesses is to some extent illusory, that it is not a condition of settled tranquillity or of peaceful repletion. There is at the outset suspense as well as suspension in the brooding heat of midnoon. The idea that the metaphorical fire of the crocus is intrinsic to the landscape is apparent also from the fact that the goddesses are not themselves associated indiscriminately with the element of fire. They all share in Œnone's imagery of water. But in terms of the symbolic properties of landscape in this scene it is clear that Pallas's affinities are with the cloud that comes from Œnone's dawn world while it is Aphroditè who is to be associated with the fiery element in the midnoon landscape. Although the landscape with its fire and the arrival of the goddesses are intimately related phenomena, they are related principally in the sense that the goddesses (with their contrasting attributes) and the landscape(s) in which they appear are complementary symbolic embodiments of one spiritual drama. The symbolic cold and heat of Pallas and Aphroditè respectively are paralleled in the contrast between the cloud of Œnone's dawn world and the fire of the crocus. Both the events of the Judgement scene and the presentation of the landscape at midnoon record a movement towards the predominance of a symbolic heat over a symbolic cold.

There is a special significance in the enactment at the level of the natural setting of the movement from the frigidity of 'purity' to the warmth of 'impurity'. The close relationship maintained throughout the poem between literal and symbolic dimensions of landscape description, together with Tennyson's representation of forces breaking out of the landscape at midnoon, have one major effect. This is to establish a fundamental correlation between the principle of development governing the transition from spiritual purity to impurity and the principle of natural development which determines the unfolding of the natural day. The warmth of midday is carefully anticipated in the account (54–55; quoted, p. 50) of the sun's light striking the virgin snow of the early morning. Tennyson's concern to establish a picture of the evaporation of morning coldness is evidenced in a draft version of the lines in a manuscript in the Huntington Library, California (HM 19501): 'Far-up the lonely morning lit the streaks / Of virgin snow' (Ricks and Day 1987–93: XXVII.160). It follows, of course, that by the time of its ascendancy in the midnoon the sun must have completed its work of dispersing the cold freshness of the morning. And there is the implication that by the same process as the natural chill of the morning is dissolved, the spiritual innocence symbolised by that morning condition is also lost. There is a recapitulation of this development in the midnoon scene itself, where we see a conflation of the dawn to noon phase of the daily cycle in the way that a morning landscape represented by the lost cloud is displaced by a landscape more appropriate to the midday in its association with the element of fire. Again it appears that just as the midday is the natural crucible in which the cold realities of the morning finally evaporate, so the spiritual bearings of Œnone's dawn world are lost and give way to the more complicated reality represented by heat and fire.

While the element of fire appears in the landscape at midnoon it is necessary for fire to combine with water in order that the poem's basic motif involving water may be completed. The realisation of the symbolic movement from frozen water to flowing water occurs on the afternoon of Œnone's song when we find elements of heat and water associated in an image of psychological and spiritual disintegration which involves not only the idea of a flowing of water but also that of its draining away. It is the scene of Œnone's intemperate desire for Paris:

> Ah me, my mountain shepherd, that my arms
> Were wound about thee, and my hot lips prest
> Close, close to thine in that quick-falling dew
> Of fruitful kisses, thick as Autumn rains
> Flash in the pools of whirling Simois.

> (198–202)

The strange and disconcerting quality of this image arises out of its combination of the autumnal (rich, fruitful, culminative) with the meaningless loss of fullness in the river. For Œnone, thought and feeling here no longer exist in a balanced and mutually supportive relation. Instead, an oddly precise intellectual control shapes an emotional loss of control. Although the exaggeration of the images points to the disturbance in Œnone's mind, there remains a rational and precisely ordered associative movement from the thought of the pressure of hot lips to the image of fruitful kisses which in turn are seen to be of an autumnal density. What is unusual is that the transition between these images of fulfilment is effected through an imagery of fluid descent and dissipation. The quick-falling *dew* becomes the thick *rains* which 'Flash' in the *pools* of the 'whirling' *river*. By the incremental development of this motif of waste, increase becomes an increase in loss and the rate of change at which the possibilities of stabilisation are undercut is dizzying. Amidst all this fluidity the word 'Flash' maintains the theme of consumption by fire through its connotation of the processes of ignition and combustion. From the winding arms of Œnone to the whirling of the Simois the passage brilliantly enacts the vertiginously self-undermining processes of intensely willed and acutely introverted experience.

The correspondence Tennyson draws in 'Œnone' between an interior, spiritual development and natural processes of change may be compared with Milton's rendering of the transition in Eden from the state of innocence to that of experience. In *Paradise Lost* there is figurative significance attached to the time of the day at which the Fall occurs. The noon is the hour at which Eve would naturally be most hungry. But, as Alastair Fowler has commented, Milton means merely 'to run excitingly close to a tragedy of necessity' (Fowler 1971: 482). However much Eve's appetitive urge might be greatest at midday, the point of the fable is that over and above her bodily nature she has a spiritual constitution which ought to remain unaffected by natural instincts. In stressing a midnoon hunger Milton connects only Eve's 'lower' nature with the rhythms of the natural world. She remains free to insist on the integrity of her spiritual being. This is demonstrated by the fact that between presenting the initial appeal of the fruit to her senses, and his presentation of her act of eating it, Milton is careful to interpose a precise and detailed account of the deliberative process through which Eve passes. In 'Œnone' it is of critical importance – as a poem avowedly dealing with the question of the contradictory demands of law and impulse – that Tennyson neither presents distinct acts of will on the parts of Paris and Œnone nor leaves room for a clear distinction between a natural and a spiritual reality. The idea that spiritual and moral values of purity have an absolute, objective grounding in a realm transcending the order of the nature is called into question as we see a close correspondence established between those values and the relative physical stability of early morning cold. Given the parallels drawn in the poem between a spiritual development and the unfolding of natural phenomena across a natural day, there is in the image of the state of purity an implication that its integrity is something which simply cannot be protected from the processes of the natural world. As a representation of the dynamic of the fall, Tennyson's Judgement of Paris in 'Œnone' moves very close indeed to a tragedy of necessity as we see an equivalence maintained between the loss of innocence and an unavoidable process of natural development. Far from being a conventional allegory of moral choice, 'Œnone' shows Tennyson engaged with the idea that the exercise of the moral faculty may be inextricably bound up with and may be conditioned and limited by the natural man to a degree not allowed for in traditional, essentially Christian, concepts of conscience and free-will.

Tennyson's use in 'Œnone' of two levels of landscape description – the literal and the symbolic – also enables him to explore a disjunction between Œnone's being and nature's literal rejuvenatory cycle. Whereas the natural warmth of the Judgement day midnoon must gradually subside, Œnone, on the afternoon when she sings her song, continues to burn as evening and darkness draw near. Before the Judgement, the harmony and completeness of Œnone's relationship with the surrounding world are stressed. The reciprocity between the two is indicated by the highly personal terms in which Œnone describes her pre-Judgement landscape (the torrent calling her from the cleft, the sense of intimacy with her pines). As we come upon her at the opening of her song we find her in the predicament of having to adjust to a distressing self-consciousness, a consciousness of her isolation and estrangement from the natural world:

> The grasshopper is silent in the grass:
> The lizard, with his shadow on the stone,
> Rests like a shadow, and the winds are dead.
> The purple flower droops: the golden bee
> Is lily-cradled: I alone awake.
> My eyes are full of tears...
> And I am all aweary of my life.

(25–30, 32)

At the same time as Tennyson's picture of Œnone's loss of pastoral bliss counterpoints the Christian myth of the Fall from Eden, it echoes a Romantic tendency to conceive of the fall as a loss of innocence resulting from man's loss of unselfconscious unity with nature.

Paul Turner notes that Œnone's grand appeal –

> Hear me, O Earth, hear me, O Hills, O Caves
> That house the cold crowned snake! O mountain brooks...

(35–36)

– 'echoes that of Prometheus in Aeschylus [*Prometheus Bound*, 88–91], and even more closely Shelley's version of it' in *Prometheus Unbound* (1819), I.25–29 (Turner 1962: 60–61). The Shelleyan echo is entirely apt to 'Œnone' since, as Harold Bloom has written, one of the major meanings of Prometheus's 'cosmic cry' is that he 'describes mankind's (and his own) situation as being a fallen one... Nature is fallen and fragmented, man is fallen from himself, experience rules, relationship is nowhere to be seen' (Bloom 1969: 100–101). Prometheus's suffering is, of course, a type of humankind's, whose cause he champions, but there is no simple opposition between Jupiter and Prometheus in Shelley's re-working of the ancient myth. Jupiter defines the negative potentialities of human nature and hence, like other actors in the drama, he embodies an aspect of Prometheus's own nature. With Prometheus's receipt of the gift of knowledge, symbolically associated according to tradition with the gift of fire, came a terrible miscreation of the human will. As the Furies – the

'torturing and conflicting throngs' sent by Jupiter but 'within' (I.493)
Prometheus – torment the Titan, the Chorus sings:

> Dost thou boast the clear knowledge thou waken'dst for man?
> Then was kindled within him a thirst which outran
> Those perishing waters; a thirst of fierce fever,
> Hope, love, doubt, desire, which consume him for ever.

> (I.542–45)

But if, as Asia says, it is not Jove 'who rains down / Evil' (II.iv.100–101),
if Jupiter as an aspect of Prometheus is not himself the evil principle,
there is no further explanation offered in the poem concerning the origin
of evil. After her impassioned request for an explanation, Asia accepts
Demogorgon's assertion that 'the deep truth is imageless' (II.iv.116).
The question regarding the cause of the fall cannot be answered,
except to know that it is *love* and not hate which is the governing
power of the universe. Shelley's poem is largely optimistic. Assuming a
fallen world at its very start it is almost entirely concerned with the
processes of redemption. We learn that while Prometheus has for ages
resisted the tyranny of Jupiter's nature, he has shared in that nature
through a resistance founded on a hateful curse. If he has kept at bay
the side of himself represented by Jupiter, in his dependence on hate
he has also been separated from Asia, who was his original love in the
pastoral golden age and who is associated with all the positive aspects
of his being. At the opening of the poem, we come upon Prometheus
just at the point when he repents of his curse. This is an act of will, an
act of imagination, creative of a transformation in his own state and in
the world at large. At the repentance is set in motion the return of Asia
to Prometheus and the same hour witnesses Jupiter's consignment to
the void, leaving room for 'Love, from its awful throne of patient
power' to fold 'over the world its healing wings' (IV.557, 561). The
point of Shelley's Romantic myth of reintegration is that man possesses
the capacity to redeem himself:

> Man...
> Whose nature is its own divine control...

> (IV.400–401)

The Shelleyan echo in Œnone's appeal underlines her situation after the
Judgement as that of a consciousness in a fallen world. In his treatment

of Œnone's experience Tennyson is also preoccupied with the question of individual responsibility for imposing shape and meaning on the world. At first almost completely overwhelmed by the change in her state, and wishing only to retreat from a confusion worse than death, Œnone nevertheless struggles to adjust to a new reality. The slowness of the pace of her song enacts the difficulty she finds in attempting to make the adjustment. The act of singing is itself therapeutic:

> I will speak, and build up all
> My sorrow with my song...
> That, while I speak of it, a little while
> My heart may wander from its deeper woe.

(38–39, 42–43)

But the affirmations of Shelley's *Prometheus Unbound* are not felt in 'Œnone' as a whole. Placing Œnone in a fallen and fragmented world and sustaining her with no fable of a sympathetic higher power, Tennyson shows equal scepticism about the idea of the individual mind's capacity to regenerate itself. Tennyson's imagery of fire in 'Œnone' bears certain specifically post-Romantic possibilities. In *The Excursion* Wordsworth celebrated the self-derived authority and autonomous life of the individual imagination by comparing it to a moon which 'Burns, like an unconsuming fire of light' (IV.1065). But the imagery of fire as a consumptive agent was to become important to writers attempting to cope with the plight of the individual consciousness that has lost a sense of participation in a whole, the consciousness that has outgrown the unselfconscious integrity of the primitive or natural state or is bereft of an inclusive system of thought and belief about the world. In 1831 Carlyle diagnosed the spiritual malady of contemporary culture as one in which self-consciousness has disrupted the completeness of man's being, and in which human energy does not pass directly into the objective realm of action but impotently consumes itself in thought:

> We stand here too conscious of many things...The Thought conducts not to the Deed; but in boundless chaos, self-devouring, engenders monstrosities, phantasms, fire-breathing chimeras.
> (Tennyson, G.B. 1984: 69, 90)

The tautology 'burning fire', in the last line of 'Œnone', points with intense economy to the manner in which the introversion of the dispossessed mind repeats and undercuts itself to result only in a sense of meagreness and deprivation:

> wheresoe'er I am by night and day,
> All earth and air seem only burning fire.

(263–64)

This last line of the poem is not merely the expression of tortured self-consciousness in a broken world. It is the fire of a scepticism which allows no possibility of respite from that world.

The metaphoric and sensuous poetic mode of 'The Hesperides', 'The Lotos-Eaters', 'Tithonus' and 'Œnone', has antecedents, as I mentioned in the opening chapter, in the poetic manner of much Romantic poetry. But there is an emergent scepticism about idealist affirmation in the Keats of the *Odes* as well as at certain points, such as 'Alastor' (1816), in Shelley's verse. Through the questioning frame of reference that controls the arguments of 'The Hesperides', 'The Lotos-Eaters', 'Tithonus' and 'Œnone', Tennyson confirms and develops this sceptical strain and turns the language of mythopoeia against itself. If the energies of scepticism enable Tennyson to recast public symbols and fables in some of his shorter poems, then the same energies galvanise those of his long poems which work with a spiritual autobiographical form. Tennyson's variations on this form, in *Maud* and even in *In Memoriam*, involve a dramatisation of the first-person voice that is central to narratives of personal development. The same principle of dramatisation is present in *The Lover's Tale*, the subject of the next chapter and which, as I noted in the Introduction, establishes an imaginative strategy that reappears in both *In Memoriam* and *Maud*. It is by means of this strategy that, in *In Memoriam*, Tennyson attempts to overcome the kinds of discontinuity laid out in works such as 'The Hesperides' and 'Œnone', and it is by the same strategy that he redefines those discontinuities and a continuing inability to resolve them in *Maud*.

4

The Archetype: *The Lover's Tale* (1832)

The story of the composition and publication of *The Lover's Tale* is, unfortunately, rather complicated. My critical discussion of the poem demands, however, a preliminary outline of the main episodes in the story (for further details, see Ricks 1987: I.325–28; Wise 1908: I.25–76; Paden 1965: 111–45).

I

The Lover's Tale was first published by Tennyson in May 1879. This *1879* version in four parts is the authorised text. But Tennyson had begun composition of the work many years before and had originally intended to include early versions of Parts I and II of *1879* in his 1832 *Poems*. These two parts even went to proof, for inclusion in the 1832 volume, but at the last minute Tennyson withdrew them. 'You must be point blank mad' wrote Arthur Hallam when he heard of his friend's decision (Kolb 1981: 688). Tennyson did not change his mind. But he did cause several copies of his incomplete two-part poem to be made up separately and privately printed (hereafter referred to as the *1832* text of the poem). After 1832 Tennyson continued to work, intermittently, on the poem. In 1835, for example, he entered revisions in a copy of *1832* which is now in the British Library (Ashley 2075; Ricks and Day 1987–93: XXV.58–88; Wise 1908: I.28–29). But it seems that it was not until 1868 that he resumed seriously intensive work on the poem. In that year he had it privately printed in three parts (hereafter *1868*), with the first two parts corresponding to Parts I and II in *1832* and *1879*, and the third part constituting a version of what was to become Parts III and IV in *1879* (Lincoln P110 and P111 in Ricks and Day 1987–93: XVIII.43–178). Once again, Tennyson decided against publication. In 1869, however, he had the entire poem (without any division into parts) printed up in early sets of proofs for his volume *The Holy Grail and Other Poems* (Lincoln P200† in Ricks and Day 1987–93: XX.123–56). On this occasion Tennyson decided against publishing what were to form Parts I, II and III of *1879*, but did manage to include in the *Holy Grail* volume – under the title 'The Golden Supper' – the section which was to form Part IV of *1879*. Finally, spurred by the bibliographer R.H. Shepherd's pirated printing in 1875 of the *1832* state of *The Lover's Tale*, Tennyson published the whole work in 1879.

Part III of *1879* presents particular problems. In his headnote to *1879* Tennyson noted, with reference to the *1832* text, that 'Two only of the three parts then written were printed, when, feeling the imperfection of the poem, I withdrew it from the press.' For a long time it was thought that Part III of *1879* was not to be identified with the early third part of the poem mentioned by Tennyson. But in an article published in 1967 Clarice Short observed that a complete autograph draft – datable to the early 1830s – of what was to become Part III in *1879* is extant in a manuscript notebook in the Houghton Library, Harvard University (Harvard Notebook 12; Ricks and Day 1987–93: II.215–16; Short 1967). My discussion of *The Lover's Tale* assumes, then, that the 1832 state of the poem comprises Parts I and II of the *1832* printed text, and the material which now forms Part III of *1879*. Though it was in three parts, the 1832 *Lover's Tale* was not a complete work and there is no evidence to suggest that Tennyson had written a conclusion at that date. The concluding Part IV of *1879* – 'The Golden Supper' – was composed in the period immediately prior to the *1868* printing. It constituted, as Tennyson observed in his *1879* headnote, a work of his 'mature life'.

Even when measured by the long gestation periods of many of Tennyson's poems (*In Memoriam*, for example), the more than thirty-five years between the 1832 state of *The Lover's Tale* and the writing up of a conclusion is a remarkably long gap. Part IV, 'The Golden Supper', has long been felt to be an awkwardly contrived sequel which does not blend convincingly with the first three parts of the poem. Clarice Short, for example, remarked that it was written 'in a different emotional country... It requires such a warping of the setting, such alteration of the social position of the characters that it seems like an excrescence upon the body of the rest of the poem' (Short 1967: 79–80).

Since I am interested in *The Lover's Tale* primarily in its relation to *In Memoriam* and *Maud* (both published, of course, well before the concoction of 'The Golden Supper') I shall speak principally of *The Lover's Tale* as it stood in 1832; in its earliest coherent, albeit incomplete, form.

In respect of Parts I and II, I shall refer to the text of *1832*, since the *1879* versions were substantially revised (though without alteration of the basic story). Most of the major modifications which appeared in final form in *1879* were initiated in the period immediately prior to the *1868* printing. They are, in other words, mostly of a date corresponding with Tennyson's 'mature' composition of a conclusion to the poem, and they reflect his distinct imaginative and conceptual orientation at that time. In respect of Part III of the poem, there are only minor textual variations between the draft material noted by Clarice Short in Harvard Notebook 12 and the text of *1879*, so in this instance I shall cite *1879*.

In his edition of Tennyson's poems, Christopher Ricks gives all variant readings from the *1832* printed text in the notes to his presentation of *The Lover's Tale* of 1879. But the following discussion refers to the *1832* text as reproduced in facsimile in *The Tennyson Archive* (Ricks and Day 1987–93: XXV.58–88). This is the British Library copy of *1832* and the facsimile provides a reading text of the poem. In the passages quoted, *1832* line numbers are cited together with the equivalent *1879* line numbers given in square brackets.[1]

II

The plot of *The Lover's Tale* as it stood in 1832 in simple enough. In Part I, we come upon the speaker – the lover-protagonist – of the poem as he relates the story of his past life to a group of unspecified companions. He is himself nameless ('Julian', *1879*) but tells how he was brought up with his foster-sister Cadrilla ('Camilla', *1879*) and of the manner in which their childhood closeness turned into his youthful love for her. We hear of his distress upon being told by Cadrilla that she was in love with another man – Lionel. The second part of the poem tells of the protagonist's withdrawal into solitude and of the unsettling of his mind following Cadrilla's revelation. The third part continues with a further account of his disturbed mental condition.

Whatever the melodrama of the literal story, there moves beneath the surface of the narrative a psychological drama whose terms Edmund Gosse was quick to identify even in the much revised *1879* version of the poem. Reviewing *The Lover's Tale* in *The Academy* for 7 June 1879, and apparently unaware that the poem had first taken shape within what was the charged Shelleyan atmosphere of Tennyson's undergraduate career, Gosse discerned in the work the influence of a 'recent reading of *Epipsychidion*' (p. 489). In one move Gosse had identified the principal influence on *The Lover's Tale*: Shelley. There was Shelley and there was also, to a lesser but not insignificant degree, Keats.

Hallam Tennyson records his father denying, in his old age, the influence of Shelley on *The Lover's Tale*: ' "As for *The Lover's Tale*, that was written before I had ever seen a Shelley"' (Tennyson, Hallam 1897: II.285). But this cannot be simply true. In the headnote to the *1832* text of *The Lover's Tale* Tennyson noted that the poem 'was written in my nineteenth year', a year which would have fallen between August 1827 and August 1828. This agrees, in part, with the surviving evidence of Tennyson's composition of the poem, where the earliest substantial draft of Part I of the poem appears in a manuscript (Harvard Notebook 8, Houghton Library, Harvard University) which Tennyson was using in 1828.[2] Tennyson's 'written' must, of course, be taken to mean 'begun' in his nineteenth year, 1827–1828: 'Since Tennyson was manifestly dissatisfied, he must have worked at it until 1832' (Ricks 1987: I.327). Tennyson went up to Cambridge in November 1827 and he could not, in the course of his first year at the University, have failed to register the intense enthusiasm for Shelley amongst many of the students, and not just members of the Apostles. In his letter of November 1828 to W.E. Gladstone (quoted p. 18), shortly after arriving in Cambridge, Arthur Hallam noted the poetic taste of the Cambridge Union: 'at the present day *Shelley* is the idol before which we are to be short by the knees' (Kolb 1981: 245). At this very early stage in his Cambridge career, Hallam claimed not to value Shelley's poetry. But six months later he was, as his Eton compatriot William Windham Farr observed, 'a furious Shelleyist' (Kolb 1981: 247). It is plain that Tennyson, too, must have begun absorbing Shelley across his first year at Cambridge, his nineteenth year. Margaret Lourie has pointed out the Shelleyan echoes in a number of poems published in Tennyson's 1830 *Poems, Chiefly Lyrical* (Lourie 1979). In particular, she notes that it is specifically from 'Alastor' that Tennyson 'borrows', in 'Recollections of the Arabian Nights', Shelley's 'vehicle for the journey downward into self' (Lourie 1979: 11). 'Recollections of the Arabian Nights' appears in draft in a manuscript, dated 'January 1828' by Tennyson, at Trinity College, Cambridge (Trinity Notebook 18; Ricks and Day 1987–93: XII.3), together with other poems identifiable as having been written in 1828 (for example, 'Among some Nations Fate hath placed too far', a sonnet which is dated 1828 in the commonplace books of Tennyson's Cambridge associates J.M. Heath and John Allen; Ricks and Day 1987–93: XXIX.7 and XV.249). Trinity Notebook 18 also contains an extensive draft of part of the 1832 *Lover's Tale* (see Appendix), a text which Paul Turner has demonstrated 'is full of Shelleyan echoes' (Turner 1976: 57).

Quite why Tennyson should have wanted to dissociate *The Lover's Tale* from Shelley is not entirely clear. It may have been an impulse to confound literary source hunters. But Tennyson also made apologies for the 'immaturity' of *The Lover's Tale* ('the boy's work', as he put it in his *1879* headnote). Somewhere, perhaps, in Tennyson's 'mature' reaction against the idea of a relationship between Shelley and *The Lover's Tale*, there may be an older, high Victorian's view of the young Romantic as the poet of adolescent enthusiasm: Matthew Arnold's ' "beautiful and ineffectual angel, beating in the void his luminous wings in vain" ' (Super 1960–77: XI.327). But whatever Tennyson's later caution, the younger Tennyson clearly felt no reservation about Shelley, as he himself said in later life. In 1880 William Allingham recorded Tennyson's response to an observation made by Aubrey de Vere:

> De V. – 'Shelley used to be a great idol of yours'.
> T. – 'O yes . . . *Alastor* was the first poem of his I read. I said, "This is what I want!" '

> (Allingham 1967: 295)

In the 1860s Tennyson had declared to Frederick Locker-Lampson: ' "Nobody admires Shelley more than I once did . . . I think I like his *Epipsychidion* [1821] as much as anything by him" ' (Tennyson, Hallam 1897: II.70). At any rate, Shelley had an impact on the 1832 *Lover's Tale*. And this is not just a matter of the large number of verbal and phrasal echoes of the kind noted by Paul Turner. It involves, as I shall show, the psychological allegory that founds the poem.

III

The Lover's Tale is the earliest of what came to be Tennyson's three long poetic disquisitions upon love. Together with *In Memoriam* and *Maud*, *The Lover's Tale* adopts a dramatic autobiographical form in order to explore the matter of love. This is love seen not just as a human emotion but as the power which (debatably) orders the universe itself. *The Lover's Tale*, much influenced by Shelley, is conditioned, probably mainly through Shelley's example, by an idealist, Platonic conception of love. When, in Section XCV of *In Memoriam*, Tennyson recounted something like a mystical encounter with the ultimate principle of reality, he described the experience as a coming upon 'that which is' (*In Memoriam*, XCV.39). The source of this formula is Plato. Churton Collins glossed the expression as: 'Ultimate reality, the Platonic Tò ὄντωχὄν' (Collins 1902: 104); while Alan Sinfield observes that three passages from Plato's *Phaedo* and his great dialogue on Love, the *Symposium*, are 'precisely recalled' (Sinfield 1976: 249). Invoking Plato at this point of *In Memoriam*, Tennyson was drawing on a familiarity with Platonic thought that would have stemmed, to a significant degree, at least, from his exposure at Cambridge in the late 1820s and early 1830s to Shelley and Shelleyan platonism. Arthur Hallam himself, as well as being an enthusiastic Shelleyist within six months of his arrival at Cambridge, was also an exponent of Plato and of Plato's understanding that, as Hallam put it in his 1831 'Essay on the Philosophical writing of Cicero', '[t]he soul of man ... partook ... of the ... nature of Divinity' (Motter 1943: 159). Nor was it just a matter of the impact on Tennyson's imagination of Shelley's Platonically oriented poetry – particularly, as we have heard Tennyson himself recalling, 'Alastor' and 'Epipsychidion'. Shelley's prose writings on love were also plainly important to him. Shelley's prose fragment 'On Love', first published in 1828 for the 1829 issue of *The Keepsake*, an annual to which Tennyson himself was to contribute 'St Agnes' Eve' in 1836 (for the 1837 issue), is a model for a crucial passage in the 1832 *Lover's Tale* (I.62–88) that was significantly altered in the *1879* text of the poem [I.*55–69, 70–85].

To take Shelley's poetry first: both 'Alastor' and 'Epipsychidion' have male protagonists who are associated with a female presence that stands as a figure of their own inmost selves. The narrator of 'Alastor' tells us about the visionary-protagonist of the poem:

> A vision on his sleep
> There came, a dream of hopes that never yet
> Had flushed his cheek. He dreamed a veilèd maid
> Sate near him, talking in low solemn tones.
> Her voice was like the voice of his own soul
> Heard in the calm of thought; its music long ...
> Knowledge and truth and virtue were her theme ...
>
> (149–54, 158)

Unfortunately, this access to the promptings of his own soul is not something which the visionary can sustain beyond the realm of dream or reverie:

> he started from his trance...
> 　　　　　　Whither have fled
> The hues of heaven that canopied his bower
> Of yesternight?...

> 　　　　　　　　　　　(192, 196–98)

In a related manner, the speaker of 'Epipsychidion' tells how his youth had been attended by intimations of an ideal Being:

> There was a Being whom my spirit oft
> Met on its visioned wanderings, far aloft,
> In the clear golden prime of my youth's dawn...
> Amid the enchanted mountains, and the caves
> Of divine sleep, and on the air-like waves
> Of wonder-level dream, whose tremulous floor
> Paved her light steps; – on an imagined shore,
> Under the gray beak of some promontary
> She met me, robed in such exceeding glory,
> That I beheld her not. In solitudes
> Her voice came to me through the whispering woods...
> Her Spirit was the harmony of truth.

> 　　　　　　　(190–92, 194–201, 216)

The speaker's growth from youth into manhood brought with it, however, a failure of this visionary haunting. However much it was desired and pursued, the vision faded:

> Then, from the caverns of my dreamy youth
> I sprang, as one sandalled with plumes of fire,
> And towards the lodestar of my one desire,
> I flitted...
> But She, whom prayers or tears then could not tame,
> Passed...

> 　　　　　　　　(217–20, 225–26)

What the speaker has lost is something intimately involved with his own identity:

> a voice said: -'O thou of hearts the weakest,
> The phantom is beside thee whom thou seekest'.

Then I – 'Where?' – the world's echo answered 'where?'
And in that silence, and in my despair,
I questioned every tongueless wind that flew
Over my tower of mourning, if it knew
Whither 'twas fled, this soul out of my soul . . .

(232–38)

There is a parallel deployment of male protagonist and anima-figure in Keats's *Endymion* (1818). G.H. Ford has noted verbal echoes of *Endymion* in *The Lover's Tale* and comments that Tennyson's poem is very 'Keatsian in tone' (Ford 1944: 24).[3] We learn in Keats's poem that the shepherd Endymion has become dissatisfied with the common lot of human kind ('The comfortable green and juicy hay / [Of] human pastures', III.4–5) and yearns for an ideal 'far / . . . past the scanty bar / To mortal steps' (II.123–25):

'tis no prize,
That toiling years would put within my grasp,
That I have sighed for; with so deadly gasp
No man e'er panted for a mortal love.

(I.523–26)

The object of Endymion's visionary desire takes, as in Shelley, a female form. It is Cynthia, moon-sister to Sun-Apollo, who in this poem images the finite self's insight into a 'completed form of all completeness' (I.606). There is nothing in nature to compare with her: 'Speak, stubborn earth, and tell me where, oh where, / Hast thou a symbol of her golden hair?' (I.608–609). Cynthia's role as an aspect of Endymion himself is highlighted on the second fleeting occasion that he sees her when, with undisguised narcissism, he glimpses her face:

A wonder, fair as any I have told –
The same bright face I tasted in my sleep,
Smiling in the clear well.

(I.894–96)

Both Shelley's and Keats's and, for that matter, as we shall see, Tennyson's use of a female figure to image some ideal potency of a male mind stands liable to the charge of an exploitation of the female which precludes engagement with the actuality of women. It is the kind of thing Marina Warner examines when, in *Monuments and Maidens: The Allegory of the Female Form* (1985), she speaks of the 'misogynist strain' which cleaves 'image and reality' and stresses 'the disjunction between women and the positive idea' they represent 'in allegory' (Warner 1987: 199). But whatever the essential misogyny of these poets' imaging of the ideal, this was the traditional Western psychological and metaphysical stratagem they employed. The Platonic background to Shelley's use of the stratagem – with the female figure in 'Alastor' sounding to the visionary like 'the voice of his own soul' (153), and a comparable figure in 'Epipsychidion' appearing to the speaker as the 'soul out of my soul' (238) – has been discussed by Carlos Baker in terms of what he calls Shelley's 'psyche-epipsyche strategy', where a female figure stands as epipsyche to a male protagonist's psyche:

> The basic assumption of the psyche-epipsyche strategy may be found under explicit discussion in the *Symposium* and *Phædrus* of Plato. Phædrus himself calls it ... 'the emulous desire for what is fine' ... the psyche-epipsyche strategy in a nutshell is the evolution by the mind of an ideal pattern towards which it then aspires ... Although the epipsyche terminology does not appear in Shelley until 1821 [with the publication of 'Epipsychidion'], the notion of a search for a true mate, a complementary heroine for the Shelleyan hero, has been born by 1815 and is well developed by 1817. The relationship is always, at its highest level, a spiritual union ... it is a form of idealism, with its roots in the romantic psychology of aspiration, and its branches extending up towards the 'light that never was on sea or land' ... Emilia [in 'Epipsychidion'] is only, or mainly, one more metaphor of the Shellyan epipsyche ... The Idea which bears the name of Emilia in *Epipsychidion* may be defined as that part of the inmost soul which participates in the world-soul. Shelley had attempted an exposition of this mystical idea in the prose fragment 'On Love'.
>
> (Baker 1948: 53–54, 218–19)

In 'On Love' Shelley observes that a human being may find within themself a principle of identity which is pure and perfect – what he terms in this prose fragment 'a soul within our soul'. The parallel to this in 'Epipsychidion' is the conception of Emilia as epipsyche; what Baker describes as 'that part of the inmost soul which participates in the world-soul'; or, as the speaker of the poem has it, this 'soul out of my soul' (238). Shelley tells us, in 'On Love', that

We dimly see within our intellectual nature a miniature as it were of our entire self, yet deprived of all that we condemn or despise, the ideal prototype of every thing excellent or lovely that we are capable of conceiving as belonging to the nature of man...a mirror whose surface reflects only the forms of purity and brightness; a soul within our soul that describes a circle around its proper paradise, which pain, and sorrow, and evil dare not overleap. To this we eagerly refer all sensations, thirsting that they should resemble or correspond with it.

(Ingpen and Peck 1926–30: VI.201–202)

Shelley sees love as a phenomenon associated with the meeting between two individuals who are acutely tuned in to the ideal prototype in each other. 'The discovery of' the 'antitype' of the 'soul within our soul', Shelley goes on, 'the meeting'

with an understanding capable of clearly estimating our own; an imagination which should enter into and seize upon the subtle and delicate peculiarities which we have delighted to cherish and unfold in secret; with a frame whose nerves, like the chords of two exquisite lyres, strung to the accompaniment of one delightful voice, vibrate with the vibrations of our own; and of a combination of all these in such proportion as the type within demands; this is the invisible and unattainable point to which Love tends.

(Ingpen and Peck 1926–30: VI.202)

The movement towards apprehending perfection within is balanced and reciprocated by a desire to find the same perfection in another. Human beings are impelled simultaneously both inwards and outwards towards the same spiritual object. This impulsion or, rather, compulsion is the magnetic energy of love which animates creation:

What is love? Ask him who lives, what is life? ask him who adores, what is God?...

Thou demandest what is love? It is that powerful attraction towards all that we conceive, or fear, or hope beyond ourselves, when we... seek to awaken in all things that are, a community with what we experience within ourselves...This is Love. This is the bond and the sanction which connects not only man with man, but with everything which exists.

(Ingpen and Peck 1926–30: VI.201)

The manner of Shelley's rhetorical expostulations at the outset of the 'On Love' fragment – 'What is love? Ask him who lives, what is life?' – is rehearsed in Tennyson's *The Lover's Tale* when the protagonist, addressing his unnamed audience, speaks of the impossibility of specifying a date when he *began* to love. Love and life for him have always implied each other:

> Ye ask me, friends,
> When I began to love. How should I tell ye? . . .
> how should I have lived and not have loved? . . .
> 'Tis even thus:
> In that I live I love; because I love
> I live: whate'er is fountain to the one
> Is fountain to the other; and whene'er
> Our God unknits the riddle of the one,
> There is no shade or fold of mystery
> Swathing the other.

> (I.141–42, 167, 174–80 [I.139–40, 165, 172–78])

This kind of vision, in which selfhood and love are indistinguishable, is central to *The Lover's Tale*. Herbert Tucker puts it well when he says that what the protagonist 'loves, in his capacity as lover, is love itself, which becomes another name for the principle of his identity' (Tucker 1988: 97). It is a vision which forms the background for lines 62–88 of Part I of the poem, where Tennyson provides a strikingly original version of the Shelleyan conception of the ideal as something found deep within the self and at the same time realised through loving communion with another. Shelley's female epipsyche reappears in these lines – ambivalently both inside and outside the mind – as the protagonist describes the way in which he and Cadrilla would gaze into each other's eyes. Tennyson also offers a variation on the figure which Shelley used in 'On Love' when he was defining the sense in which a 'miniature' version of the self, shorn of all imperfection, may be glimpsed deep within the soul:

> Eye feeding upon eye with deep intent;
> And mine with love too high to be exprest,
> Arrested in its sphere, and ceasing from
> All contemplation of all forms, did pause
> To worship mine own image, laved in light,
> The centre of the splendours, all unworthy

Of such a shrine – mine image in her eyes
By diminution made most glorious,
Moved with their motions, as those eyes were moved
With motions of the soul, as my heart beat
Time to melody of her's. Her face
Was starry-fair, not pale, tenderly flushed
As 'twere with dawn. She was darkhaired, darkeyed:
Oh, such dark eyes! a single glance of them
Will govern a whole life from birth to death,
Careless of all things else, led on with light
In trances and in visions: look at them,
You lose yourself in utter ignorance;
You cannot find their depth; for they go back,
And farther back, and still withdraw themselves
Quite into the deep soul, that evermore
Freshspringing from her fountains in the brain,
Still pouring thro', floods with redundant light
Her narrow portals.
                        Trust me, long ago
I should have died, if it were possible
To die in gazing on that perfectness
Which I do bear within me...

(I.62–88 [I.*55–69, 70–85])

The passage enacts a series of transactions between lover and loved-one in which the possibility of making a literal distinction between them is suspended. The protagonist speaks of his contemplation of the ideal object of his love as an exercise in self-contemplation ('To worship mine own image', I.66). At the same time, he speaks as if capitulating himself to the object of his love ('such dark eyes...You lose yourself... You cannot find their depth', I.75, 79, 80). The two perspectives are not held in clearly contrasting frames of reference but, throughout the passage, modulate into each other. The large modulations are reinforced by the way in which difference between lover and loved-one is erased as the possessives that locate the protagonist and the pronouns that identify the loved-one give way at points to a definite article that subsumes the two: '*the* soul', '*the* deep soul' (I.71, 82). As lover and loved-one interfuse in these lines, the identity that is asserted between them is the common identity that comes of losing the separate, mundane self to the deep, the general soul.

The implication of lover in loved-one and vice-versa recurs throughout *The Lover's Tale*. The protagonist tells us at one point, for example, that 'my love/Grew with myself' (I.161–62 [I.159–60]). In its immediate sense this denotes the protagonist's own capacities of love, but the possessive formulation elides a few lines later with the same construction used in reference to Cadrilla: 'she, my love, is of an age with me' (I.192 [I.190]). The perfection and fullness found through the mutual implication is referred, throughout the poem, to a metaphysical principle defined by the capitalised abstraction 'Love'. The protagonist relates the way in which 'Love,/Warm in the heart' (I.154–55 [I.152–53]) cannot 'remember/Love in the womb' (I.155–56 [153–54]). The time of the protagonist's greatest happiness with Cadrilla is defined in terms of the same abstraction:

> On that day,
> Love waking shook his wings . . .
> > and blew
> Fresh fire into the sun . . .
> > we saw . . .
> > > a land of Love,
> Where Love was worshipped upon every height . . .
> > but how should earthly measure mete
> The Heavenly-unmeasured or unlimited Love . . .
>
> > > (I.306–309, 318, 321–22, 464–65 [I.310–13,
> > > 321, 325, *326, 463–64])

The merging of lover and loved-one within this principle of Love is, at the same time, part of an identification of lover with loved-one taking place even at the literal level of the narrative. '[M]y love/Grew with myself': the protagonist's capacities of love and, as it turns out, the literal life-story of both himself and Cadrilla. As the narrative has it, Cadrilla – the foster-sister – indeed grew with the protagonist. She was the daughter of the protagonist's mother's sister, who had died in childbirth. Both protagonist and Cadrilla were born on the 'same morning', under 'the selfsame aspect of the stars' (I.194–95 [I.192–93]):

> So were we born, so orphaned. She was motherless
> And I without a father. So from each
> Of those two pillars which from earth uphold
> Our childhood, one had fallen away, and all

> The careful burthen of our tender years
> Trembled upon the other. He that gave
> Her life, to me delightedly fulfilled
> All lovingkindnesses...
>   She was my fostersister...
>   one common light of eyes
> Was on us as we lay: our baby lips
> Kissing one bosom, ever drew from thence
> The stream of life, one stream, one life, one blood...

> (I.214–21, 229, 232–35 [I.212–19, 227, 230–33])

Paul Turner notes that in making Cadrilla the 'lover's foster-sister' Tennyson was following Shelley's example in *The Revolt of Islam* (1818) where 'Cyntha is Laon's' foster-sister (Turner 1976: 57). The stylised, symmetrical patterning of the life-stories of Cadrilla and the protagonist forms part, as do Shelley's repeated incest or quasi-incest motifs, of a fable of some primordial psychic and spiritual integrity. Of his happiest, most lovingly replete, time with Cadrilla the protagonist enthusiastically reminds his listeners that he is, after all, recounting a mythic condition, a condition that exceeded the descriptive power of language itself:

>   Sooner Earth
> Might go round Heaven...
> Than language grasp the infinite of Love.
>   Oh day, which did enwomb that happy hour,
> Thou art blessèd in the years, divinest day!

> (I.472–73, 475–77 [I.471–72, 474–76])

Tennyson's development in *The Lover's Tale* of the narrative of Cadrilla as anima-figure also shares significant features in common with the narrative development of the parallel idea in Shelley and Keats. Carlos Baker observes that in Shelley:

> The separation of epipsyche from psyche produces death, whether actual or symbolic. The lamp is shattered, or at any rate is incapable of giving light because the energising power is not there.

> (Baker 1948: 55)

In 'On Love' Shelley spoke of the loss of the compulsion towards an object of love, the loss of the psyche's desire to fuse with epipsyche, as follows:

So soon as this want or power is dead, man becomes the living sepulchre of himself, and what yet survives is the mere husk of what once he was.

(Ingpen and Peck 1926–30: VII.202)

There is an associated kind of observation in 'Alastor'. In that poem, the fleeting glimpse of the ideal imaged in the appearance of the veiled maid destroys for the visionary all sense of value in the ordinary self and world. Once the vision of the veiled maid has passed, nature alone appears cold, vulgar and empty, bereft of any higher life. It becomes a mirror-image of the spiritual void that the visionary experiences within himself:

> Roused by the shock he started from his trance –
> The cold white light of morning, the blue moon
> Low in the west, the clear and garish hills
> The distinct valley and the vacant woods,
> Spread round him where he stood. Whither have fled
> The hues of heaven that canopied his bower
> Of yesternight? The sounds that soothed his sleep,
> The mystery and the majesty of Earth,
> The joy, the exultation? His wan eyes
> Gaze on the empty scene as vacantly
> As ocean's moon looks on the moon in heaven...

(192–202)

Similarly, the speaker of 'Epipsychidion', during a youth attended by the spiritual 'Being', experienced himself and the natural world as instinct with mystical power:

> There was a Being whom my spirit oft
> Met on its visioned wanderings...
> Amid the enchanted mountains...
> In solitudes
> Her voice came to me through the whispering woods,
> And from the fountains, and the odours deep
> Of flowers, which...
> Breathed but of *her* to the enamoured air;
> And from the breezes whether low or loud,
> And from the rain of every passing cloud...
> And from all sounds, all silence.

(190–91, 194, 200–203, 205–207, 209)

But when the 'soul out of my soul' has 'fled' (238), the self and the world are husks of what they had been, the external world only reiterating to the speaker the absence of the ideal within himself: 'Then I – "Where?" – the world's echo answered "where?"' (234). The world of nature uninformed by spirit is empty, effectively dead.

The problem for the 'Alastor' visionary is that the intimation of the ideal represented by the glimpse of the veiled maid is something which destroys for him all sense of significance in the merely natural universe and he pursues his vision quite literally beyond the bounds of natural life. Because of his vision, he wants the totality of spirit and he wants it now. His unqualified desire for a completed form of all completeness beyond the inadequacies of human and natural reality can be satisfied only by what he thinks of as a lifting of the veil, only by passing himself literally through the 'dark gate of death' (211). But the poem is poised uneasily between an affirmation of this ending as defining a true, objectively grounded fulfilment of the unfinished self of the protagonist, on the one hand, and an anxiety that the subjective vision may have been no more than a meaningless, self-consumptive and self-destructive delusion, on the other. An anxiety that the visionary's obedience 'to the light / That shone within his soul' (492–93), his passing out of life, may be no more than a negation, no more than the natural death of a natural creature suffering from delusions of spiritual grandeur.

Such uncertainty does not govern the fantastic ending of Keats' *Endymion*, where Endymion is envisioned as being about to undergo a 'change' from his 'mortal state' so that he can be 'spiritualized' (IV.992, 991, 993). A.C. Bradley commented that Endymion's 'pursuit of the goddess leads not to extinction but to immortal union with her' (Bradley 1909: 241). Even so, earlier in Keats' poem, when Endymion's vision of Cynthia has vanished, he experiences a falling away from the pure ideal into a natural world defined by the principle of death:

> all the pleasant hues
> Of heaven and earth had faded: deepest shades
> Were deepest dungeons; heaths and sunny glades
> Were full of pestilent light; our taintless rills
> Seemed sooty, and o'er-spread with upturned gills
> Of dying fish . . .
>   If an innocent bird
> Before my heedless footsteps stirred and stirred
> In little journeys, I beheld in it

A disguised demon, missionéd to knit
My soul within under-darkness...

(I.691–96, 698–702)

When Endymion has seen Cynthia once more, her departure is again associated with death:

A wonder, fair as any I have told –
The same bright face I tasted in my sleep,
Smiling in the clear well. My heart did leap
Through the cool depth. It moved as if to flee,
I started up – when lo! refreshfully,
There came upon my face in plenteous showers
Dew-drops...
Bathing my spirit in a new delight.
Aye, such a breathless honey-feel of bliss
Alone preserved me from the drear abyss
Of death, for the fair form had gone again.

(I.894–900, 902–905)

The topic of death is not absent from *The Lover's Tale*. Tennyson's protagonist tells his listeners that on his happiest day with Cadrilla the two of them had ascended 'the hill of woe',

so called,
Because the legend ran that, long time since,
One rainy night, when every wind blew loud,
A woeful man had thrust his wife and child
With shouts from off the bridge, and following plunged
Into the dizzy chasm below...

(I.363–68 [I.365–72])

It was on this hill that the protagonist experienced his most fulfilled hour and it was this hill that Cadrilla suggested be renamed ' "The Hill of Hope" ' (I.454 [I.452]). After the recounting of the 'delighted hour' (I.462 [I.461]) we are reminded of the deaths of the wife and child:

We trod the shadow of the downward hill;
We past from light to dark. On the other side
Is scooped a cavern and a mountainhall,

> Which none have fathomed. If you go far in,
> (The country people rumour,) you may hear
> The moaning of the woman and the child,
> Shut in the chambers of the rock...
>   the cavernmouth,
> Half overtrailèd with a wanton weed,
> Gives birth to a brawling stream, that stepping lightly
> Adown a natural stair of tangled roots,
> Is presently received in a sweet grave
> Of eglantines...
>   Lower down
> Spreads out a little lake, that, flooding, makes
> Cushions of yellow sand; and from the woods
> That belt it rise three dark, tall cypresses;
> Three cypresses, symbols of mortal woe,
> That men plant over graves.
>
>   (I.513–19 [I.505–11], I.522–27 [I.514–19],
>   I.531–36 [I.523–28])

The protagonist declares that had he died at the moment of his richest hour with Cadrilla he would not have encountered death as a 'gap or jump in nature' (Hulme 1936: 3), because death would only have taken him to that greater spiritual reality of which he had had a 'foretaste' in his spiritual communion with Cadrilla:

> Had I died then, I had not seemed to die,
> For bliss stood round me like the lights of Heaven,
> That cannot fade, they are so burning bright...
> Oh had the Power from whose right hand the light
> Of Life issueth, and from whose left hand floweth
> The shadow of Death, perennial effluences...
>   had he stemmed my day with night, and driven
> My current to the fountain whence it sprang, –
> Even his own abiding excellence, –
> On me, methinks, that shock of gloom had fall'n
> Unfelt...
>   bearing on thro' Being limitless
> The triumph of this foretaste, I had merged
> Glory in glory, without sense of change.
>
>   (I.484–86 [I.484–85], I.493–95 [I.487–89], I.498–502
>   [I.492–96], I.510–12 [I.504^505])

Despite, however, Cadrilla's suggestion that the hill of 'woe' be renamed the hill of 'Hope', the protagonist recalls: 'Nevertheless, we did not change the name' (I.456 [I.454]). This ominous signal, together with the account of the lovers' journey from light to dark past the cavern of death, prepares us for the development in the story where Cadrilla tells the protagonist of her love for Lionel. At the literal level of the tale the protagonist is the disappointed lover. But the full significance of his reaction to Cadrilla's confidence emerges at the level at which she represents his own higher or ideal self, that part of his soul which participates in 'Being Limitless'. At this level of the psycho-drama, Cadrilla's attachment to another man amounts, in Shelleyan terms, to the divorce of psyche from epipsyche. The speaker's reaction to Cadrillas's news is cast in terms of a symbolic death:

> it seemed as tho' a link
> Of some tight chain within my inmost frame
> Was riven in twain: that life I heeded not
> Flowed from me, and the darkness of the grave,
> The darkness of the grave and utter night,
> Did swallow up my vision: at her feet,
> Even at the feet of her I loved, I fell,
> Smit with exceeding sorrow unto Death.
>
> (I.598–605 [I.583–90])

Recalling the loss of his beloved, his communication with the ideal, the protagonist in the present wishes he could have ceased being in the manner that a mere creature of nature ceases being:

> Would I had lain
> Until the pleachèd ivytress had wound
> Round my worn limbs, and the wild briar had driven
> Its knotted thorns thro' my unpaining brows,
> Leaning its roses on my faded eyes.
> The wind had blown above me, and the rain
> Had fall'n upon me, and the gilded snake
> Had nestled in this bosomthrone of Love,
> But I had been at rest for evermore.
>
> (I.631–39 [I.606–14])

In Part II of the poem we understand that the protagonist indeed retreated to a savage solitude, looking to achieve some kind of peace through oblivion in nature:

> From that time forth I would not see her more;
> But many weary moons I lived alone –
> Alone, and in the heart of the great forest...
> > the merry linnet knew me,
> The squirrel knew me, and the dragonfly
> Shot by me like a flash of purple fire.
> The rough briar tore my bleeding palms; the hemlock,
> Browhigh, did strike my forehead as I past...

> (II.1–3 [II.1–3], II.15–19 [II.15–19])

But there was no peace. The protagonist was caught in a nightmare world between an unspiritualized nature and an unavailable ideal. He was driven delirious by an inability to penetrate behind the mortal screen of nature, an inability to lift the veil on the ideal which had been lifted in his relationship with Cadrilla:

> Chiefly I sought the cavern and the hill
> Where last we roamed together...
> > Sometimes
> All day I sat within the cavernmouth,
> Fixing my eyes on those three cypresscones
> Which spired above the wood; and with mad hand
> Tearing the bright leaves of the ivy-screen,
> I cast them in the noisy brook beneath,
> And watched them till they vanished from my sight
> Beneath the bower of wreathèd eglantines:
> And all the fragments of the living rock...
> > in mine agony
> Did I make bare of all the deep rich moss...
> > So gazed I on the ruins of that thought
> Which was the playmate of my youth – for which
> I lived and breathed...
> The precious jewel of my honoured life,
> Erewhile close couched in golden happiness,
> Now provèd counterfeit...

> (II.32–33 [II.32–33], II.35–43 [II.35–43], II.49–50
> [II.46–47], II.70–72, 77–79 [II.67])

Not that the protagonist failed to have dreams of Cadrilla during his exile in the wilderness. But in these dreams she appeared in strangely altered form. The general pattern is as follows:

> Oftentimes
> The vision had fair prelude, in the end
> Opening on darkness, stately vestibules
> To caves and shows of Death...

> (II.129–32 [I.122–25])

The protagonist records in detail the several stages of one of his dream-visions:

> Alone I sat with her...
> her eloquent eyes...
> Filled all with pure clear fire, thro' mine down rained
> Their spiritsearching splendours...
> those fair eyes
> Shone on my darkness...
> the light
> Which was their life, burst through the cloud of thought
> Keen, irrepressible.

> (II.145 [II.138], II.149 [II.142], II.151–52 [II.144–45],
> II.162–63 [II.155–56], II.168–70 [II.161–63])

The dream-vision moves to a room 'Hung round with paintings of the sea, and one / A vessel in mid-ocean' (II.172–73 [II.165–66]). As the protagonist and Cadrilla gaze at this boat, 'each heart / Grew closer to the other' (II.190–91 [II.183–84]), until the 'painted vessel, as with inner life, / Gan rock and heave upon that painted sea' (II.195–96 [II.188–89]):

> round and round
> A whirlwind caught and bore us; mighty gyres
> Rapid and vast, of hissing spray winddriven
> Far thro' the dizzy dark. Aloud she shrieked –
> My heart was cloven with pain. I wound my arms
> About her: we whirled giddily: the wind
> Sung: but I clasped her without fear: her weight
> Shrank in my grasp, and over my dim eyes,
> And parted lips which drank her breath, down hung

> The jaws of Death: I, screaming, from me flung
> The empty phantom: all the sway and swirl
> Of the storm dropt to windless calm, and I
> Down weltered thro' the dark ever and ever.

(II.200–212 [II.193–205])

With Cadrilla transformed, unlike the visionary 'phantom' who stands 'beside' the speaker in 'Epipsychidion' (233), into a tautologically *empty* phantom – divested of spiritual content and gothically denoting death – Part II of *The Lover's Tale* concludes.

Again, Shelley offers a precedent for Tennyson's representation of Cadrilla under a darker aspect in the second part of *The Lover's Tale*. In provoking the visionary to pursue her beyond the bounds of natural life, in inciting him to a form of suicide, the veiled maid of 'Alastor' can assume an unattractive aspect. As far as the earthly self is concerned, the ideal figure of the 'Alastor' youth's vision can appear a threateningly destructive power. The problems are increased with the anxiety that the visionary figure may have no objective ground, that it may be no more than a subjective fantasy. If the ideal promise of the veiled maid is illusory, empty, then the demise of the worldly self that she invites turns her into an agent not of higher life but of annihilation only. As such, she can be seen not simply as questionable but as dangerous. In line 297 of 'Alastor' she is described as the 'fair *fiend*' (my italics). A little earlier, as the impossible object of the visionary's desire, she has been associated with treachery as well as with the demonic:

> He eagerly pursues
> Beyond the realms of dream that fleeting shade;
> He overleaps the bounds. Alas! Alas!
> Were limbs, and breath, and being intertwined
> Thus treacherously? Lost, lost, for ever lost,
> In the wide pathless desert of dim sleep,
> That beautiful shape!...
>   At night the passion came,
> Like the fierce fiend of a distempered dream,
> And shook him from his rest, and led him forth
> Into the darkness...

(205–11, 224–27)

A similar ambivalence in respect of the minds' aspirations towards the ideal appears in a short poem, 'Oh! there are spirits of the air', that Shelley published in the same 1816 volume that included 'Alastor':

> Ah! wherefore didst thou build thine hope
>   On the false earth's inconstancy?
> Did thine own mind afford no scope
>   Of love, or moving thoughts to thee? . . .
>
> Thine own soul still is true to thee,
> But changed to a foul fiend through misery
>
> This fiend, whose ghastly presence ever
>   Beside thee like thy shadow hangs,
> Dream not to chase; – the mad endeavour
>   Would scourge thee to severer pangs.
>
>   (19–22, 29–34)

Comparably, in Tennyson's protagonist's separation from Cadrilla, in his discovery of the 'precious jewel of [his] honoured life, / . . . Now provéd counterfeit' (II.77, 79 [II.*67]), hanging in a dream like a death's head over his 'lips which drank her breath' (II.208 [II.*201]), the female figure of the ideal is transmuted into a ghastly presence ironically and grotesquely mocking his desire for the ideal.

Mockery of the protagonist's yearnings for the ideal also forms the theme of the third part of *The Lover's Tale*. In the second part of the poem the protagonist had, on one occasion, dreamt of Cadrilla as dead and of how he had clasped a figure standing near him in her funeral procession – only to discover with horror that the figure was Lionel. In Part III, the protagonist has again

> The vision of the bier. As heretofore
> I walked behind with one who veiled his brow.
>
>   [III.11–12]

This time, however, the tolling of the funeral bell quickens pace and is transformed into 'four merry marriage-bells' [III.21]. Cadrilla rises from her bier to be embraced by Lionel. The vision points (with appropriately orgiastic overtones) to a celebration of purely naturalistic rebirth. From the point of view of the protagonist's spiritual hopes it constitutes a parodic image of resurrection. He is left, finally, as bereft as at the end of Part II:

> A long loud clash of rapid marriage-bells.
> Then those who led the van, and those in rear,
> Rushed into dance, and like wild Bacchanals
> Fled onward to the steeple in the woods:
> I, too, was borne along and felt the blast
> Beat on my heated eyelids...
>   she from out her death-like chrysalis,
> She from her bier, as into fresher life,
> My sister, and my cousin, and my love,
> Leapt lightly clad in bridal white – her hair
> Studded with one rich Provence rose...
>   the man who stood with me
> Stept gaily forward, throwing down his robes,
> And claspt her hand in his: again the bells
> Jangled and clanged: the stormy surf
> Crashed in the shingle: and the whirling rout
> Led by those two rushed into dance, and fled
> Wind-footed to the steeple in the woods,
> Till they were swallowed in the leafy bowers,
> And I stood sole beside the vacant bier.
>
>   [III.23–28, 41–45, 50–58][4]

IV

Shelley may also have influenced what appears to be a different attempt by Tennyson, in his drafting of *Lover's Tale* material in Harvard Notebook 8, to envisage a loved-one of dual, contradictory aspect. As I have noted, Harvard Notebook 8 contains the earliest major pre-*1832* draft of Part I of *The Lover's Tale* (details in Appendix). This draft is not extensive but it is possible to reconstruct from the partially damaged manuscript a complete version, comprising 111 lines, of Part I of the poem. This draft contains only the most basic elements of the story as it was to be formulated in *1832*. The first 64 lines or so are taken up with the unnamed speaker's recollection (there is an implied audience) of the coastal landscape of his youth. Apart from much description of the physical appearance of the landscape we learn in these 64 lines simply that the speaker suffers pain and sorrow in his present estrangement from the state of 'Love' and 'Hope' (64) which had characterised the scenes of his youth. That state was defined by his relationship with Cadrilla. But a mere 11 lines (65–76) deal directly with the special closeness between the speaker and his beloved. In the remainder of this 111-line draft we are given to understand, in very general terms, that whatever the speaker may have wished or hoped for in respect of Cadrilla did not happen. Something went badly wrong and it is apparent that the speaker and his loved-one became separated. From the present perspective of the poem the speaker is understood to spend his time looking back in memory to the period of his youth and the time he spent with Cadrilla. The draft comes to an end with the same line as was to conclude Part I in *1832* and *1879*: 'And Memory fed the soul of Love with tears'. Almost none of the narrative detail of Part I of *1832* is present in this 111-line draft. Precisely what went wrong in the lovers' relationship is never specified and there is no mention of Lionel. Most noticeable, however, is that there is nothing of the psychological interiority which is such a characteristic feature of the *1832* poem. The Harvard Notebook 8 draft of Part I of *The Lover's Tale* is very likely to date from 1828, perhaps 1827–1828 (see p. 74 and Appendix), and it is possible to speculate, in respect of the lack of interiority in the draft lines, that it originates from a phase just before Tennyson had begun to assimilate Shelley in his first year at Cambridge. This would be no more than speculation, though it would restore some credence, at least, to Tennyson's comment that *The Lover's Tale* was written before he had read Shelley.

At any rate, immediately following the draft of Part I in Harvard Notebook 8 is a hauntingly beautiful, unfortunately incomplete, draft passage which certainly does have a high degree of psychological interiority and which Clarice Short in 1967 identified, because of parallels 'in tone and substance', with *The Lover's Tale* (Short 1967: 79). This identification seems justified. The passage, which is in blank verse like *The Lover's Tale*, displays a preoccupation with a beloved of dual aspect. It shows an interiorized loved-one, Platonically ideal ('Intense Idea', 9), much desired, and at the same time threatening to the one who desires. The following is intended as a reading text of the passage and does not record all the features of the manuscript (see Appendix, p. 218):

> Fair face! fair form, sole tenant of a brain
> Peopled with griefs whose blackness cannot mar
> Your lustre, when fatigued with things less fair

> These eyes roll inward, gazing as they gazed
> Upon the archetype in happier hours.
> Beautiful permanence! indwelling light
> Unvanishing! which never transient thought
> Supplants or shades, for thou dost glow through all,
> Intense Idea; though I close the lids
> Of mental vision on thee thou dost burn
> As sunlight, through them: Slumber is no veil
> For thou art up and broad awake in dreams,
> O deeply loved: yet like a cruel foe
> Fast-centred in the heart thou hast undone
> Which must exist for ever. Can it lose
> Thy presence, when this head is low in dust?
> And won unto thyself and sendest thence
> Sharp arrows, from the fort which was mine own
>
> (1–18)

The meaning, indeed the sense, of the last four lines of this passage are somewhat obscure, though they appear to develop the sentiment of the preceding lines where the 'fair form' is a principle not only loved but also experienced as an enemy. As can be seen from the transcription in the Appendix, this is a working draft and it is possible that the lines do not constitute a fully worked out expression.

Tennyson's expression 'Fair face! fair form' recalls Keats' formulations in *Endymion*: 'A wonder, fair ... The same bright face ... the fair form' (I.894–95, 905). But what is more interesting are two verbal parallels ('archetype', 5, and 'must exist forever', 15) with words used in a passage by Shelley in his 'Discourse on the Manners of the Ancients'. In this piece Shelley is speaking of the 'object' of 'sentimental love' (Ingpen and Peck 1926–30: 228). As in Shelley's fragment 'On Love', this object is at once interior and external to the lover. It is the Platonic 'deep soul', as Tennyson put it in *1832* (I.82), which is to be discovered simultaneously within lover and loved-one:

> This object, or its archetype, forever exists in the mind, which selects among those who resemble it, that which most resembles it; and instinctively fills up the interstices of the imperfect image, in the same manner as the imagination moulds and completes the shapes in clouds ...
>
> (Ingpen and Peck 1926–30: 228)

If Tennyson is drafting, in the 'Fair face! fair form' lines, something in connection with *The Lover's Tale*, the passage would parallel the movement of the poem that is represented by Part II of *1832*. There is an affinity between Cadrilla's 'fair eyes/... forms which ever stood/Within the magic cirque of memory' (II.162–64 [II.155–57]), and which 'Shone' on the speaker's 'darkness' (II.163 [II.156]) in Part II of *1832*, and the idea of the 'Fair face! fair form' (1) burning through the 'blackness' (2) of the speaker's grief in the Harvard Notebook 8 passage – just as there is a parallel between Cadrilla as a figure associated with 'jaws of Death' (II.209 [II.202]) in *1832* Part II and the 'Fair face' which turns into a 'cruel foe' (13) in the Harvard Notebook 8 passage. It would be tempting to see the 'Fair face' passage as a direct continuation of the early version of *1832* Part I in Harvard Notebook 8. But its degree of psychological interiority, while it matches elements in the *1832* text of the poem, seems too developed to fit easily with the largely external narrative of the early draft of Part I. In any case, if Tennyson was indeed influenced by Shelley in the 'Fair face!' passage, the drafting of these lines would have taken place some time after the likely 1827–28 date of the drafting in the notebook of what was to become Part I of *1832*. Because the relevant lines from Shelley's 'Discourse on... the Ancients' did not appear in full until 1840, when Mary Shelley published Shelley's *Essays, Letters from Abroad, etc.* Tennyson's own copy of this edition is in the Tennyson Research Centre at Lincoln (Campbell 1971–73: No. 2023). Prior to Mary Shelley's publication of Shelley's *Essays*, Thomas Medwin had published, in 1832, extracts from Shelley's 'Discourse on... the Ancients' in *The Athenæum* and in 1833 he reproduced them in his collection *The Shelley Papers*. One of these extracts is of Shelley's comments in the 'Discourse' on love, but the text of the passage quoted above is, at its opening, slightly modified, missing out the words 'forever exists': 'The mind selects among those who most resemble it, that which is most its archetype, and instinctively fills up the interstices...' (*Athenæum*, 29 September 1832, 633). It is possible that in the early 1830s Tennyson read this extract published by Medwin and was influenced by it. But what is perhaps more possible, given the verbal parallels between Shelley's text and Tennyson's 'Fair face! fair form' lines, is that he read and was influenced by Shelley's *Discourse* in Mary Shelley's edition and that, in his intermittent work on *The Lover's Tale* in the years following the publication of *1832*, before he resumed intensive work on the poem in 1868, he returned to a notebook which he had used to draft *Lover's Tale* material at its inception in order to experiment with ideas that related to the poem at a later stage of its development. Tennyson would have been trying out a variation on what was the substance of Part II in *1832*, with the protagonist still haunted by the loved-one in both positive and negative ways. There is evidence of further material apparently relating to *The Lover's Tale* on stubs following the 'Fair face!' passage in Harvard Notebook 8. But from this point it is impossible to reconstruct the half-lines from any other version of the poem. We are left with an indwelling light that is loved but seen as a cruel foe and whose role or station after death seems (in the last four lines of the 'Fair face!' passage) to be the subject of some uncertainty. Just as the draft of Part I in Harvard Notebook 8 does not tell us exactly what went wrong in the speaker's relationship with Cadrilla, so the poetically startling 'Fair face!' passage is tantalisingly inconsequential.

V

Inconsequence is a feature of the incomplete three-part *Lover's Tale* of 1832. Equally, however, even the 'completed' *Lover's Tale* text of *1879* never escapes the charge of not really being finished. Part IV of *1879*, the sequel of Tennyson's 'maturity', is told in the third person. The idea is that the speaker, unable to continue his story at the end of Part III, leaves to a friend, one of the company he has been addressing, the task of completing the tale of his past affair with Camilla. We hear that when the protagonist emerged from his solitude in the woods and was living in his mother's house, he discovered that Camilla, some eleven months after her marriage to Lionel, had apparently died:

> All that looked on her had pronounced her dead.
> And so they bore her . . .
> And laid her in the vault of her own kin.

(IV.35–36, 39)

The protagonist, desiring to see his love one last time, entered her tomb: there to discover she was not actually dead. Taking her to his home, he nursed her back to health. He then threw a banquet, ostensibly to mark his own final departure from the land of his youth. At this banquet, the protagonist asked the guests to

> solve me . . . a doubt.
> I knew a man, nor many years ago;
> He had a faithful servant, one who loved

> His master more than all on earth beside.
> He falling sick, and seeming close on death,
> His master would not wait until he died,
> But bad his menials bear him from the door,
> And leave him in the public way to die.
> I knew another, not so long ago,
> Who found the dying servant, took him home
> And fed, and cherished him, and saved his life.
> I ask you now, should this first master claim
> His service, whom does it belong to? him
> Who thrust him out, or him who saved his life?

> (IV.251–64)

Lionel's answer is that:

> By all the laws of love and gratefulness,
> The service of the one so saved was due
> All to the saver . . .

> (IV.275–77)

The protagonist then brings the revived Camilla into the banquet hall and, once the guests, particularly Lionel, have recovered from the shock, says

> in her you see
> That faithful servant whom we spoke about,
> Obedient to her second master now . . .

> (IV.338–40)

But the protagonist does not insist on her obedience to him. In a spirit of generous self-sacrifice he restores her to her husband, Lionel:

> Take my free gift, my cousin, for your wife;
> And were it only for the giver's sake,
> And though she seem so like the one you lost,
> Yet cast her not away so suddenly,
> Lest there be none left here to bring her back . . .

> (IV.360–64)

Following this, the protagonist 'past for ever from his native land' [IV.384] and took up residence in the foreign place where he is found telling his story at the opening of the poem.

Part IV is 'founded upon a story in Boccaccio', as Tennyson declared in a headnote when he published what was to become Part IV of *1879* as 'The Golden Supper' in the 1869 *Holy Grail* volume. The tale is from *The Decameron* (10th Day, 4th Tale), and tells the story which Tennyson copied in Part IV of *The Lover's Tale*. It is the story of a knight, Gentil Carisendi, who was in love with Catalina, the wife of another man, Niccoluccio Caccianimico. She did not reciprocate the man's affection but one day, Niccoluccio being away and she being with his child, she collapsed and apparently died. Gentil Carisendi secretly went to see her body, interred in a vault, where he discovered she was, in fact, still alive. He carried her to his mother's house where Catalina gave birth to a son. Afterwards, Gentil Carisendi ordered a great entertainment at his house. At this feast he told the assembled company a story of a man who had a very trustworthy servant. The servant was taken ill and was thrown out into the street in that condition by his master. A stranger rescued the servant and nursed him back to health. Gentil Carisendi asked the guests at the feast who had the right to the servant. Niccoluccio answered that it must be the stranger who rescued him. Carisendi then revealed Catalina to the company, saying that, according to Niccoluccio's response to the story, Catalina should now belong to him, who rescued her. But, instead, out of the goodness of his heart, he restored Catalina and her child to Niccoluccio, thereafter settling down to live near the reunited husband and wife. The way that Tennyson's protagonist leaves Camilla and Lionel and rides away for ever at the end of Part IV of *1879* is a deviation from the story of Gentil Carisendi, though Tennyson at one stage had thought to follow Boccaccio a little more closely in this respect. In the privately printed *1868* trial edition of the poem, and in a trial edition of the 1869 *Holy Grail* volume, Tennyson added seventeen lines to the conclusion as it was to stand in *1879*. In these lines we hear that the protagonist is, in fact, going to 'return' to the 'land of love,/...see his lady once again;/...and play with all her boys' (15–17; Ricks and Day 1987–93: XVIII.90; XX.156).

Not that Tennyson's adaptation of Boccaccio relates only to Part IV of the 1879 poem. The Boccaccio story appears to have been in Tennyson's mind from a very early stage in his composition of *The Lover's Tale*. In the trial edition of the *Holy Grail* volume Tennyson provided a headnote in which he describes, not just the lines that were to become Part IV of *1879*, but the entire poem 'as founded upon a story by Boccaccio'

(Ricks and Day 1987–93: XX.124). This ascription of the relevance of Boccaccio to the poem as a whole is supported by an 1868 entry in the Diary (now in the British Library: MS. Eg. 3766) of Mrs Marian Bradley, wife of G.G. Bradley who was headmaster of Marlborough College, where Tennyson's son Hallam was at school. In January 1868 the Bradleys were visiting the Tennysons and in her diary entry for 24 January Mrs Bradley wrote:

> At dinner at Farringford... AT asked me... what I thought of his publishing it [*The Lover's Tale*] 'Someone is sure to do it someday' he said. I said I thought it very full and rich... but that the parentheses were long & the form would require altering to make it generally understandable & readable, & there was some that could be cut out with advantage – He said 'Oh I can't pick it to pieces & make it up again, it is not worth that...'. He then told me that it would not be easy to understand the allusions unless I knew the Tale in Boccaccio from which it was taken...

On 25 January Mrs Bradley records:

> A long afternoon before dinner talking with Emily Tennyson two chief topics – her boys & her desire to get 'The Lover's Tale' re-written... I hope AT will throw himself into it – he was telling us how much better he feels mentally, spiritually & bodily when engaged on some long Poem... I took the opportunity of urging him to lose no time in beginning 'The Lover's Tale'... E[mily] T[ennyson] thought he might re-set the poem & add to 'The Fragment' 'a sequel as heard from other lips in after years' – something of the sort.

Tennyson had obviously lent Mrs Bradley an early version of the poem in which he had not yet embarked on the major revisions which define the text from *1868* through *1879*.[5] The important point is that Tennyson spoke of this version of the poem, which preceded the writing of what was to become Part IV of *1879*, as finding its source in the Boccaccio story.

Another piece of external evidence which emphasises the bearing of the Boccaccio story on *The Lover's Tale* at an early stage of its development is a note written by Tennyson in proofs, now at the Tennyson Research Centre, of *The Lover's Tale* as originally set for the 1832 volume of *Poems*. The note refers to a passage in Part II of the poem where the speaker is wondering, with respect to a dream he has had of his loved-one's death, whether:

> the cleareyed Spirit,
> Being blasted in the Present, grew at length
> Prophetical and prescient of whate'er
> The Future had in store ...

(II.136–39 [II.129–32])

Tennyson's note reads:

> This & some few other passages in the Poem allude to a circumstance in the sequel, which is in a great measure founded on the beautiful tale of Gentil Carisendi in The Decameron.
> (Lincoln P108 (A); Ricks and Day 1987–93: 269)

The note was not adopted in the *1832* private-printing of *The Lover's Tale* but it is in an early hand and, even if inscribed in this set of proofs at a date later than the *1832* private-printing, it is unlikely that it was inserted at a much later date.

The passage referred to in Tennyson's note in the Lincoln P108 (A) proofs itself suggests that, at the time Tennyson had written the first three parts of the poem he was already thinking of a continuation which would have involved at least the idea of Cadrilla's apparent death. Another point of contiguity between the first three and the fourth parts of *The Lover's Tale* is the theme of resurrection which informs the protagonist's dream-vision of Cadrilla's regeneration in Part III quite as much (albeit in different terms) as the representation of her restoration to life in Part IV. This motif is also implicit in the protagonist's description of himself after Cadrilla has told him of her love for another:

> I was shut up with Grief;
> She took the body of my past delight,
> Narded, and swathed, and balmed it for herself,
> And laid it in a newhewn sepulchre
> Where man had never lain. I was led mute
> Into her temple like a sacrifice ...

(I.705–10 [I.669–74])

The allusions in this passage are to the Gospels, especially John, XIX.40–41, and to Isaiah, LIII.7. The identification is with Christ and preludes the protagonist's 'raising' of Cadrilla / Camilla from the tomb in Part IV.

If Tennyson had the Boccaccio story in mind from the outset of writing *The Lover's Tale,* one can speculate that his original idea might have been to show, in a concluding part of the poem, that the protagonist could effect the 'resurrection' of Cadrilla and then bless the union of Cadrilla and Lionel in a spirit of higher love – a principle of Love which inheres in but is at the same time larger than the individual. Something like this might be distantly implied in the extra seventeen lines which conclude the poem in the trial editions of *1868* and of the 1869 *Holy Grail* volume, where the protagonist returns to the land of love and to some kind of coexistence with Cadrilla and her family. It is harder to see how it is implied at all in Part IV of *1879,* except that the protagonist here, as in Boccaccio, does a far, far nobler thing in sacrificing his interests in favour of those of Cadrilla and Lionel and then proceeds to get out of their lives altogether.

The real problem with envisaging how *The Lover's Tale* might have concluded if Tennyson had finished it, with the Boccaccio story in mind, in the early 1830s is that Part IV in *1879* gives so few clues as to how Tennyson might originally have conceived the dynamics and atmosphere of the conclusion. Part IV in *1879* is a purely external narrative with none of the psychological and spiritual interiority of the early first three parts of the poem. A. Dwight Culler has made this point:

'The Golden Supper' is a purely external narrative of actions, whereas the first three parts of the tale are concerned exclusively with the world of emotion.

Parts I–III . . . are not properly a tale but a Romantic exploration of the psychology of the teller.

(Culler 1977: 36)

It is its externality which makes Part IV fail to ring true as a concluding movement of the poem. An interiorised treatment of Cadrilla's 'resurrection' and of the protagonist's emotional and spiritual generosity towards her and Lionel might have turned the section into a convincing idealist affirmation about a large principle of love, with psychological and spiritual reintegration taking place in some way at a higher level than individual character or interest. Such an affirmation would certainly not have constituted a sceptical vision. But, in any case, it did not happen. The poem is no more genuinely complete in 1879 than it had been in 1832.

What is important for this study, however, is that the formal completion of the narrative in *1879* in terms which do not fulfil the psychological and metaphysical orientations of the first three parts of the poem in their early state has obscured the relevance of those orientations to *In Memoriam* and *Maud*. It was in these two works rather than in the text of *1879* that some of the principal themes of the incomplete *Lover's Tale* of 1832 were to be successfully developed. They were developed in these two poems, however, in markedly different directions.

5

The Archetype that Waits: 'Oh! that 'twere possible', *In Memoriam*

'We do not profess perfectly to understand the somewhat mysterious contribution of Mr Alfred Tennyson, entitled "Stanzas"', declared the *Edinburgh Review* for October 1837. The stanzas referred to were those of the lyric beginning 'Oh! that 'twere possible', published earlier in the year in *The Tribute*, an anthology edited by Lord Northampton. 'Oh! that 'twere possible' is indeed a strange piece, but the obscurities which puzzled the *Edinburgh* reviewer conceal an important connection between *The Lover's Tale* of 1832 and both *In Memoriam* and *Maud*.

I

The stanzas from *The Tribute* read in numerous respects like a concentrated version of *The Lover's Tale*. There is none of the elaborate narrative of the earlier poem. Only a speaker in the present preoccupied with a lost loved-one. But some of the basic psychological and metaphysical formulae of *The Lover's Tale* re-emerge, shorn of narrative complications and encumbrances, in the 1837 lyric:

> Oh! that 'twere possible,
> After long grief and pain,
> To find the arms of my true-love
> Round me once again!

(1–4)

But it is not possible: insofar as there is a literal story in this lyric, the loved-one is dead: 'Alas for her that met me, / That heard me softly call'

(49–50). And yet her ghost haunts the speaker in the present of the lyric. More properly, it should be said, her ghosts: since she comes, on the one hand, as ominous 'shadow' (11) and, on the other, as 'phantom fair and good' (91). Thus it is that George Marshall can speak of the way in which the 'mourner' of 'Oh! that 'twere possible' is 'governed by the dual aspect of the spiritual presence of the dead loved one' (Marshall 1963: 229). 'Spiritual presence' is better, in fact, than ghost. In the closing stages of the poem, the speaker identifies the 'good' spirit of the lyric as the 'phantom' of 'the maiden, that I lost' (91, 79). 'Fair and kind' and 'lovely by my side' is this phantom (86, 88). But it is not some 'literal' gothic ghost. It has its origin in the speaker's mind. 'Would' that 'the happy Spirit' *would* 'descend / In the chamber or the street / As she looks among the Blest' (71–73) reflects the speaker, but:

> But she tarries in her place,
> And I paint the beauteous face
> Of the maiden, that I lost,
>   In my inner eyes again . . .
>
> I can shadow forth my bride
> As I knew her fair and kind . . .
>   In the silence of my life –
>   'Tis a phantom of the mind.
>
>   (77–80, 85–86, 89–90)

Similarly, the contrasting manifestation of the lost beloved, the 'shadow' or 'abiding phantom cold' (11, 35) which the speaker describes as 'ghastly sister' (94) of the 'phantom fair' (91), is also a power of the speaker's mind. This 'ghastly' presence first 'flits before' the speaker in the third stanza (11), and in the fourth it

> . . . leads me forth at Evening,
> It lightly winds and steals
> In a cold white robe before me . . .
>
>   (17–19)

This might also be a property of paranormal romance, a dramatisation of the 'visible but impalpable form of a dead person' (*OED*). But the lyric undermines clear distinctions between speaker and shadow. The nightly emaciations of the speaker in the fifth stanza, for example, 'Half the night

I waste in sighs' (23), prelude a progressive reduction of the speaker to a wraith of himself, a blurring of contrast between himself and the condition of the shadow. Thus, the 'abiding phantom cold' which in the sixth stanza attends the speaker at dawn and wakefulness is followed in the seventh by the speaker rising only to be lost within a phantasmagoric city scene:

> Then I rise: the eave-drops fall
> And the yellow-vapours choke
> The great city sounding wide;
> The day comes – a dull red ball
> Wrapt in drifts of lurid smoke,
> On the misty river-tide.
>
> (36–41)

And where, in the fourth stanza, we hear that the shadow 'winds and steals' through the city, in the eighth the speaker himself 'steals' through the unreal city with the insubstantiality of the shadow that accompanies him:

> Through the hubbub of the market
> I steal a wasted frame;
> It crosseth here, it crosseth there –
> Through all that crowd, confused and loud,
> The shadow still the same . . .
>
> (42–46)

In stanza three we hear that the shadow 'flits' (11) before the speaker. In the tenth stanza the confusions of speaker and shadow are intensified as the 'eye' which 'flits' in the second line of the stanza reads simultaneously as the eye of the speaker and of the shadow. The point of view of the depleted and depressed psyche is punningly elided here – through the homonym 'eye' / 'I' – with the gaze of the shadow itself:

> Then the broad light glares and beats,
> And the sunk eye flits and fleets,
> And will not let me be.
>
> (55–57)

As *sister* of that potency of the speaker's mind which is cast as the 'phantom fair', it is not surprising that the loved-one's 'shadow' should be cast as haunting the speaker as an individual may be tracked by his or her own shadow; or as an individual possesses and is possessed by the reflections of his or her own mind.

The speaker emphasises that the shadow is not simply identical with the loved-one he has lost: 'Not thou, but like to thee' (12). The shadow is a kind of negative image of her. In the eleventh stanza, he tries to dismiss this image:

> Get thee hence...
> Mix not memory with doubt,
> 'Tis the blot upon the brain
> That *will* show itself without.

> (65, 68–70)

The blot within the mind externalised in the shadow involves a doubt about the memory of the beloved as 'fair and kind' (86). The doubt defined by a shadow which is the ghastly sister of the positive image calls in question whether the memory of the beloved as 'fair and good' (91) has any veracity. It is something that calls in question whether the primordial state of perfect fulfilment which is imaged in memory –

> We stood tranced in long embraces,
> Mixt with kisses sweeter, sweeter,
> Than any thing on earth.

> (8–10)

– is only wish fulfilment. A part of the fear inspired by the shadow is that conceptions of the ideal may be no more than fantasy. It is the fear that death may not lead to an ideal state associated with 'light' (108). It is at once the speaker's doubt about the nature of his desire to be at one with the lost beloved. At one point the speaker's yearning for her seems like an infantile, regressive desire for the womb:

> Always I long to creep
> To some still cavern deep,
> And to weep, and weep and weep
> My whole soul out to thee.

> (61–64)

The speaker's doubt – that which causes his 'anguish' to hang 'like shame' – is whether his image of the ideal may be just a glamourisation of despair, a glossing-over of what Christopher Ricks calls a 'suicidal wish for oblivion' (Ricks 1989: 133). The ideal here would collapse into its opposite. Wordplay in the lyric allows the possibility of the illusoriness of the distinction that the speaker insists upon, the possibility that the distinction is just a rationalisation of a death-wish. For all that it seeks at one level to make an absolute contrast between them, traces of the one sister are continually surfacing in the other. The poem witnesses, throughout, the two spirits collapsing lexically into one another. The 'Archetype' of the fair phantom is 'Clad in light' (107–108) but the shadow '*lightly* winds' its 'white' winding-sheet (18–19). The phantom fair should represent a different principle from that signalled by the 'shadow' but, in the speaker's imagining of them, the two phantoms fall surreptitiously together: 'I can *shadow* forth my bride / As I knew her fair . . .' (85–86). And when we assume that the long-wished-for rest of the tenth stanza is to be provided by the *fair* spirit, 'Always I long to creep / To some *still* cavern deep', we should recall the grave stasis that in the eighth verse typifies 'The shadow *still* the same'. One dislocation between stanzas works to great effect in dissolving any certainty of separation between the two phantoms of the lyric. When the eleventh stanza opens, 'Get thee hence, nor come again, / Pass and cease to move about – / Pass, thou death-like type of pain', we can read *in* a connection with the 'shadow'. But we might equally read the lines as referring to the impulse just recounted at the end of the tenth stanza, 'Always I long . . . / . . . to weep . . . / My whole soul out to thee'; and that 'thee' may address a loved-one as shadowy as she is fair.

The speaker struggles against this fusion, this implication that his ideal is no more than a dressing-up of a suicidal proclivity:

> I paint the beauteous face
> Of the maiden, that I lost,
> In my inner eyes again,
> Lest my heart be overborne
> By the thing I hold in scorn,
> By a dull mechanic ghost
> And a juggle of the brain.

(78–84)

But resistance is hard when the dark wish is involuntary. The desire for oblivion is deeper than the speaker's capacity to control:

> 'Tis a phantom fair and good;
>   I can call it to my side,
>   So to guard my life from ill,
>   Though its ghastly sister glide
>   And be moved around me still
> With the moving of the blood,
>   That is moved not of the will.

(91–97)

Matters are even worse when the compulsion appropriates the faculty of choice itself: 'Tis the blot upon the brain / That *will* show itself without' (69–70).

The speaker of 'Oh! that 'twere possible' insists on maintaining the contrast between dark and light shadows right to the end of the lyric:

> Let it pass, the dreary brow,
>   Let the dismal face go by.
> Will it lead me to the grave?
>   Then I lose it: it will fly:
> Can it overlast the nerves?
>   Can it overlive the eye?
> But the other, like a star,
> Through the channel windeth far
>   Till it fade and fail and die,
> To its Archetype that waits,
> Clad in light by golden gates –
> Clad in light the Spirit waits
>   To embrace me in the sky.

(98–110)

But these lines do not resolve anything. The claim that there is an archetype of light which waits does not dispel the unanswered questions about the abiding phantom cold, whose negativity *may* indeed abide, even after death: 'Can it overlast the nerves? / Can it overlive the eye?' There is a rhetorical separation between the two ghosts or presences which does not dispel the anxiety, felt throughout the poem, that they may in fact not be separable. It is an anxiety that there may be no transcendental authority for the duality of light and dark. An anxiety that a value system based on such a duality may have no ultimate ground.

There are clear affinities between the 'dual aspect of the spiritual presence of the dead loved one' in 'Oh! that 'twere possible' (Marshall 1963: 229) and the spiritual presence of Cadrilla after the protagonist has lost her in *The Lover's Tale*. The positive aspect of the imagined loved-one in 'Oh! that 'twere possible', the 'phantom fair and good' with 'beauteous face', recalls Cadrilla as she appears with 'face / . . . starry-fair' and eyes which govern life 'with light' in Part I of *The Lover's Tale*, and as she appeared with 'fair eyes', 'forms' shining on the 'darkness' of the bereft protagonist in Part II. (Likewise, the 'Archetype' of the fair phantom of the mind in 'Oh! that 'twere possible' recalls the 'archetype' that haunts the speaker's mind in the 'Fair face! fair form' passage in Harvard Note-book 8; the word 'archetype', notably, being used by Tennyson on only these two occasions in his entire work.) Conversely, the 'shadow' that is associated with death in the 1837 lyric – the 'phantom cold', 'ghastly sister' of the 'phantom fair and good' – recalls Cadrilla as the 'empty phantom' identified with the 'jaws of Death' in *The Lover's Tale*.

The protagonist at the end of Part II of *The Lover's Tale* flings the 'empty phantom' from him – although in his dream the action does not prevent him from falling down 'thro' the dark ever and ever'. This concluding image of Part II, where the speaker discovers himself in a love-embrace with the spectre of Death, highlights an important feature of *The Lover's Tale*. Throughout the poem there is a sense in which the protagonist is half in love with death. The impulse towards death is treated more indirectly in *The Lover's Tale* than in 'Oh! that 'twere possible.' But the idea shadows the following lines in *The Lover's Tale*, where the ideal persona within negotiates with the suicidal impulse:

> . . . Time and Grief abode too long with Life,
> And, like all other friends i' the world, at last
> They grew aweary of her fellowship:
> So Time and Grief did beckon unto Death,
> And Death drew nigh and beat the doors of Life;
> But thou didst sit alone in the inner house,
> A wakeful portress, and didst parle with Death, –
> 'This is a charmèd dwelling which I hold';
> So Death gave back, and would no further come.

(I.105–13 [I.103–11])

From his 'farthest lapse', his 'latest ebb', Cadrilla's 'image, like a charm of light and strength' pushes the protagonist back towards life (I.89–90 [I.86–87]). In her positive aspect in *The Lover's Tale* the image of Cadrilla foreshadows the 'phantom fair and good' which the speaker in 'Oh! that 'twere possible' conjures to protect himself from the 'ill' of the good phantom's 'ghastly sister'. But in neither poem is the disjunction between the two images or potentialities overcome. The speaker in the incomplete *Lover's Tale* of 1832 is restored by the positive image of Cadrilla to a life that is yet 'deserted and barren'. The speaker in 'Oh! that 'twere possible' is not certain of his chances of exorcising the abiding 'phantom cold'. Tension remains high in both poems. The poem of 1832, in its incompleteness, and the lyric of 1837 equally rest with an unresolved negotiation between the dark and the light.

Negotiation between the dark and the light continues in both *In Memoriam* and *Maud*. But in these two poems Tennyson was to move beyond the irresolutions of the earlier poems. In *In Memoriam* he tilted the scales in favour of the light. In *Maud* he was to reverse the affirmations of the poem of 1850 and emphasise a more negative direction.

It is well known that 'Oh! that 'twere possible' was 'the "germ" of *Maud*' (Ricks 1987: II.20) and that the 1837 lyric was partially incorporated into the poem of 1855 (II.141–238). But 'Oh! that 'twere possible' also 'has many links with *In Memoriam*' (Ricks 1987: II.20). The lyric was first written in 1833–1834, following the death of Arthur Hallam. In its original form (as it appears in two drafts in the Commonplace Book of J.M. Heath; Ricks and Day 1987–93: XXIX.48–49, 68–69) it is usually taken to represent 'Tennyson's immediate poetic response to the death of Arthur Hallam' (Marshall 1963: 228).

The links between 'Oh! that 'twere possible' and *In Memoriam* range from correspondences in verbal and imagistic detail to parallels between the larger themes of the two works. Joyce Green, for example, has noted how the imagery of the city in 'Oh! that 'twere possible' is 'closely akin' to that throughout section VII of *In Memoriam* (Green 1951: 671). But the most comprehensive discussion of the parallels was made by George O. Marshall, whose observations include the point that

> Such affectionate expressions as 'the arms of my true love/Round me once again' and 'tranced in long embraces' [ll. 3–4, 8] are matched in *In Memoriam* by 'A little while from his embrace' [CXVII.3] and 'That yet remembers his embrace' [LXXXV.111]. 'The hand, the lips, the eyes' [I.25] is paralleled by 'Sweet human hand and lips and eye' [CXXIX.6].
>
> (Marshall 1963: 228)

On the affinities between the overall themes of the two poems, Marshall comments that in the 1837 lyric the lover's 'contemplation' of the 'good spirit' and his 'hope for a reunion with its archetype that waits to embrace him in the sky' –

> suggests the hope Tennyson expressed in *In Memoriam* for a reunion with the spirit of Hallam after death . . .
>
> By expressing his own despair in 'Oh! that 'twere possible' in terms of the grief of a lover over a dead woman, and not of a man for a man as in *In Memoriam*, Tennyson sought an emotional release by objectifying his emotions. Even so, the expressions of love in the early lyric are hardly more passionate than those in *In Memoriam*.
>
> (Marshall 1963: 227–28)

'Let go by the paraphernalia of the two ghosts, and the heavenly hopes', says Christopher Ricks of 'Oh! that 'twere possible'. Instead, let us remember only 'what is here effortlessly memorable' of Tennyson's reaction to the death of his friend: 'a broken cry, a suicidal wish for oblivion, for dissolution, for dissolving into tears' (Ricks 1989: 133). But the two ghosts are not mere trapping. The affinities between *The Lover's Tale* and 'Oh! that 'twere possible' suggest that the hauntings are elements in a deeply founded imaginative structure. Most important, these affinities tell us that this imaginative paradigm predates the death of Tennyson's friend. 'Oh! that 'twere possible' may represent a response to the loss of Hallam, its pathos excited by that loss, but the work shows Tennyson interpreting the basic fact of the loss according to a pre-formulated plan.

What is true of 'Oh! that 'twere possible' may also be seen to be true of *In Memoriam*. The links between *The Lover's Tale* and 'Oh! that 'twere possible', on one hand, and between the lyric from *The Tribute* and *In Memoriam* on the other, invite inquiry, in the next section, into the senses in which Hallam's death and Tennyson's response to it in *In Memoriam* are, to a significant extent, grafted onto a conceptual and imaginative strategy that had been developed several years before the 'disastrous day' (*In Memoriam*, LXXII.26), 15 September 1833, of Arthur Hallam's death.

II

In Memoriam asks large questions about the nature of God and the significance of human life in the face of death. As I observed in the first chapter, Tennyson does not adopt in the poem a strictly Christian perspective for examining these questions. To the extent that the poem displays a spiritual conviction, Tennyson's sympathies are with a way of thinking that internalises spiritual impulse within the world and, most important, within the human mind. Tennyson put the case explicitly, if, at this stage of the poem, inquiringly, in section LV:

> The wish, that of the living whole
> > No life may fail beyond the grave,
> > Derives it not from what we have
> The likest God within the soul?

(LV.1–4)

Tennyson glossed the last line of this verse: 'The inner consciousness – the divine in man' (Tennyson, Hallam 1913: 948).

Again, in section XCV of *In Memoriam*, it is the interiority of the poet's encounter with 'Ultimate reality, the Platonic *Tò ὄντωςὄν*' (Collins 1902: 104), which is foregrounded:

> But when those others, one by one,
> > Withdrew themselves from me and night,
> > And in the house light after light
> Went out, and I was all alone,
>
> A hunger seized my heart; I read
> > Of that glad year which once had been,
> > In those fallen leaves which kept their green,
> The noble letters of the dead:
>
> And strangely on the silence broke
> > The silent-speaking words, and strange
> > Was love's dumb cry defying change
> To test his worth; and strangely spoke
>
> The faith, the vigour, bold to dwell
> > On doubts that drive the coward back,
> > And keen through wordy snares to track
> Suggestion to her inmost cell.
>
> So word by word, and line by line,
> > The dead man touched me from the past,
> > And all at once it seemed at last
> The living soul was flashed on mine,

And mine in this was wound, and whirled
    About empyreal heights of thought,
    And came on that which is, and caught
The deep pulsations of the world,

Æonian music measuring out
    The steps of Time – the shocks of Chance –
    The blows of Death. At length my trance
Was cancelled, stricken through with doubt.

(XCV.17–44)

In these lines, the approach to ultimate reality, to 'that which is' (39), is through the poet's memory. And the moment of mystical apprehension is born of a meeting of souls, the poet's and another: 'all at once it seemed at last/The living soul was flashed on mine' (35–36). In respect of the second line here, Tennyson took a deliberate step to avoid the implication of an individual spiritual encounter with the dead Hallam, when, in an edition of *In Memoriam* separately published in 1872, he altered the reading as it had stood since 1850, '*His* living soul' (my italics), by the substitution of the definite article. Tennyson, perhaps recalling the 'seemed' (35) and the 'doubt' (44) which, together, had qualified and stricken his enrapture, was reservedly laconic about 'The living soul': 'The Deity, maybe', he said (Tennyson, Hallam 1913: 952). 'The first reading', Tennyson went on to say, '"His living soul", troubled me, as perhaps giving the wrong impression' (Tennyson, Hallam 1913: 952). Hallam Tennyson observed: 'With reference to the later reading, my father would say: "Of course the greater Soul may include the less"' (Tennyson, Hallam 1913: 952).

Above all, Tennyson wants in *In Memoriam* to be able to identify 'that which is', the spiritual ground of life – what he calls, variously, across the poem, 'Him' (XXVI.10), the 'general Soul' (XLVII.4), the 'Power . . . / Which makes the darkness and the light' (XCVI.18–19), even, conventionally, 'God' (CXXX.11) – with love; or, more properly, 'Love', which appears throughout the poem as both the name and the attribute of God as well as encompassing the human participation in that principle. Anxiety in the poem does not centre only around the issue that God might not exist. On occasion, even when the reality of a transcendent power is taken as given, Tennyson allows for the potentially alien nature of such a power, if it is not to be identified with Love. In section XXVI, for example, he pictures an absolute which neither guarantees the spiritual survival of human life nor recognises the spiritual reality of Love. Suicide, indeed, might be desirable in the face of an amoral and nihilistic

God. Tennyson glossed 'that eye which watches guilt' in line 5 of the section as 'The Eternal Now, I AM' (Tennyson, Hallam 1913: 945):

> And if that eye which watches guilt
>   And goodness, and hath power to see
>   Within the green the mouldered tree,
> And towers fallen as soon as built –
>
> Oh, if indeed that eye foresee
>   Or see (in Him is no before)
>   In more of life true life no more
> And Love the indifference to be,
>
> Then might I find, ere yet the morn
>   Breaks hither over Indian seas,
>   That Shadow waiting with the keys,
> To shroud me from my proper scorn.
>
> (XXVI.5–16)

The idea of an absolute spiritual Love which sustains the universe and endorses the meaning of human life is challenged most distinctively in *In Memoriam* by Tennyson's well-known engagement with contemporary geological and biological science. As a traditional, religiously based perspective on human life was undermined in the course of its intellectual and cultural development, the nineteenth century could induce nightmares. And this is what happened to Tennyson when, in the 1830s, he read Charles Lyell's *Principles of Geology* which had first been published, in three volumes, between 1830 and 1833 (see Lang and Shannon 1982–90: I.145; Tennyson, Hallam 1897: I.162). Charles Lyell, whose ideas grew out of Enlightenment thinking on geological matters and whose work is the foundation of modern geological science, argued that the earth is very, very old indeed. He showed that the geological story, as recorded in the earth's strata, is comprehensible only if unimaginably huge lengths of time are taken into account. Lyell ran into opposition from those who held to the tradition that the earth was less than six thousand years old (in the 1650s Archbishop James Ussher of Armagh had calculated from family genealogies in the Bible that the world was created in 4004 BC). Intellectually, Tennyson accepted Lyell's thesis and evidence. At the same time, he could not rest easy with everything that Lyell said. Lyell set out to prove that past changes in the earth's surface, observable in the morphology of rocks, were not signs of great catastrophes in the geological history of the earth, as had been proposed by the French naturalist Georges Cuvier (1769–1832), who proposed a series of immense cataclysms to explain discontinuities in the geological record. The title-page of the first volume of *Principles of Geology* described the book as 'an Attempt to Explain the Former Changes of the Earth's Surface by Reference to Causes now in Operation'. Lyell showed that the world as we know it is the result of a natural process of erosion and igneous activity that has always been in operation, which is still in operation and will continue to be so. He placed great emphasis on the significance of water-erosion and deposition in the geologic process. Lyell's insight touched Tennyson's imagination vividly in *In Memoriam*, where two of the most evocative lyrics, sections XXXV and CXXIII, picture the power of water-erosion and deposition in forming and deforming entire land-masses. But however he sought to demythologise the processes of the inorganic world, Lyell adopted, in the *Principles* of 1830–1833, an oddly contradictory vision of the organic. He theorised that species are specially and successively created by the 'Author of Nature' to fit changing physical environments. His proposal was that each species 'had its origin in a single pair, or individual, where an individual was sufficient' and that species have been 'created in succession at such times and in such places as to enable them to multiply and endure for an appointed period, and occupy an appointed space on the globe' (Lyell 1997: 252):

> We must suppose, that when the Author of Nature creates an animal or plant, all the possible circumstances in which its descendants are destined to live are foreseen, and that an organisation is conferred upon it which will enable the species to perpetuate itself and survive under all the varying circumstances to which it must be inevitably exposed.
>
> (Lyell 1997: 200)

These species are, moreover, engaged in an 'universal struggle for existence' in which 'the right of the strongest eventually prevails' (Lyell 1997: 225). It is not only individual life-forms that die in this mutually destructive struggle between organisms. The geological record shows that complete species become extinct: 'the successive destruction of species must...be part of the regular and constant order of Nature' (Lyell 1997: 265). And Lyell does not exempt human kind from the possibility of extinction. Most important, Lyell's notion in the 1830s of the gradual extinction of some species and the continuous creation of new ones did not involve any evolutionary thesis. The creation of new species did not come about through the transmutation of existing species. There was nothing developmental, still less progressive, in Lyell's vision of an organic world that is caught in a state of endless warfare. There is no thread of growth. There is nothing like a celebration of human beings as standing at the top of an ascending scale. In Lyell, the organic world lives in a condition of directionless and purposeless violence. Tennyson was appalled by this vision of what in *In Memoriam* he called 'Nature, red in tooth and claw' (*In Memoriam*, LVI.15) and he wrote about it in that poem to striking effect across the three sections LIV, LV and LVI.

In section XXXV Tennyson tries to make sense of his loss of Hallam in the context of Lyell's vision of the instability of the physical world. Lines 8–12 of the section key in to the desolating processes and vistas of geological time. What is desolated by a sense of those processes is faith in Love as a lasting reality – and, by implication, faith in any human sense of value. The potency of the poetic sensibility itself is qualified. Lines 8–12 work with a cadence of attrition as they exemplify the way in which the rich imaginings of the ear can be imaginings even of impoverishment:

> Yet if some voice that man could trust
>   Should murmur from the narrow house,
>   'The cheeks drop in; the body bows;
> Man dies: nor is there hope in dust':
>
> Might I not say? 'Yet even here,
>   But for one hour, O Love, I strive
>   To keep so sweet a thing alive':
> But I should turn mine ears and hear
>
> The moanings of the homeless sea,
>   The sound of streams that swift or slow
>   Draw down Æonian hills, and sow
> The dust of continents to be;
>
> And Love would answer with a sigh,
>   'The sound of that forgetful shore
>   Will change my sweetness more and more,
> Half-dead to know that I shall die'.
>
> (XXXV.1–16)

Comparably, Lyell's thesis influenced the way that Tennyson sees, in sections LV and LVI, a divorce of interest between God and the organic world. Lyell's perspective did not posit any special connection between the animate world, including humanity, and some divine spiritual reality. Lyell's vision is of a series of successive creations, none of them going anywhere. The significance of the individual in this vision is nil. So, too, is the significance of entire species (which Tennyson refers to as 'types'). In section LV Tennyson registers his concern at the irrelevance of the individual in relation to the species:

> Are God and Nature then at strife,
> That Nature lends such evil dreams?
> So careful of the type she seems,
> So careless of the single life...

(LV.5–8)

In LVI he records an equal distress that, as the fossil evidence in cliff and quarry indicates, species themselves are transitory. Tennyson's special horror is that the human species, bereft of a caring God and with no purpose to its existence, will one day become extinct:

> 'So careful of the type?' but no.
> From scarpèd cliff and quarried stone
> She cries, 'A thousand types are gone:
> I care for nothing, all shall go.'
>
> ...And he, shall he,
>
> Man, her last work, who seemed so fair,
> such splendid purpose in his eyes...
>
> Who trusted God was love indeed
> And love Creation's final law –
> Though Nature, red in tooth and claw
> With ravine, shrieked against his creed –
>
> Who loved, who suffered countless ills,
> Who battled for the True, the Just
> Be blown about the desert dust,
> Or sealed within the iron hills?
>
> No more? A monster then, a dream,
> A discord...
>
> O life as futile, then, as frail!
> O for thy voice to soothe and bless!
> What hope of answer, or redress?
> Behind the veil, behind the veil.

(LVI.1–4, 8–10, 13–22, 25–28)

The sense of threat to idealist imagining presented by Lyellian geology and the disturbance generated by the idea of the endless replacement of species are especially acute in this section. Commenting on the lyric, Isobel Armstrong has noted that 'implicitly the biological Type elides with the theological Type' (Armstrong 1993: 263). The Platonic ground that, in *The Lover's Tale* and in 'Oh! that 'twere possible', had sustained the idea that human reality is founded in a divine principle of Love is undermined by the Lyellian notion of a God who is indifferent to the fate of all species, including, pre-eminently, humanity. Lyell's is not a God to endorse the archetype of Love which a part of Tennyson is so anxious to affirm.

By the closing sections of the poem the voice of *In Memoriam* will recover nerve and re-assert 'love' as 'Creation's final law'. In section CXXVI:

> Love is and was my King and Lord,
>   And will be, though as yet I keep
>   Within his court on earth...
> And hear at times a sentinel
>   Who moves about from place to place,
>   And whispers to the worlds of space,
> In the deep night, that all is well.
>
> (CXXVI.5–7, 9–12)

The figure of the dead Hallam is germane to this re-affirmation. In section CXXX:

> Thy voice is on the rolling air;
>   I hear thee where the waters run;
>   Thou standest in the rising sun,
> And in the setting thou art fair.
>
> (CXXX.1–4)

The conception of Hallam in these lines exceeds just the memory of a dead friend, however close that friend might have been. The third line of this verse recalls the Book of Revelation, XIX.17: 'And I saw an angel standing in the sun' (Ricks 1987: II.450). The dead 22-year old is addressed as a kind of cosmic force. A part of the treatment of the figure of Hallam in *In Memoriam* involves an idealisation of him as the vehicle by which the poet communes with a transcendental spirit of love. This idealisation of Hallam irritated the reviewer of *In Memoriam* in *The Times* for 28 November 1851: 'Instead of a memorial we have a myth...The lost friend stalks along a giant of 11 feet, or moves a spiritual being, with an Eden-halo, through life.'

It is through the mythologisation of Hallam that the links between *In Memoriam* and *The Lover's Tale* emerge particularly clearly.

III

In *The Lover's Tale* the mythologisation of the protagonist's happiest day with Cadrilla includes the following elements:

>   On that day the year
>   First felt his youth and strength, and from his spring
>   Moved smiling toward his summer. On that day,
>   Love waking shook his wings...
>   and blew
>   Fresh fire into the Sun; and from within
>   Burst thro' the heated buds, and sent his soul
>   Into the songs of birds...
>   Up the rocks we wound...
>   As mountain brooks
>   Our bloods ran free: the sunshine seemed to brood
>   More warmly on the heart than on the brow.
>   ...looking back, we saw...
>   a land of Love,
>   Where Love was worshipped upon every height...
>   From verge to verge it was a holy land...

> (I. 304–11, 313–18, 321–22, 327 [I.*297–315,
> 317, 319–22, 325, *326, 330])

Of his happiest hour on his happiest day, the protagonist tells us that:

>   Methought all excellence that ever was
>   Had drawn herself from many thousand years,
>   And all the separate Edens of this earth,
>   To centre in this place and time.

> (I.546–49 [I.538–41])

This representation of a time of marvellous fulfilment – a time when death itself seemed transcended ('Had I died then.../...On me, methinks, that shock of gloom had fall'n/Unfelt.../I had merged/Glory in glory, without sense of change'; I.487, 501–502, 511–12 [I.486, 495–96, 504^505]) – is summed up in the talismanic triad of words, 'Love', 'Life' (I.494 [I.488]), and 'Hope' (I.454 [I.452]).

The model of the protagonist's fabulous past in *The Lover's Tale* appears again in the early stages of *In Memoriam* when the poet recounts, across sections XXII–XXV, his past relationship with Hallam:

> The path by which we twain did go...
>> Through four sweet years arose and fell...
>
> And we with singing cheered the way,
>> And, crowned with all the season lent,
>> From April on to April went,
> And glad at heart from May to May...
>
>> (XXII.1, 3, 5–8)

> And all we met was fair and good,
>> And all was good that Time could bring,
>> And all the secret of the Spring
> Moved in the chambers of the blood;
>
> And many an old philosophy
>> On Argive heights divinely sang,
>> And round us all the thickets rang
> To many a flute of Arcady.
>
>> (XXIII.17–24)

These lines re-envisage the *Lover's Tale* conceit of the 'bloods' of the lovers that 'ran free' in their primal 'spring' (I.316, 305 [I.320, *297–310]). In Tennyson's image in *In Memoriam* of a state of lost integrity the cycle of nature is resolved into a perpetual spring. Winter is skipped entirely in the idealisation of the four years of friendship between the poet and the dead friend. And where the protagonist of *The Lover's Tale* characterises his old relationship with his beloved in terms of the Biblical story of paradise ('all the separate Edens of this earth', I.540), the voice of *In Memoriam* refers to the classical image of a pastoral paradise.

Tennyson draws back a little, in section XXIV, from presenting his relationship with Hallam when alive according to the conventions of Arcadian fantasy. But in section XXV – using the capitalised abstractions 'Life' and 'Love', recalling *The Lover's Tale* – he again idealises the satisfactions of the lost condition; except that this time the idealisation is less according to the conventions of a literary mode and more within his own imaginative frame of reference:

> And was the day of my delight
>> As pure and perfect as I say? . . .
>
> If all was good and fair we met,
>> This earth had been the Paradise
>> It never looked to mortal eyes
> Since our first sun arose and set.

(XXIV.1–2, 5–8)

> I know that this was Life, – the track
>> Whereon with equal feet we fared . . .
>
> Nor could I weary, heart or limb,
>> When mighty Love would cleave in twain
>> The lading of a single pain,
> And part it, giving half to him.

(XXV.1–2, 9–12)

Heightening the literal fact of his relationship with Hallam into an image of a matchless state that has been lost, Tennyson reinvents the figure of the protagonist's original relationship with Cadrilla – a relationship signifying the uninterrupted exchange between being and Being – in *The Lover's Tale*.

If sections XXII–XXV show Tennyson beginning to present his relationship with Hallam on earth in terms which are larger than those of strict autobiography, then they also show him describing the death of his friend and the fracturing of their relationship in terms of the fable of the fall. In *The Lover's Tale* the protagonist is displaced from his Eden after he and Cadrilla 'trod the shadow of the downward hill' and 'past from light to dark' (I.513–14 [I.505–506]). It is following this descent that Cadrilla tells the protagonist of her love for Lionel. The protagonist has intimations of what she is going to say before she has finished speaking:

> Hope was not wholly dead,
> But breathing hard at the approach of Death,
> Updrawn in expectation of her change . . .

(I.590–92 [I. 573–74, 574^75])

When the news is out the protagonist suffers a symbolic death: 'The darkness of the grave and utter night, / Did swallow up my vision . . . / . . . I fell, / Smit with exceeding sorrow unto Death' (I.602–605 [I.587–90]).

Miltonic allusions underline the way in which Tennyson establishes, in his presentation of the protagonist's trauma, a psychological parallel to the story of the Fall. The 'change' that 'Hope' is about to suffer in I.592 echoes, as did the use of the word in line 223 of 'Œnone', the 'change' that Eden suffers after the eating of the Forbidden Fruit in *Paradise Lost* (X.213; XI.193). There is an echo of Milton, too, in the convulsion that Earth suffers in *The Lover's Tale* after the protagonist has fallen 'with exceeding sorrow unto Death'. In Milton, at the moment Adam ate the 'fair enticing fruit' (*Paradise Lost*, IX.996) –

> Earth trembled from her entrails, as again
> In pangs, and nature gave a second groan,
> Sky loured and muttering thunder, some sad drops
> Wept at completing of the mortal sin ...

(IX.1000–1003)

– while, in *The Lover's Tale*, as the protagonist 'fell' (I.604 [I.589]),

> Then had the Earth beneath me yawning given
> Sign of convulsion, and thro' horrid rifts
> Sent up the moaning of unhappy Spirits
> Imprisoned in her centre, with the heat
> Of their infolding element; had the Angels,
> The watchers at Heaven's gate, pushed them apart,
> And from the golden threshold had downrolled
> Their heaviest thunder – I had lain as still,
> And blind, and motionless, as then I lay!

(I.606–14 [I.591–96])

The poet of *In Memoriam* relates his lapse from 'pastoral' bliss after the loss of Hallam in the following terms:

> But where the path we walked began
>   To slant the fifth autumnal slope,
>   As we descendèd following Hope,
> There sat the Shadow feared of man,
>
> Who broke our fair companionship ...

(XXII.9–13)

> Now, sometimes in my sorrow shut...
>> Alone, alone, to where he sits,
> The Shadow cloaked from head to foot...
>
>> I wander, often falling lame,
>> And looking back to whence I came,
> Or on to where the pathway leads;
>
> And crying, How changed from where it ran
>> Through lands where not a leaf was dumb;
>> But all the lavish hills would hum
> The murmur of a happy Pan...

(XXIII.1, 3–4, 6–12)

And just as the protagonist of *The Lover's Tale* falls into division after the loss of Cadrilla, alienated from the energy of absolute love, so, after the loss of Hallam, the poet of *In Memoriam* loses relationship with spiritual reality:

>> Thy spirit ere our fatal loss
>> Did ever rise from high to higher...
>
> But thou art turned to something strange,
>> And I have lost the links that bound
>> Thy changes; here upon the ground,
> No more partaker of thy change.

(XLI.1–2, 5–8)

>> I falter where I firmly trod,
>> And falling with my weight of cares
>> Upon the great world's altar-stairs
>> That slope through darkness up to God,
>
>> I stretch lame hands of faith, and grope,
>> And gather dust and chaff...

(LV.13–18)

Some further insight into the special role Hallam is allotted in the earlier stages of *In Memoriam* is yielded by section IV of the poem:

>> To Sleep I give my powers away;
>> My will is bondsman to the dark;

> I sit within a helmless bark,
> And with my heart I muse and say:
>
> O heart, how fares it with thee now,
>   That thou should'st fail from thy desire,
>   Who scarcely darest to inquire,
> 'What is it makes me beat so low?'
>
> Something it is which thou hast lost,
>   Some pleasure from thine early years.
>   Break, thou deep vase of chilling tears,
> That grief hath shaken into frost!

(VI.1–12)

Tennyson commented on the image in the last two lines here: 'Water can be brought below freezing point and not turn into ice – if it be kept still; but it if be moved suddenly it turns into ice and may break the vase' (Tennyson, Hallam 1913: 943). 'The same fact', Elaine Jordan has noted, was used by Goethe in *Dichtung und Wahrheit*, Book XIII:

The circumstances of both uses of the image are significantly similar – the unexpected death of a young friend of promise shocks the author out of a prolonged mood of inactive melancholy into composition. Tennyson's extension of the image – freezing water expands as it turns to ice so that its container may be broken – leaves its metaphorical meaning more vague. It could suggest suicide, or the mere relief of weeping, or the relief... of giving grief some sort of expressive form, in elegy...

'While my thoughts were thus employed, the death of young Jerusalem took place... The plan of *Werther* was instantly conceived. The elements of that composition seemed now to amalgamate, to form a whole, just as water, on the point of freezing in a vase, receives from the slightest concussion the form of a compact piece of ice.'

(Jordan 1968: 414)

Certainly, but what is particularly interesting about Tennyson's lines is that they suggest that the loss of Hallam is not, in one sense, the primary loss of the poem. Hallam's death succeeds a prior loss: 'Some pleasure from thine early years'. These must be years earlier than the four blissful ones which Tennyson spent with Hallam because the reservoir of 'chilling tears', shed over the loss of this pleasure, was filled before the death of

Hallam. Grief over that death caused the already existing heart sickness to crystallise in – among other things, perhaps – the writing of *In Memoriam*. Quite what this early pleasure consisted of is not elaborated upon. Tennyson never worked, in the manner of Wordsworth, with a legend of the spiritual wholeness of his own childhood. In *The Lover's Tale* Tennyson constructed a fable of lost integrity without autobiographical points of reference. In *In Memoriam*, the working myth is the period of his friendship with Hallam. Not, of course, that it was not an exceptional friendship. Nor that Tennyson did not suffer intense and prolonged grief at its loss. But Tennyson's motivation in speaking of his life with Hallam across sections XXII–XXV in highly idealised, quasi-mythological terms is illuminated by the statements in section IV of the poem. Just as the loss of the 'pleasure' of the poet's early years is accommodated to the experience of the loss of Hallam, so the image Tennyson creates out of the literal fact of his relationship with Hallam incorporates the significance of the lost pleasure, the unconstrained condition, of his own early years. There are two levels of reference to Hallam throughout *In Memoriam*. The first is the autobiographical and the real. The other, running concurrently and sometimes overlapping with the first, is the mythological. The *Times* reviewer was wrong to say that in *In Memoriam* we have myth *instead* of memorial. What we have is memorial *and* myth. To the extent that grief over the loss of Hallam incorporates an earlier sense of loss, the figure of Hallam, even at this very early stage of the poem, functions, at a 'mythic' level, as an emblem of a dimension of the poet's own psyche. Towards the very end of *In Memoriam* this function of the figure of Hallam is articulated with the full metaphysical machinery of the poem behind it.

In section CXXX the poet apprehends the dead Hallam as a potency now mixed with the divine and hence with the power that drives nature:

> Thy voice is on the rolling air;
> I hear thee where the waters run;
> Thou standest in the rising sun,
> And in the setting thou art fair.

> What art thou then? I cannot guess;
> But though I seem in star and flower
> To feel thee some diffusive power,
> I do not therefore love thee less:

> My love involves the love before;
> My love is vaster passion now;

> Though mixed with God and Nature thou,
> I seem to love thee more and more.

> Far off thou art, but ever nigh;
> I have thee still, and I rejoice;
> I prosper, circled with thy voice;
> I shall not lose thee though I die.

Where, in section XLI, the poet had lost connection with the 'spirit' of Hallam that 'Did ever rise from high to higher' (XLI.1–2), here that spirit is reapprehended as part of the highest, absolute spirit. What is important is that the very apprehension, the engagement with the spirit of Hallam, confirms the spiritual capacity of the poet himself and merges it with the spiritual object that it contemplates. Hearing, seeing and feeling Hallam as some diffusive power in nature is to hear, see and feel the divine. It is also the poet apprehending, through the capacity to identify, that part of himself which shares in the nature of the divine. At the level of the spiritual, at the level of the soul or the ideal self, there is no distinction between the poet and the dead Hallam. Hallam as a portion of 'that which is' emblematizes the 'likest God within the soul' (LV.4) of the poet himself. The poet's reunion with Hallam in section CXXX, his intuition of a Hallam who is diffused in God, defines simultaneously a re-engagement with his own highest self, a recognition of that part of himself which partakes of the absolute in which Hallam is now mixed. The apotheosized Hallam in section CXXX is one and the same as the apotheosized poet's soul. And the romanced version of the poet's relationship with Hallam on earth across sections XXII–XXV of the poem, accommodating the notion of the 'pleasure' of the poet's early years, figures the poet's ideal being in a manner parallel to the apotheosized Hallam at the end of the poem. It is as this kind of mythologised figure, whose condition implies that of the poet himself, that the Hallam of *In Memoriam* is generically descended from the figure of Cadrilla in *The Lover's Tale*.

Hallam is occasionally presented in *In Memoriam* under an idiom strongly reminiscent of that used to describe Cadrilla in *The Lover's Tale*. In the earlier poem, the lost Cadrilla's eyes had enlivened the protagonist's distress: 'those fair eyes / Shone on my darkness' (II.162–63 [II.155–56]); while in the 'Fair face! fair form' passage in Harvard Notebook 8 the preternatural aspect of the face is not dimmed by the 'blackness' of the speaker's 'grief' (2). Section LXX of *In Memoriam* ends (15–16) with an image of the dead Hallam calming the poet's disturbance: 'through a lattice on the soul / Looks thy fair face and makes it still' (a draft reading of line 16 in the Lincoln Manuscript of *In Memoriam* had: 'Look thy fair eyes & make it still'; Lincoln M1: Ricks and Day 1987–93: XVI.43). Again, the interior shining of the face recurs in section CXVI of *In Memoriam*, where we hear that 'the face will shine / Upon me' and alleviate 'regret for buried time' (9–10, 1). The reviewer of *In Memoriam* in the *Times* was irritated by what he called 'the tone of – may we say so! – amatory tenderness' pervading the poem: 'Very sweet and plaintive these verses are; but who would not give them a feminine application?' (28 November 1851). In details of the lovers' language, as well as in the 'reiterated metaphor of man and wife' in *In Memoriam* (Ricks 1989: 206), emerge traces of the male–female orientation of Tennyson's prototypical, metaphysical allegory of the bereft lover in *The Lover's Tale*.

There is also an ambivalence in Tennyson's expression 'My love' (*In Memoriam*, XCVII.1) which recalls the use of the same expression – with double reference to both the protagonist and Cadrilla – in *The Lover's Tale*. Distinctions between lover and loved-one are suspended in the opening stanza of section XCVII. It is open whether the poet is speaking of the dead friend or of himself and his own capacities:

> My love has talked with rocks and trees;
>   He finds on misty mountain-ground
>   His own vast shadow glory-crowned:
> He sees himself in all he sees.

(1–4)

Tennyson glossed these lines: 'Like the spectre of the Brocken' (Tennyson, Hallam 1913: 952). A.C. Bradley observed that 'the "spectre" is the observer's shadow thrown on a bank of mist' (Bradley 1915: 194). The significance of Tennyson's lines is illuminated by Coleridge's allusion to the phenomenon in the poem which he entitled 'Constancy to an Ideal Object':

> The woodman winding westward up the glen
> At wintry dawn, where o'er the sheep-track's maze
> The viewless snow-mist weaves a glist'ning haze,
> Sees full before him, gliding without tread,
> An image with a glory round its head;
> The enamoured rustic worships its fair hues,
> Nor knows he makes the shadow, he pursues!

(26–32)

Tennyson, by contrast, is fully aware of the fact that he makes the shadow he pursues. Since the form of address embraces both himself and Hallam, Tennyson's image of the spectre of the Brocken allows the blending of his own ideal self and the soul of Hallam in a common ground of love.

IV

The irresolutions of *The Lover's Tale* and 'Oh! that 'twere possible' are, overtly, overcome in *In Memoriam*. Where *The Lover's Tale* was never properly completed and where 'Oh! that 'twere possible' ends openly with unanswered questions, *In Memoriam* asserts finally that it has successfully countered all the dubieties voiced in the course of the poem. As the poet intuits the spiritual reality of the dead Hallam, so he achieves his own psychic and spiritual regeneration, engaging once more the spiritual reality that informs his own and Hallam's being. Though *In Memoriam* is soaked in nostalgia, the speaker of the poem is not presented, at the last, as caught in a state of regret, like the protagonist of the unfinished *Lover's Tale*. As in Shelley's 'Alastor' and 'Epipsychidion' the motivating principle of *In Memoriam* is the mind's desperate search for reintegration, for reunion with the lost archetype or epipsyche. The poem finally confirms that reunion, thereby completing the narrative paradigm that may have been projected and desired but was never closed in either *The Lover's Tale* or 'Oh! that 'twere possible'.

The phantoms fair and good in *The Lover's Tale* and in the lyric from *The Tribute* are matched with shadows of a contradictory significance. Shadows do not entirely disappear from *In Memoriam*. The poet speaks in section XCVII of 'My love' seeing 'himself in all he sees'. But if the reflection of XCVII is glory-crowned, there nevertheless remain in the poem hints of a darker possibility. A fear that the ideal object of the mind may be no more than, as it was put in *The Lover's Tale*, an 'empty phantom' (II.210 [II.203]), surfaces in section CVIII. Here the spectre of solipsism provokes the anxiety that there may be no more than a mortal meaning to all idealist projections of the mind:

> What find I in the highest place,
> But mine own phantom chanting hymns?
> And on the depths of death there swims
> The reflex of a human face.

(CVIII.9–12)

Not a divine face. Not a shining face. But such anxieties are not allowed
to govern the general conclusion of *In Memoriam*. The poem at its end
lays principal emphasis on the positive aspect of the phantom as it had
appeared in *The Lover's Tale* and 'Oh! that 'twere possible'. In 'Oh! that
'twere possible' the speaker recalls the 'hand, the lips, the eyes' of his
lost beloved who haunts him as the 'phantom fair and good; / I can
call ... to my side' (91–92). In *In Memoriam* the fair figure of the lost
beloved is similarly possessed:

> Known and unknown; human, divine;
>> Sweet human hand and lips and eye;
>> Dear heavenly friend that canst not die,
> Mine, mine, for ever, ever mine ...

> (CXXIX.5–8)

The overt resolution of *In Memoriam* does not, however, mean that
the dark ghosts of the earlier two poems have convincingly been laid.
There is evidence within *In Memoriam* itself to suggest that its positive
ending was somehow forced. Section LVII speaks of a leave-taking,
a leave-taking from the act of writing elegy itself:

> Peace; come away: the song of woe
>> Is after all an earthly song:
> Peace; come away: we do him wrong
> To sing so wildly: let us go ...

> Methinks my friend is richly shrined;
> But I shall pass; my work will fail.

> Yet in these ears, till hearing dies,
>> One set slow bell will seem to toll
>> The passing of the sweetest soul
> That ever looked with human eyes.

> I hear it now, and o'er and o'er,
>> Eternal greetings to the dead;
>> And 'Ave, Ave, Ave', said,
> 'Adieu, adieu' for evermore.

> (LVII.1–4, 7–16)

In 1892 Joseph Jacobs commented that 'From comparison of LVIII,
it would seem that *In Memoriam* was originally intended to cease

with LVII' (Jacobs 1892: 92). In LVIII, the poet, looking back on the 'adieus' of the last line of LVII, says that the 'high Muse' admonished him not to trouble his 'brethren' by ending on a gloomy note and insisted that he carry on writing so that he might reach a 'nobler' conclusion:

> In those sad words I took farewell:
>   Like echoes in sepulchral halls,
>   As drop by drop the water falls
> In vaults and catacombs, they fell . . .
>
> The high Muse answered: 'Wherefore grieve
>   Thy brethren with a fruitless tear?
>   Abide a little longer here,
> And thou shalt take a nobler leave'.
>
> (LVIII.1–4, 9–12)

It is certainly possible to read the transition from section LVII to LVIII as suggesting that Tennyson once thought of finishing on a sombre note but that a sense of responsibility led him to continue writing toward something more positive. In the early 1870s Tennyson himself said to James Knowles that 'I thought' the last stanza of LVII 'was too sad for an ending' (Ray 1968: 39). It would have been a very Victorian sense of responsibility that led Tennyson to countenance not an elegiac-tragic ending but a comic one, in the sense of the reconciliations of Shakespearian comedy. Or, if not Shakespeare, then Dante. Tennyson said: 'It was meant to be a kind of *Divina Commedia*, ending in happiness' (Tennyson, Hallam 1897: I.304). It is as if there were a dimension of artifice imposed on the personal expression of loss. Tennyson did say that the 'different moods of sorrow as in a drama are dramatically given' (Tennyson, Hallam 1897: I.304). To James Knowles he also said: 'It's a very impersonal poem as well as personal . . . It's too hopeful . . . more than I am myself' (Ray 1968: 37, 41). Section LVIII implies, at least, that there is something self-consciously willed about the latter direction of the poem. And to the extent that that direction – towards an affirmation of divine love and purpose in the universe – that 'nobler leave', is a willed imposition, it involves some peculiar statements on Tennyson's part. In one of the lyrics that Tennyson placed towards the end of the poem, for instance, we find this:

Whatever I have said or sung,
>   Some bitter notes my harp would give,
>   Yea, though there often seemed to live
> A contradiction on the tongue,

Yet Hope had never lost her youth;
>   She did but look through dimmer eyes;
>   Or Love but played with gracious lies,
> Because he felt so fixed in truth.

(CXXV.1–8)

The problem with these stanzas is that they deny the authenticity of the poem's earlier misery. In so doing they deprive themselves of gravity. By dismissing the pain and despair in the opening part of the poem as a falsehood, even a 'gracious' one, the poem arrives at its final position by playing Judas to itself. The imputation of the lie carries no authority. Indeed, it might be thought to impute itself. The will to impose order, the will to complete union with the archetype, by denying so much of the poem in the earlier stages of its development contradicts imaginative integrity. As T.S. Eliot said of the poem: 'Its faith is a poor thing, but its doubt is a very intense experience' (Eliot 1953: 183).

The imaginative insufficiency of many of the closing sections of *In Memoriam* means that there is a special kind of irresolution to the poem. Formally it insists on having tied-up ends. Imaginatively the negative side is, at many points, simply denied rather than creatively overcome and transcended. And one of the principal things that is unaccommodated in several of the concluding sections of *In Memoriam* is the imaginative depth of Tennyson's grasp of contemporary science. Tennyson was not just playing with Lyell and his geology. *In Memoriam* shows, indeed, that his imagination, however much it wanted to be able to endorse the spiritually positive vision that he willed into being at the end of the poem, remains addicted to the humanly reductive, critical perspectives of a science that had its roots in the rationalism of the Enlightenment. The extent to which the happy ending reads like a willed imposition is itself an index of the extent to which Tennyson had internalised and was unable to jettison the sceptical implications of a scientific, rationalistic understanding of the world. A reminder of the underlying addiction appears in section CXXIII of the poem. Like the late discovery, in section CVIII, that in the highest place there is only the reflex of his own mortal face, in section CXXIII there is a resurgence

of the secular scientific vision which empties experience of spiritual
hiding places:

> There rolls the deep where grew the tree.
>   O earth, what changes hast thou seen!
>   There where the long street roars, hath been
> The stillness of the central sea.
>
> The hills are shadows, and they flow
>   From form to form, and nothing stands;
>   They melt like mist, the solid lands,
> Like clouds they shape themselves and go.
>
> (CXXIII. 1–8)

Once this kind of Lyellian perspective has been learned, it seems it cannot
be unlearned, however hard another part of the mind might try. The
rational understanding which underpins the fertile poetry of the first
two stanzas of this section throws spiritual assertion, in the final stanza
of the section, onto the defensive, unconvinced and unconvincing:

> But in my spirit will I dwell,
>   And dream my dream, and hold it true;
>   For though my lips may breathe adieu,
> I cannot think the thing farewell.
>
> (CXXIII.9–12)

The inequity in imaginative power between the deeply grasped empirical
geology in the first two stanzas of section CXXIII and the retreat into
spiritual dreaming in the last stanza can up to a point, but only up to
a point, be seen as a microcosm of *In Memoriam* as a whole. The concluding
stanzas of the Epilogue to *In Memoriam* show that Tennyson 'had assimilated a good deal' of the doctrine of the Scottish writer Robert Chambers in
order to cope, not so much with Lyell's geology, but at least with Lyell's
vision of purposeless violence in the organic world (Killham 1958: 256).
In *Vestiges of the Natural History of Creation* (1844) Chambers engaged in
those pre-Darwinian debates about evolution which again found their
source in Enlightenment thought, including that of Jean Baptiste
Lamarck (1744–1829). Chambers's book was, as John Killham has noted,
a 'thoroughgoing advocacy of an evolutionary theory of the origin of
species' (Killham 1958: 252), in which he offered a vision of organic

nature not as something caught in a state of directionless process, but as a system that was developing in accordance with divine plan: 'Chambers' theory of evolution adumbrated the possibility that the evidences of physical development of man from lower species were not reason for despair, but simply proof of God's majestic scheme of continuous creation' (Killham 1958: 258). Chambers' speculative evolutionism tried to explain suffering in the world as part of a larger plan which would redeem all in the end:

> It may be that...there is a system of Mercy and Grace behind the screen of nature, which is to make up for all casualties endured here...it is necessary to suppose that the present system is but a part of the whole, a stage in a Great Progress, and that the Redress is in reserve.
> (Chambers 1969: 384–85)

He also went so far as to suggest that human beings themselves may evolve further as part of the 'Great Progress':

> Is our race but the initial of the grand crowning type? Are there yet to be species superior to us in organization, purer in feeling, more powerful in device and act, and who shall take a rule over us!... There may then be occasion for a nobler type of humanity, which shall complete the zoological circle on this planet, and realize some of the dreams of the purest spirits of the present race.
> (Chambers 1969: 276)

It was in significant part these kinds of comment which enabled Tennyson to bring *In Memoriam* to a positive conclusion, to envisage optimistically a future 'crowning race' of humanity (Epilogue, 128), which would be the realisation of God's plan for creation as a whole. Chambers helped Tennyson finish his poem in a way that, if not Christian, at least managed to combine an evolutionary perspective with something like a spiritual teleology. Chambers's wording permeates the vision at the very end of the Epilogue, where Tennyson, celebrating the marriage of his sister Cecilia to his friend Edmund Lushington, imagines a child born of the marriage:

> A soul shall draw from out the vast
> And strike his being into bounds,

And, moved through life of lower phase,
      Result in man, be born and think,
      And act and love, a closer link
Betwixt us and the crowning race

Of those that, eye to eye, shall look
      On knowledge; under whose command
      Is Earth and Earth's, and in their hand
Is Nature like an open book;

No longer half-akin to brute,
      For all we thought and loved and did,
      And hoped, and suffered, is but seed
Of what in them is flower and fruit;

Whereof the man, that with me trod
      This planet, was a noble type
      Appearing ere the times were ripe,
That friend of mine who lives in God,

That God, which ever lives and loves,
      One God, one law, one element,
      And one far-off divine event,
To which the whole creation moves.

                (Epilogue, 123–44)

A comparable perspective had informed section CXVIII:

           They say,
The solid earth whereon we tread

In tracts of fluent heat began,
      And grew to seeming-random forms,
      The seeming prey of cyclic storms,
Till at the last arose the man:

Who throve and branched from clime to clime,
      The herald of a higher race,
      And of himself in higher place,
If so he type this work of time

Within himself . . .
                  and show
That life is not as idle ore,

But iron dug from central gloom,
 And heated hot with burning fears,
 And dipt in baths of hissing tears,
And battered with the shocks of doom

To shape and use. Arise and fly
 The reeling Faun, the sensual feast;
 Move upward, working out the beast,
And let the ape and tiger die.

(CXVIII.7–17, 19–28)

The vision of the Epilogue offers an ideologically distinctly biased reading of evolutionary process. It, like section CXVIII, is instinct with a discourse of progress that is necessarily political. Tennyson's idea of evolution in these two sections, his idea of a continuous, unilinear ascent, slowly 'working out the beast', is part and parcel of the gradualism which, more often than not, he espoused in social and political matters. This politically conservative preference for gradual change is highlighted in the hostility he shows in *In Memoriam* to what he sees as 'The blind hysterics of the Celt', which he contrasts with the 'freedom' that resides in the 'regal seat / Of England' (CIX.16, 14–15); or in his hostility to what he describes as the French predilection for revolutionary, cataclysmic change: 'The red fool-fury of the Seine' (CXXVII.7). Tennyson's evolutionary vision and his social and political prejudices imply each other here. Working out the beast and letting the ape and tiger die are the same as avoiding and feeling superior to blind hysterics and red fool-fury. The message is that England, in its Imperial sobriety, has already evolved further than either Ireland or France.

The ideological imaginary that governs Tennyson's understanding of evolution in the Epilogue to *In Memoriam* at once governs his presentation of the figure of Hallam. The figure of the archetype is now absorbed into an Idea of a humanity which has not, as yet, even appeared on earth. So that the by now completely mythologised Hallam is seen as a 'type' of a future 'crowning race' of superior beings (Epilogue, 138, 128). Tennyson may, up to a point, be seen as responding to Chambers' conjectural evolutionism in the spirit of the 'spirit' that dreams its 'dream' in the last stanza of CXXIII. The dream of the Epilogue, with its imaginary, Chambers-like construction of evolutionary progress and its hyper-idealised beloved, may be seen to sidestep the perception born of Lyell's hard science that 'The hills are shadows... /... and nothing stands' (CXXIII.5–6). It may be seen to pass over the phantom that has no spiritual content in section CVIII. And yet, and it is a big 'yet', we should not lose sight of the fact that even Tennyson's leap into faith betrays a deep need for something like scientific authority. In drawing on Chambers in the Epilogue Tennyson went, in one fundamental respect, a great deal further than the Lyell of the 1830–33 *Principles*. Tennyson accepts, as Lyell had not, the idea of evolution. Neither Tennyson, nor Chambers before him, knew what Darwin was to explain in his 1859 *Origin of Species*: that is, the mechanism, natural selection, by which evolution proceeds. But Tennyson nevertheless takes on board, at the end of *In Memoriam*, the world-altering concept of the transmutation of species. In so doing, he is confronting the anxieties which even the early Lyell had sought to avoid in his opposition to Lamarckian ideas of evolution in the 1830–33 *Principles*. What is important is that, after having been gravely disconcerted by the insights of rational science upon reading Lyell's *Principles*, Tennyson does not react in any crass way against scientific perspective in his conclusion to *In Memoriam*. Tennyson may write, in section CXX, 'What matters Science unto men?' (CXX.7), but the conclusion of *In Memoriam* shows that it continues to matter a great deal to him. The Epilogue bases its optimism on a reading of evolutionary process itself. This should not be underestimated. The reading may appear in the twenty-first century to be unacceptably over-determined. But the overdetermination should not obscure the reality of Tennyson's imaginative incorporation of one of the most conceptually revolutionary ideas in human thought. Nor should it obscure for us Tennyson's craving to be able to identify spiritual hope in a broadly scientific frame of reference.

The optimism that the closing stages of *In Memoriam* were to salvage from the writings of Robert Chambers was not something that Tennyson was to sustain in the years immediately following the publication of the poem. In *Maud* it was the turn of Tennyson's sceptical imagination entirely to overwhelm idealist hankering and of the empty phantom to claim its due.

6
That Abiding Phantom Cold: *Maud*

Tennyson's *Maud. A Monodrama* was originally titled *Maud or the Madness* (Tennyson, Hallam 1897: I.402; Shatto 1986: 22). It seems that Tennyson was still toying with the idea of this title even after its first, 1855, publication simply as *Maud*, since 'or the Madness' is added in his hand on the title page of a copy of the first edition now in the University of Virginia Library (Ricks and Day 1987–93: XXX.298). The addition of 'A Monodrama' to the title was made in an 1875 edition of Tennyson's *Works*. Both Tennyson's subtitle and his original title are relevant to a reading of *Maud*; the first in respect of the poem's form and the second in respect of its subject.

I

Many of Tennyson's contemporaries were perplexed by the formal features of the poem. Tennyson himself called *Maud* 'a drama, i.e. a monodrama and one sui generis' (Lang and Shannon 1982–90: III.47). It was, he said, 'a drama in lyrics. It shows the unfolding of a lonely, morbid soul, touched with inherited madness' (Van Dyke 1920: 97). He also commented that the 'peculiarity of this poem is that different phases of passion in one person take the place of different characters' (Tennyson, Hallam 1897: I.396). Many contemporary readers found it difficult to follow the dramatic narrative of the poem. It can still be awkward, since the narrative connection between lyrics that show different phases of passion often has to be inferred. The problem is there from the start. In the very first lines of *Maud* we are plunged, without narrative explication, into the midst of one of the protagonist's phases of passion. Eric Griffiths has commented on this opening:

> The speaker has an odd way of, as it were, button-holing the absence
> of his interlocutor. The opening of the poem is very frank and

communicative, too much so, in fact, for no conversation could comfortably start as this poem starts:

> I hate the dreadful hollow behind the little wood,
> Its lips in the field above are dabbled with blood-red heath,
> The red-ribbed ledges drip with a silent horror of blood,
> And Echo there, whatever is asked her, answers 'Death'.

> (I.1–4)

Nothing can be answered to these lines. (What could you say – 'Oh, really, how fascinating' or 'Yes, yes, so do I, so do I'?) '*The* dreadful hollow', '*the* little wood': the definite articles press on us the obsessive predominance of these places in the speaker's imagination but as yet the reader, not knowing the story, has no idea which hollow and wood are of such concern, and so even less idea why they matter.

> (Griffiths 1989: 158)

One of the most impressive things about *Maud* is the way that it sustains – across the entire poem – the intense, anxious pace established in its opening stanza. It is a pace achieved by the way in which Tennyson repeatedly casts the protagonist's imagination at least one step beyond the reader's grasp. The reader does, at points, catch up, in passages where he or she is allowed to breathe, passages which partly explain what is happening. But then she or he is thrown back into the position of having to catch up again and yet again. Even in sequences where we have understood what is going on, the speaker's shifting feelings and reflections frequently follow each other with dizzying speed. The formal properties of *Maud* are not seriously problematic a century and a half later, for readers who have had to negotiate the fragmentations and non-sequiturs of much twentieth-century modernist and postmodernist writing. In its relative dislocation the work anticipates those movements, even though a plain narrative sequence in the poem *is* recoverable. For many readers in the mid-nineteenth century, however, it was an unacceptable challenge.

When the review in the *Press* for 11 August 1855 used the word 'incoherent' of the poem, it was articulating a widely held reaction. The reviewer in the *Morning Post* of 2 August had observed that either of the two vowels in the title of the poem could be excised in order to get an idea of its nature. 'As it is a new form of Poem altogether, the critic not being able to make it out, went at it', Tennyson commented ruefully in October 1855 (Lang and Shannon 1982–90: II.133).

II

The form of the poem should not be taken in isolation from its subject: madness. Madness and a ringing of the changes on a variety of kinds of internal and external disorder. The formal dislocations in *Maud* are symptomatic of the poem's engagement with disturbance. It is disturbance in every sphere. In the first Part or movement of the poem there is the protagonist's troubled perception of discord in the natural world. The nightmare vision of 'Nature, red in tooth and claw' in *In Memoriam* (LVI.15) reappears in the protagonist's horrified understanding that violence in nature is something which cannot be redeemed by religious sentiment:

> For nature is one with rapine, a harm no preacher can heal;
> The Mayfly is torn by the swallow, the sparrow speared by the shrike,
> And the whole little wood where I sit is a world of plunder and prey.
> (I.123–25)

The vision of rapine is widened to embrace the mid-nineteenth-century political scene in Europe: 'Shall I weep if a Poland fall? shall I shriek if a Hungary fail? / Or an infant civilisation be ruled with rod or with knout?' (I.147–48). The protagonist also has an extreme revulsion against mid-nineteenth-century British capitalist society where, as he sees it, an overt peace masks vicious internal malpractice. Economic prosperity at home he deems a false peace, an euphemism for

> Civil war, as I think, and that of a kind
> The viler, as underhand, not openly bearing the sword...
>
> Peace sitting under her olive, and slurring the days gone by,
> When the poor are hovelled and hustled together, each sex,
>   like swine,
> When only the ledger lives, and when only not all men lie;
> Peace in her vineyard – yes! – but a company forges the wine.
>
> And the vitriol madness flushes up in the ruffian's head,
> Till the filthy by-lane rings to the yell of the trampled wife,
> And chalk and alum and plaster are sold to the poor for bread,
> And the spirit of murder works in the very means of life,

And Sleep must lie down armed, for the villainous centre-bits
Grind on the wakeful ear in the hush of the moonless nights,
While another is cheating the sick of a few last gasps, as he sits
To pestle a poisoned poison behind his crimson lights.

(I.27–28, 33–44)

'[T]hese hexameters', George Eliot commented in 1855, are 'grating in sound...undeniably strong in expression, and eat themselves with phosphoric eagerness into our memory, in spite of our will' (Eliot 1963: 193).

At moments, in the early stages of *Maud*, the protagonist affects detachment from the scenes of plunder and prey which so clearly appal him: '*I* have not made the world, and He that made it will guide' (I.149). But this is wishful, desperate thinking. He is more deeply driven by a conviction that there is no spiritual principle directing the world. His perception of a destructive force of competition in natural and human realms is conditioned, as in *In Memoriam*, by contemporary scientific thinking about the world. It is this conditioning, in particular, which provokes scepticism about whether reality is ordered by a caring, loving, reconciling power. Just as man, nature's 'last work, who seemed so fair' under the old dispensation is reduced to 'A monster...a dream, / A discord' under the new order of science in section LVI of *In Memoriam* (9, 21–22), so in *Maud* the 'sad astrology, the boundless plan' (I.634), which Tennyson identified as 'modern astronomy' (Tennyson, Hallam 1913: 958), turns the stars into 'tyrants in...iron skies':

> Innumerable, pitiless, passionless eyes,
> Cold fires, yet with power to burn and brand
> His nothingness into man.

(I.635–38)

Nor is it just the modern science of astronomy which renders the universe devoid of spiritual meaning and indifferent to human life. Nature as 'rapine' is coloured by Lyellian thought:

> the whole little wood where I sit is a world of plunder
>   and prey.
> We are puppets, Man in his pride, and Beauty fair in her flower;
> Do we move ourselves, or are moved by an unseen hand
>   at a game
> That pushes us off from the board, and others ever succeed?

(I.125–28)

Discord and alienation characterise the relations between the protagonist's family and that of Maud's. It seems that the protagonist's father and Maud's father had together been involved in some business enterprise, some 'vast speculation' (I.9). The failure of the enterprise had somehow benefitted Maud's father whilst ruining the protagonist's:

> that old man, now lord of the broad estate and the Hall,
> Dropt off gorged from a scheme that had left us flaccid
>   and drained.

> (I.19–20)

'Villainy somewhere!' thinks the protagonist (I.17) and he holds Maud's father morally responsible for the violent (apparently self-inflicted) death suffered by his own father following the collapse of the business scheme. As the Mayfly is torn by the swallow, so the protagonist speaks of 'the feud, / The household Fury sprinkled with blood / By which our houses are torn' (I.715–16). For the protagonist the spirit of division inheres in the universe, from competition for survival in nature, through international relations, the capitalism of mid-Victorian Britain, to the relations between families. '[T]he spirit of Cain' (I.23) defines existence and there is no New Testament restitution. It is a fallen universe, a universe of schism, hate, despair and death, from which the protagonist, in the earlier sections of the poem, finds no respite: 'the drift of the Maker is dark, an Isis hid by the veil' (I.144).

Above all, the spirit of feud defines not merely the external world and the external relations of things, but the protagonist's own being. Amidst all the external disorder, he is himself psychologically disturbed:

> A wounded thing with a rancorous cry,
> At war with myself and a wretched race,
> Sick, sick to the heart of life, am I.

> (I.363–65)

There is a disarming frankness about some of the protagonist's images of his own disintegration:

> Living alone in an empty house . . .
> Where I hear the dead at midday moan . . .
> And my own sad name in corners cried . . .

> (I.257, 259, 261)

The protagonist's sickness involves a fixation with death. He remembers the occasion of his father's death:

> I remember the time, for the roots of my hair were stirred
> By a shuffled step, by a dead weight trailed, by a whispered fright,
> And my pulses closed their gates with a shock on my
>   heart as I heard
> The shrill-edged shriek of a mother divide the shuddering night.
>
> (I.13–16)

At times, the protagonist's obsession with death is both involuntary and explicitly elicited from the scene described:

> I heard no sound where I stood
> But the rivulet on from the lawn
> Running down to my own dark wood;
> Or the voice of the long sea-wave as it swelled
> Now and then in the dim-gray dawn;
> But I looked, and round, all round the house I beheld
> The death-white curtain drawn;
> Felt a horror over me creep,
> Prickle my skin and catch my breath,
> Knew that the death-white curtain meant but sleep,
> Yet I shuddered and thought like a fool of the sleep of death.
>
> (I.516–26)

The automatic way in which thoughts of death surface in the protagonist's imagination captures the deepest level of his obsession, where his fixation with death touches a death-wish:

> What! am I raging alone as my father raged in his mood?
> Must *I* too creep to the hollow and dash myself down and die...
>
> O, having the nerves of motion as well as the nerves of pain,
> Were it not wise if I fled from the place and the pit and the fear?
>
> (I.53–54, 63–64)

III

Maud is a monodrama. We have only the protagonist's lens of perception. This does not mean that everything he sees has a reality only in his mind. We take as fact, within the fiction of the poem, that the speaker's father is dead and that his death was in some way related to a financial venture which had gone wrong. The protagonist's views on the rapaciousness of contemporary British capitalism – 'Civil war' (I.27) – are grounded in observation of a world outside the fiction of the poem. Tennyson had read his friend Charles Kingsley's 1850 *Alton Locke*, with its descriptions of the appalling conditions of mid-nineteenth-century slum life. He had had 'long talks with Charles Kingsley and F.D. Maurice about the terrible conditions in the rapidly growing industrial cities with their vile housing, sweated labour, dirt, disease and misery' (Tennyson, Charles 1968: 281). Tennyson himself, in a letter to Arthur Gurney of 6 December 1855, spoke of his protagonist as having a 'vein of insanity', but he also noted:

> I do not mean that my madman does not speak truths too: witness this extract from the letter of an enlightened German, quoted in one of our papers about the state of England, and then think if he is all wrong when he calls our peace a war, and worse in some respects than an open civil war – 'Every day a murder or two or three – every day a wife beaten to death by her husband – every day a father or mother starving their children, or pinching, knocking, and kicking them into a state of torture and living putrefaction'.
>
> (Lang and Shannon 1982–90: II.137–38)

Similarly, we take it as given that contemporary science had, for many thinking Victorians, undermined the credibility of any spiritual doctrine that sought to neutralise the degradations of the world in a vision of ultimate divine benevolence. Despair is a comprehensible kind of response in such a situation.

For all this, however, the protagonist does have 'vein of insanity' and our reading of his vision is always affected by doubts about its reliability. The sense that there is a large element of deluded overreaction in the protagonist's reactions to the world is unavoidable. What is interesting, however, is that the protagonist himself is given, in some measure at least, to know this: 'What! am I raging alone...?' (I.53). It is on this glimmering self-knowledge that his attempt to struggle away from the place, the pit, and the fear is based. What makes the attempt so impossibly hard is that he is living at a time when he cannot seek support for a more positive vision in any external structure or framework of belief. Such structures having been undermined, he exists in a world where responsibility for imposing a satisfactory order and meaning upon experience falls entirely on himself. The prospect of his finding a centre, a resting-place either within or without, is bleak. The confusion of inner and outer disorders, each reflecting and exacerbating the other, seems from the outset a tragic formula. Hallam Tennyson reported his father as saying: ' "This poem is a little *Hamlet*" ' (Tennyson, Hallam 1897: I.396). The figure of Hamlet was often invoked by Victorians in order to image the contemporary *maladie du siècle*, the perturbed subjectivism blighting individual consciousness in a world where long-cherished systems of thought and belief had been eroded. In the 'Preface' to the first edition of his Poems (1853) Matthew Arnold described his portrayal of Empedocles in his 1852 poem 'Empedocles on Etna':

> I intended to delineate the feelings of one of the last of the Greek religious philosophers... living on into a time when the habits of Greek thought and feeling had begun fast to change, character to dwindle, the influence of the Sophists to prevail. Into the feelings of a man so situated there entered much that we are accustomed to consider as exclusively modern; how much, the fragments of Empedocles himself which remain to us are sufficient at least to indicate. What those who are familiar only with the great monuments of early Greek genius suppose to be its exclusive characteristics, have disappeared: the calm, the cheerfulness, the disinterested objectivity have disappeared; the dialogue of the mind with itself has commenced; modern problems have presented themselves; we hear already the doubts, we witness the discouragement, of Hamlet and of Faust.
>
> (Super 1960–77; I.1)

The Arnold of 'Dover Beach' (1867), cheerlessly stranded in a nineteenth-century world which has neither 'certitude, nor peace, nor help for pain' (1.34), appeals to love as a kind of last resort against chaos. In so doing he evinces a typically Victorian response, as Walter E. Houghton notes:

> At its extreme, the intellectual struggle could result... in a sick state of skeptical negation. Without a theory of life or action to sustain the will to live, lost in a wasteland of loneliness and despair, the sensitive mind could turn to love as the only value left to hold onto. Here at least was an anchor for the soul and a refuge from cosmic and social isolation. 'Scepticism is my spirit', cries out Symonds. 'In my sorest needs I have had no actual faith, and have said to destruction,

"Thou art my sister". To the skirts of human love I have clung, and I cling blindly. But all else is chaos'.

(Houghton 1973: 388–89)

Maud is no exception to this cult of redemptive love. The protagonist of the poem reaches a position where he celebrates Maud as: 'my love, my only friend'; 'her whose gentle will has changed my fate' (I.599, 621). The consequence of his claim to have found love is large. It is not just that it is personally reinvigorating. The love that the protagonist speaks of between himself and Maud extends outwards to include an idea of the reunion of their families and an implication that the principle of reintegration works its way back up the scales – through the divisions in society and nature – to the point where the fracture at the heart of the cosmos is healed. At the same time as associating a 'sad astrology' (I.634) with modern astronomy, Tennyson noted that 'of old astrology was thought to sympathise with and rule man's fate' (Tennyson, Hallam 1913: 958). The universe as conceived before modern science took, in other words, intimate notice of human life. Tennyson also noted that in his discovery of love the protagonist replaces the demythologised universe of modern astronomy with a 'newer astrology' and 'describes' the stars 'as "soft splendours"' (Tennyson, Hallam 1913: 958). Through the love he insists upon the protagonist claims to have overcome both self-alienation and alienation from the world. He also asserts that, by the same means, an alien universe is transformed into a sympathetic one; into a universe which, suffused with love, is in step with and pays proper attention to the mortal condition:

> Here will I lie, while these long branches sway,
> And you fair stars that crown a happy day
> Go in and out as if at merry play,
> Who am no more so all forlorn,
> As when it seemed far better to be born
> To labour and the mattock-hardened hand,
> Than nursed at ease and brought to understand
> A sad astrology . . .
>
> But now shine on, and what care I,
> Who in this stormy gulf have found a pearl
> The countercharm of space and hollow sky . . .
>
> Beat to the noiseless music of the night!
> Has our whole earth gone nearer to the glow
> Of your soft splendours that you look so bright?

> *I* have climbed nearer out of lonely Hell.
> Beat, happy stars, timing with things below...
>
> (I.627–34, 639–41, 675–79)

So the protagonist affirms the regenerative power of love. It is because of love that he declares he will 'Not die; but live a life of truest breath, / And teach true life to fight with mortal wrongs' (I.651–52). Tennyson commented that these lines enshrine the 'central idea' that is explored in *Maud*: 'the holy power of Love' (Tennyson, Hallam 1897: I.404). It is as the object of the protagonist's love that Maud assumes a place comparable to that occupied by Arthur Hallam in *In Memoriam* and by Cadrilla in *The Lover's Tale*. Hallam Tennyson notes that 'My father liked reading aloud this poem, a "Drama of the Soul", set in a landscape glorified by Love' (Tennyson, Hallam 1913: 956). In the context of such a drama the figure of Maud, while possessing a notional literal reality, functions principally to dramatise a dimension of the protagonist's own mind. The psychological interdependence of lover and loved-one in *Maud* was commented upon by Roy Basler in 1944:

> It has been observed that *Maud* is hardly an indicative title for the poem, in as much as the heroine is never materialised, but appears only through the hero's highly wrought vision. Yet one who follows Tennyson's theme cannot carp at a title so justly given; for Maud, the object of desire, is most realistically presented (psychologically speaking) as the dominant force in the drama which involves the inner conflict between the phases of the hero's soul... From the beginning to the end of the poem, she largely controls... the hero's psychic quest for the meaning of existence. The hero means nothing intelligible, either to the reader or to himself, except through her.
>
> (Basler 1944: 147–48)

In the first part of *Maud* the protagonist's discovery of someone to be loved *by* is presented as indistinguishable from the discovery of his own capacity *for* love. Maud becomes a figure of that higher self which the protagonist claims to apprehend in himself. Maud's status as an ideal object is emphasised through the high-flown associations and the more-than-natural descriptive terms which accumulate around her. She is an 'Oread' (I.544), the visible embodiment of a divine agent; or she has a 'grace that, bright and light as the crest / Of a peacock, sits on her shining head' (I.552–53), where one of the associations of peacocks is the incorruptible soul. The Cadrilla whose 'fair eyes / Shone' in *The Lover's Tale* (II.162–63 [II.155–56]), and the Hallam whose 'face', Tennyson declares, 'will shine / Upon me' in *In Memoriam* (CXVI.9–10), are both recalled in this preternatural 'shining' of Maud in the 1855 poem. Comparably, the protagonist, speaking of Maud, tells us that the 'Dark cedar', which he describes in section XVIII of the poem, is 'haunted by the starry head / Of her whose gentle will has changed my fate' (I.620–21). The conjunction between this somewhat surreal icon of Maud as a ghostly 'starry head' and the reference to Maud's will is symptomatic of the conjunction that takes place in the poem as a whole between the figure of Maud and the protagonist's psyche. Throughout the poem there is no real distinction between the wills of lover and loved-one. It is, for example, because of the love he feels for Maud that the protagonist agrees to accept Maud's view of her brother as 'rough but kind' (I.753). Previously, the brother has been disliked as the son of the man responsible for the death of the protagonist's father. Maud's brother has also snubbed the protagonist and, we are told, resisted Maud's wish that there should be a reconciliation between the two families. But the protagonist agrees to forgo resentment and align himself with Maud's better will:

> Well, rough but kind; why let it be so:
> For shall not Maud have her will? . . .
>
> So now I have sworn to bury
> All this dead body of hate,
> I feel so free and so clear . . .

> (I.766–67, 779–81)

For Maud to have her will is the same thing as a generous act of will on the part of the protagonist. Because what he is doing in these lines is, as he insists, putting away that part of himself which has been fixated with death and consumed with hatred at least as far back as the death of his father (recalled in the metaphor of the 'dead body' in line 780). The essential identity of the wills of the protagonist and of Maud – or the imaging of the protagonist's higher will through that of Maud – is suggested by other passages in both Parts I and II of the poem. In Part I the protagonist tells how Maud made him 'divine amends' (I.202) through bestowing upon him 'a smile so sweet' (I.201):

> And thus a delicate spark
> Of glowing and growing light

> Through the livelong hours of the dark
> Kept itself warm in the heart of my dreams...

(I.204–207)

The imagery of this inner spark of light reappears in Part II, when the protagonist speaks of Maud's love as the condition of – indeed identifies that love with – the reality of his own will:

> as long, O God, as she
> Have a grain of love for me,
> So long, no doubt, no doubt,
> Shall I nurse in my dark heart,
> However weary, a spark of will
> Not to be trampled out.

(II.100–105)

In Part III of the poem the protagonist wills a regeneration of his own dark heart. The poem, however, does not endorse his confidence in that regeneration.

IV

The protagonist claims regeneration twice. His celebration of a fulfilled love for Maud is the first. The second appears in the third part of the poem where he tells of 'a hope for the world in the coming wars' (III.11). The protagonist's commitment to the imminent war against Russia, what history calls the Crimean War, takes place some time after he has assaulted and killed Maud's brother in the garden where, at the end of Part I of the poem, he last meets Maud. In his violence against Maud's brother the protagonist forfeited any chance he might have had of developing his relationship with *Maud*: 'there rang on a sudden a passionate cry, / A cry for a brother's blood: / It will ring in my heart and ears, till I die, till I die' (II.33–35). We learn, indeed, that Maud has died in the interval between the event in the garden and our coming upon the protagonist on the Breton shore at the outset of Part II. But the protagonist connects the prospective war which he enthuses about in Part III with his love for Maud. In his biography of Tennyson, Robert Bernard Martin gives a conventional account of this link made by the protagonist between his love and his concluding assertion of the regenerative potential of war:

> When her brother discovers Maud and the narrator in the garden at midnight, a duel ensues, and the brother is killed. Maud dies, and the protagonist goes mad, is confined to an asylum in Brittany, and at last is cured of his madness by a purified love of the dead Maud that leads him to a more generalised love of mankind, which finally manifests itself by his going to the Crimea to fight on the side of the right.
>
> (Martin 1980: 384)

This summary echoes the outline of *Maud* given by Tennyson's son. In the text of this account included in his *Memoir* of his father, Hallam Tennyson gives only the reference to *Hamlet* as a verbatim quotation of Tennyson himself:

> As he said himself, 'This poem is a little *Hamlet*', the history of a morbid poetic soul, under the blighting influence of a recklessly speculative age. He is the heir of madness, an egotist with the makings of a cynic, raised to sanity by a pure and holy love which elevates his whole nature, passing from the height of triumph to the lowest depth of misery, driven into madness by the loss of her whom he has loved, and, when he has at length passed through the fiery furnace, and has recovered his reason, giving himself up to work for the good of mankind through the unselfishness born of a great passion.
>
> (Tennyson, Hallam 1897: I.396)

This summary can be read, as *Maud* itself has often been read, as meaning that both poem and poet sanction the protagonist's claim, in the concluding part of the poem, to have found health in war fever. In his ending of *Maud* Tennyson has been taken to task for being emotionally, morally and politically at fault. Isobel Armstrong, commenting on *In Memoriam* and *Maud*, writes that 'Both sanction conservative, not to say reactionary endings' (Armstrong 1993: 283). Many, by no means all, but many contemporary reviewers of the poem saw Tennyson, through his protagonist, culpably endorsing the case for war. In the *Saturday Review* for 3 November 1855, for example, Goldwin Smith observed:

> To the glorification of war as a remedy for the canker of peace, the common sense of the nation, even the most warlike part of it, has

answered, that war, though to be faced, and even to be accepted with
enthusiasm, for other ends, is not to be incurred for this... To wage
'war with a thousand battles and shaking a hundred thrones', in
order to cure a hypochondriac and get rid of the chicory in coffee, is
a bathos... In Milton, Byron, Shelley, Wordsworth, a passionate cry
for a just war would have seemed like the foam on the wave – in
Mr. Tennyson it seems a little like the foam without the wave.

(Jump 1967: 186–87, 190)

Smith engages what was a national debate about the war in the Crimea.
One example of the debate was a piece, in *Blackwood's Edinburgh Magazine*
for November 1854 (LXXVI), which influenced Tennyson in his writing of *Maud*. The item was entitled 'Peace and War: A Dialogue', and
parallels between it and *Maud* were noted by Robert Schweik in 1960
(Schweik 1960).

The Platonic-type dialogue in *Blackwood's* was between a Quaker and
a member of the 'Peace Society' called Irenaeus (derived from the Greek
word for 'peace') and Tlepolemos (who was an Homeric hero and whose
name means 'enduring of war') respectively. Irenaeus, the Quaker, mouths
the kinds of sentiment about the value of peace that the protagonist of
Tennyson's poem scorns. The Quaker as despised peace-man appears
not only in lines 327–33 of Part II, but also in Part I, where it is a Quaker
who 'preach[es] our poor little army down, /... This broad-brimmed
hawker of holy things, / Whose ear is crammed with his cotton, and
rings / Even in dreams to the chink of his pence' (I.367, 370–72). But it
is Tlepolemos' justification of war that is most fully echoed in the *Maud*
protagonist's thoughts. Tlepolemos makes the same distinction as the
protagonist between the moral honour of open war and the moral dis-
honour of conflict, corruption and depredation within a commercial
society only technically at peace:

Malice and hatred in human hearts are far more odious in the eyes of
Heaven than wounds and death. These are part of natural evil, while
those are part of moral evil...

What is called peace is too often a misnomer: only another name for
intestine and most uncivil war. It is war at home, civil or uncivil,
I especially deprecate...

What do you say to the struggle of society to get on, to get rich...
This is the everyday life of a peaceful commercial society; this is
peace, if you like, but seasoned... with envy, hatred, malice, and all

uncharitableness... Does mercantile speculation stir up no evil passions? What do you say to the railway mania of 1847?... war has never, and will never, afflict society with the anxiety, the madness, the degradation... which that railway mania did... In the worst cases there have been two rival camps of the worst kind, each striving to outstarve the other, capital fighting with savings... and the victory eventually belonging, not to the strongest battalions, but the longest purse; peace at length restored, but heart-burnings innumerable perpetuated. Talk of the horrors of war! – these... are the horrors of peace... Not only your wine merchant drugs your port, but your grocer sands your sugar... your baker puts alum in your bread... To so great a degree has this system of falsification been carried, that, on the evidence of a leading medical journal, we appear to eat, drink, and smoke little else but solid, liquid and gaseous lies.

(*Blackwood's* 1854: LXXVI.593–96)

The indignation of Tennyson's protagonist is a heightened version of the same. Not only are there details like the 'chalk and alum and plaster... sold to the poor for bread' (I.39), but there is the broad critique of a marauding capitalist peace:

Why do they prate of the blessings of Peace? we have made them
    a curse,
Pickpockets, each hand lusting for all that is not its own;
And lust of gain, in the spirit of Cain, is it better or worse
Than the heart of the citizen hissing in war on his own hearthstone?

But these are the days of advance, the works of the men of mind,
When who but a fool would have faith in a tradesman's ware or
    his word?
Is it peace or war? Civil war, as I think, and that of a kind
The viler, as underhand, not openly bearing the sword.

(I.21–28)

The protagonist enters the open war against Russia for the same higher reasons ('I embrace the purpose of God...', III.59) as are advanced by Tlepolemus in the *Blackwood's* dialogue: 'To set peace above right is to set the seen above the unseen, – the present life of man above his more glorious destiny' (*Blackwood's* 1854: 593).

So Tennyson, in *Maud*, was directly entering the debate of the times. Tlepolemus seems to have the advantage in the *Blackwood's* dialogue.

But to read Tennyson's poem as if it were a straightforward transcription of the Blackwood's essay, with Tennyson supporting his protagonist's vigour for war, would be to overlook the dramatic ironies of the work and the critical relationship the poem has with issues of its time.

Not all of Tennyson's contemporary commentators saw the poet as endorsing his protagonist's final position. In an analysis much favoured by Tennyson, published in the year that *Maud* first appeared, George Brimley emphasised that Tennyson had written a work 'which demands to be judged, not by the intrinsic goodness and beauty of the actions and emotions depicted, but by their relation to character' (Jump 1967: 196). Brimley was sensitive to the fundamental dramatic nature of the poem. This is something that Tennyson, stung by some of the reviews of *Maud*, was always to emphasise. In the last year of his life, he gave Henry Van Dyke a trenchant explanation of the distorted and pathological mentality of the poem's protagonist:

> You must remember always, in reading it, what it is meant to be – a drama in lyrics. It shows the unfolding of a lonely, morbid soul, touched with inherited madness . . . The things which seem like faults belong not so much to the poem as to the character of the hero.
>
> He is wrong, of course, in much that he says. If he had always been wise and just he would not have been himself. He begins with a false comparison – 'blood-red heath'. There is no such thing in nature; but he sees the heather tinged like blood because his mind has been disordered . . . He is wrong in thinking that war will transform the cheating tradesman into a great-souled hero, or that it will sweep away the dishonesties and lessen the miseries of humanity. The history of the Crimean War proves his error. But this very delusion is natural to him: it is in keeping with his morbid, melancholy, impulsive character to see a cure for the evils of peace in the horrors of war.
>
> (Van Dyke 1920: 97)

It is true that this is a second-hand report. Yet the terms are not merely different from, they are also much sharper than Hallam Tennyson's account of the poem in the *Memoir* (p. 151). It is also true that Henry Van Dyke was talking to the poet long after the publication of *Maud* and the end of the Crimean War. Tennyson may have been adjusting his explanation with the wisdom of extended hindsight. But there is first-hand evidence of Tennyson saying similar things, with clear and discriminating conviction, not long after the appearance of *Maud* (on 28 July 1855) and before the formal conclusion of the war against

Russia. In his letter to Archer Gurney of 6 December 1855 Tennyson stressed the intrinsic instability of the protagonist and the conjunction of this instability with the iniquities of the times:

> Now I wish to say one word about *Maud* which you and others so strangely misinterpret. I have had Peace party papers sent to me claiming me as being on their side because I had put the cry for war into the mouth of a madman. Surely that is not half so wrong a criticism as some I have seen. Strictly speaking I do not see how from the poem I could be pronounced with certainty either peace man or war man. I wonder that you and others did not find out that all along the man was intended to have an hereditary vein of insanity, and that he falls foul on the swindling, on the times, because he feels that his father has been killed by the work of the lie, and that all through he fears the coming madness. How could you or anyone suppose that if I had to speak in my own person my own opinion of this war or war generally I should have spoken with so little moderation. The whole was intended to be a new form of dramatic composition. I took a man constitutionally diseased and dipt him into the circumstances of the time and took him out on fire.
>
> (Lang and Shannon 1982–90: II.137–38)

Tennyson never stopped defending *Maud*. One more example: in her 'Memories of Tennyson' Blanche Warre Cornish recalled one of the poet's innumerable readings of the work:

> Whenever lines occurred about war, war the purifier, war the unifier, Tennyson stopped to say that the critics had misunderstood him . . . The poem was a dramatic monologue. The sentiments were in the mouth of a madman. He wished he had called the poem as first planned, *Maud or the Madness*. 'Anyone can see that the words about war represent a mood. But the critics are nothing'.
>
> (Page 1983: 115)

The various inflexions of 'madness' which emerge in these passages where Tennyson refers (or is reported as having referred) to *Maud* are not always easy to tie down. In the notes on the poem which Tennyson left his son, Tennyson commented that in Part III the hero is 'Sane but shattered' (Tennyson, Hallam 1897: I.405). This is not enormously helpful, since it is difficult to know quite what significance to place on the word 'shattered'. The more especially when we recall that, in the variation on these terms reported by James Knowles, Tennyson seems to have used 'shattered' to mean not exactly sane: 'He is not quite sane – a little shattered' (Ray 1968: 45). Perhaps Tennyson was overstating the case, or Blanche Warre Cornish misrepresenting the precise discrimination he was making, when he told her that the sentiments about war were in the mouth of a madman. In the poem the representation of an utter madness is restricted to section v of Part II. Generally speaking, however, in Tennyson's comments on the protagonist as he appears at other points (particularly at the opening and close) of the poem, the suggestion is that he is represented as not completely sane. It is a disordered mind, placed either somewhere near or on the edge of the clinically definable madness that is specifically represented in section v of Part II. It is the representation of the condition of near madness which gives the poem some of its peculiar force. The condition imposes a qualifying, relativist perspective on the protagonist's utterances at the same time as allowing a special element of truth in his visions. Tennyson can attribute his half-mad protagonist with insight into psychological and social realities which, perhaps because of the challenge they might represent to orthodox perspectives, he might have found difficult to attribute to a character supposed in all conventional senses to be sane: 'I do not mean that my madman does not speak truths too' (Lang and Shannon 1982–90: II.138).

Roy Basler delivered a compelling psychological assessment of the relativity of the protagonist's sanity at the end of *Maud* when he said that the protagonist

> has not in Part III gained a normal psychic balance, although he (and perhaps the unwary reader) may think he has. He is not completely cured of psychic illness, but has merely exchanged one obsession, self-destruction, for another, self-sacrifice in a noble cause. The extent of his sanity in Part III is wholly relative to his new obsession. Although his condition is nowise as acute as it had been in the madhouse scene, it is still psychopathic, and acceptance of what he says and does must be relative to his condition.
>
> (Basler 1944: 154)

The imbalance of the speaker's mind is demonstrated, of course, in the textures of the verse itself. It is present in the opening section of the poem in every poetic effect – from the obsessive rhythms to the nightmarish colourings (the 'flickering half-light between the sane and the insane'; Nicolson 1923: 125) – which Tennyson chose to exploit. To Henry Van Dyke, Tennyson chose merely to highlight one of the earliest signals of disorder: the detail of the 'false comparison' as the protagonist speaks of the 'blood-red heath' (I.2). But signals of disturbance are many and various. Sometimes the representation of psychological disturbance touches something very dark indeed. His own malignant potential is something that the protagonist, with the perversely egocentric honesty of the psychotic, admits to in lines 527–36 of Part I:

> So dark a mind within me dwells,
>   And I make myself such evil cheer,
> That if *I* be dear to some one else,
>   Then some one else may have much to fear;
> But if *I* be dear to some one else,
>   Then I should be to myself more dear.
> Shall I not take care of all that I think,
> Yea even of wretched meat and drink,
> If I be dear,
> If I be dear to some one else.

The emphasis on the protagonist's derangement casts a relative light most significantly on what the protagonist has to say about war. In the opening section of the poem he feverishly castigates an imperfect peace: 'Is it peace or war? better, war! loud war by land and by sea, / War with a thousand battles, and shaking a hundred thrones' (I.47–48). And, if Tennyson knows that the idea of waging such a war in order to get rid of the chicory in coffee is a bathos – 'He is wrong in thinking that war will transform the cheating tradesman into a great-souled hero' (Van Dyke 1920: 97) – then the point would apply equally to the protagonist's glorification of war in the closing passages of the poem. Those passages bear not only the same sentiments but the same grating rhythms and the same overcolouring to which we were introduced at the outset. The glorifications of war at the beginning and end of the poem are linked also through the figure of Maud, and a doubt about the glorification lies at the heart of that linking.

In the early sections of the poem the protagonist views Maud herself in different ways. She *first* appeals to him when he hears her singing a martial ballad:

> A passionate ballad gallant and gay,
> A martial song like a trumpet's call!
> Singing alone in the morning of life,
> In the happy morning of life and of May,

> Singing of men that in battle array,
> Ready in heart and ready in hand,
> March with banner and bugle and fife
> To the death, for their native land.

$$(I.165–72)$$

This Maud of the martial song can be distinguished from the Maud of love, the Maud with whom the protagonist falls in love; a love which, he tells us, restores his psychological health by displacing his early, anxious isolation: 'My own heart's heart ... / I have climbed nearer out of lonely hell' (I.672, 678). The Maud of the martial song reappears in Part III of the poem. Just as Maud sang her song of war 'In the happy morning of life and of May' (I.168), so, in Part III, the protagonist invokes the spirit of a martial Maud at the time when the constellation 'Gemini' (III.7), which rises in late spring, is in the ascendant:

> like a silent lightning under the stars
> She seemed to divide in a dream from a band of the
>   blest,
> And spoke of a hope for the world in the coming wars –
> 'And in that hope, dear soul, let trouble have rest,
> Knowing I tarry for thee', and pointed to Mars
> As he glowed like a ruddy shield on the Lion's breast.

$$(III.9–14)$$

The appeal of the Maud of the martial song in Part I, Maud's initial appeal to the protagonist, answered to that imbalance with which the protagonist censored peace and eulogised war in the first forty-eight lines of the poem – a phase in which the protagonist's mind was what Tennyson called 'disordered' (Van Dyke 1920: 97) and in which the protagonist speaks of himself as having been 'raging' (I.53). If that initial eulogy of war is an expression of disorder and rage, then a question certainly arises about whether the glorification of war in the final part is equally such an expression. Tennyson himself seems to have allowed that a reading of the protagonist's concluding affirmations might be governed by a reading of the disease at the opening of the poem: 'Take this with the first where he railed at everything – He is not quite sane' (Ray 1968: 45).

Perhaps, however, the love that the protagonist claims to have experienced between his initial condition in the poem and his position in

Part III makes a difference to his enthusiasm for war in the final part. Certainly, the protagonist himself presumes that there is a difference between his 'raging' at the opening of the poem and what he claims is the purity and truth of his enthusiasm for war in Part III. The protagonist's dream of the dead Maud presides over this enthusiasm:

> She seemed to divide in a dream from a band of the blest,
> And spoke of a hope for the world in the coming wars . . .
>
> And it was but a dream, yet it yielded a dear delight
> To have looked, though but in a dream, upon eyes so fair,
> That had been in a weary world my one thing bright;
> And it was but a dream, yet it lightened my despair
> When I thought that a war would arise in defence of the right . . .
>
> And as months ran on and rumour of battle grew,
> 'It is time, it is time, O passionate heart', said I
> (For I cleaved to a cause that I felt to be pure and true),
> 'It is time, O passionate heart and morbid eye,
> That old hysterical mock-disease should die'.
>
> (III.10–11, 15–19, 29–33)

The protagonist's *own* reading of the trajectory of his life is what is reproduced in Hallam Tennyson's account of the poem in the *Memoir*, where the protagonist, at first a 'morbid poetic soul', then experiences 'a pure and holy love' and, at last, in his closing commitment to war, gives himself up 'to work for the good of mankind through the unselfishness born of a great passion' (Tennyson, Hallam 1897: I.396). Yet there is something questionable not only about the protagonist's raging for war but about both his claim to have been regenerated through love *and* his linking of the purity he supposes he found in love with the purity of motive that he claims in his excitement about war. The issue turns on the matter of passion.

V

In the opening stages of the poem the world of feud, rapine and death perceived by the protagonist is characterised by him as a world of unregenerate passion. 'Put down the passions', he declares intemperately,

> Put down the passions that make earth Hell!
> Down with ambition, avarice, pride,

> Jealousy, down! cut off from the mind
> The bitter springs of anger and fear;
> Down too, down at your own fireside,
> With the evil tongue and the evil ear,
> For each is at war with mankind.

(I.375–81)

All the harmful energies which the protagonist finds in the world and in himself are focussed in his mind around the image of his father's violent death. It is through this image that the deepest level of his fixation with destructive passion appears. At the heart of his passionate intolerance of passion is a preoccupation with the unreason that dips towards self-violence. Feeding his insistence upon the morbidity of passion is a shameful sense of the isolated passion of the suicide. It is guilty fear of this proclivity in himself which determines his negative view of nearly all forms and manifestations of passion.

Love itself is bound up with the protagonist's experience of self-destructive passion. He remembers his mother's scream – 'The shrill-edged shriek' (I.16) – on the night of his father's death. It is a cry of love that is fused in the protagonist's mind not only with death but with suicide. And, of course, not only his father's suicide:

> Must *I* too creep to the hollow and dash myself down and die
> Rather than hold by the law that I made, nevermore to brood
> On a horror of shattered limbs and a wretched swindler's lie?
>
> Would there be sorrow for *me*? there was *love* in the passionate shriek,
> Love for the silent thing that had made false haste to the grave –

(I.54–58)

The negative associations which love has for the protagonist account for his initial 'fight', as Tennyson put it, against his 'growing passion' for Maud (Tennyson, Hallam 1897: I.402). He tells us how he caught sight of Maud as she passed in a carriage and the control he is striving to impose on his own feelings finds expression in the image he constructs of her:

> a cold and clear-cut face...
> Faultily faultless, icily regular, splendidly null,
> Dead perfection, no more; nothing more, if it had not been

> For a chance of travel, a paleness, an hour's defect of the
>   rose...
> From which I escaped heart-free, with the least little touch
>   of spleen.

(I.79, 82–84, 87)

But that little touch of spleen betrays the pointlessness of his attempt to rein in his passion. It is an impulse of the blood which reminds us of an important difference between *Maud* as a poem and *In Memoriam*. In *Maud*, as not in *In Memoriam*, the theme of love involves an exploration of specifically sexual love. It *involves* such an exploration. It is not reduced to such an exploration. There *is* an individual case history treated in *Maud*. But this case history has more than just an individual and local scope or significance. Tennyson is finally concerned in *Maud*, as in *In Memoriam*, with questions concerning the nature of love as a universal category. But the incorporation of the sexual dimension in the individual experience of human love is central to Tennyson's sceptical attitude in *Maud* towards the idea that absolute spiritual regeneration is possible in the human condition. Through mixing a presentation of the sheer worldliness and irrationality of the sexual drive with a presentation of an impulse towards spiritual purity, Tennyson avoids an over-simplification of human spiritual aspiration. Tennyson's protagonist acts out a model of human nature which contrasts negatively with idealist models of that nature.

It is not possible to distinguish between individual and wider implications in the representation of the protagonist's spleenful reaction to Maud. In that passage, sexual desire and anger at the heart of such desire, together with a fear of sexual rejection (a fear that generates its own resentments), inform what A.S. Byatt has called the 'perfectly placed strained flippancy' of the lines (Armstrong 1969: 82). In the verse which follows, the 'cold and clear-cut face' of the preceding passage returns to infect the protagonist with a passion that the imposed image was intended to freeze:

> Cold and clear-cut face, why come you so cruelly meek,
> Breaking a slumber in which all spleenful folly was drowned,
> Pale with the golden beam of an eyelash dead on the cheek,
> Passionless, pale, cold face, star-sweet on a gloom profound;
> Womanlike, taking revenge too deep for a transient wrong
> Done but in thought to your beauty, and ever as pale as before
> Growing and fading and growing upon me without a sound,
> Luminous, gemlike, ghostlike, deathlike, half the night long...

(I.88–95)

Attempting to repress sexual feeling, the protagonist had succeeded in willing only a type of death ('an eyelash dead on the cheek...'). The image of immobility itself implies the negative power of the energy the image was supposed to discipline. Embarrassment and guilt about his own sexual responses surface in the protagonist's awareness of a 'wrong / Done but in thought to your beauty'. But rage does not disappear even as it is acknowledged. There is still accusation and blame: 'Womanlike...'. And the impulse to destroy is fused with the impulse to be destroyed. The dream exposes the subliminal proximity in the human psyche of erotic desire and a yearning for annihilation not only of the other but of the self. In the closing lines of the dream-passage, intimations of the death of the self – intimations which embrace, but which are not contained by, the memory of the death of the father and of the mother's reaction – are woven into the protagonist's sensory responses to the external world. They are also there in the references to the dead daffodil and to the dead Orion. The daffodil, a member of the narcissus family, denoting a man destroyed by love of his own reflexion; and Orion, a hero blinded and destroyed through his own aggressive sexual impulses. The protagonist is, of course, implicitly aware of the unregeneracy of his own human nature and of the solipsistic and self-negating character of his passion:

> Growing and fading and growing, till I could bear it no more,
> But arose, and all by myself in my own dark garden ground,
> Listening now to the tide in its broad-flung shipwrecking roar,
> Now to the scream of a maddened beach dragged down by
>   the wave,
> Walked in a wintry wind by a ghastly glimmer, and found
> The shining daffodil dead, and Orion low in his grave.

(I.96–101)

Desperately aware of the gravity of these cadences, the protagonist would prefer to nullify all passion in himself and to divorce himself from a world of unaccommodated passion:

> The passionate heart of the poet is whirled into folly and vice.
> I would not marvel at either, but keep a temperate brain;
> For not to desire or admire, if a man could learn it, were more
> Than to walk all day like a sultan of old in a garden of spice...

Be mine a philosopher's life in the quiet woodland ways,
Where if I cannot be gay let a passionless peace be my lot...

(I.139–43, 150–151)

There has, however, been that one expression of passion which the protagonist has *not* seen as disturbed and potentially self-destructive. This is the open and public war he had affirmed in the opening stages of the poem – 'war! loud war' (I.47) – and which he reasserts in the closing part:

I stood on a giant deck and mixed my breath
With a loyal people shouting a battle cry...

And many a darkness into the light shall leap...
And the heart of a people beat with one desire;
For the peace, that I deemed no peace, is over and done,
And now by the side of the Black and the Baltic deep,
And deathful-grinning mouths of the fortress, flames
The blood-red blossom of war with a heart of fire.

(III.30–35, 46, 49–53)

What distinguishes the heartfelt desire for war from other, inadmissible, impulses of the passionate heart? Appalled by death in nature and in a society nominally at peace, the protagonist does not consciously flinch from the chances of death in war. The passion of war is legitimate, he says, because it flows in the service of the just and the good. In stating this, in Part III, he effectively repeats the distinction he had made in Part II, in the midst of his phase of complete madness following his assault on Maud's brother, between violence in personal relations and violence exercised in the *public* interest:

Friend, to be struck by the public foe,
Then to strike him and lay him low,
That were a public merit, far,
Whatever the Quaker holds, from sin;
But the red life spilt for a private blow –
I swear to you, lawful and lawless war
Are scarcely even akin.

(II.327–33)

But the vantage point of clinical insanity from which the protagonist is speaking in this section cannot be disregarded. It is not clear
that a valid distinction is being made. The protagonist makes a simplistic
equation between the just and the public, and the unjust and the private.
He confuses things as he establishes a straightforward equation between
categories that are not simply interchangeable. There is no admission
that publicly sanctioned violence may be seen to be wrong and no sense
that private and public may not easily be separable.

The protagonist thinks that his distinction between lawful and lawless
violence grows out of his love for Maud whom, at a fairly early point in
his obsession with her, he had heard singing a martial song. But to
accept his terms here would be to forget his enthusiasm for war at a
time before he had become intensely preoccupied with her. In that
enthusiasm he had simply made a bald, emotional appeal to war as a
save-all from the failings of peace. He undertook no subtle discrimin-
ations. Nor is the crudeness of this early appeal by a mind touched with
hysteria refined in the arbitrary and confused distinctions drawn by the
protagonist in his state of complete madness in Part II. In Part III it is
convenient for him that he perceives the Czar of Russia as a 'giant liar'
(III.45) and Britain as defending the right. But the original, undiscrimi-
nating and disordered rage for war remains the fundamental motivation
in this section. As Goldwin Smith observed in November 1855:

> To the hero of *Maud* himself, indeed, the justice of the war is only a
> parenthesis between more real motives –
>
>> And as months ran on, and rumour of battle grew,
>> 'It is time, it is time, O passionate heart', said I,
>> (For I cleaved to a cause that I felt to be pure and true),
>> 'It is time, O passionate heart and morbid eye,
>> That old hysterical mock-disease should die'.
>
> The relief of the passionate heart and morbid eye is his first object.
> What he wants is not a just and necessary war, but war in itself.
>
> (Jump 1967: 186)

Controlling the protagonist's idea of war in Part III is the same fundamentally naive equation between the private and the unjustified, on
one hand, and the public and the justified, on the other, as had directed
his deliberations in Part II. Any war would have served the purpose if it
had fulfilled two primary requirements in the protagonist's mind. First,
the need for a common public belief and second, no less important, the
need for the speaker to fuse his own private attitude with that common

belief. Beneath the 'ethical blather' (Basler 1944: 154) in Part III, the driving assertions are of the unity of public opinion with regard to war and the alignment of the speaker himself with that opinion. Both assertions are crucial to the protagonist's equation of the public with the virtuous. It is through the achievement of a common body of opinion and through an identification of the private opinion with the public, essentially irrespective of any matter of principle, that the protagonist sees a path to salvation. In forcing that path the protagonist is shown as wilfully disregarding the fact that there was not, at the time, an absolute unity of public opinion about the prospective conflict in the Crimea, as is indicated by the dialogue about 'Peace and War' in *Blackwood's Edinburgh Magazine* for November 1854.

In his insistence upon a clear pattern of public belief and upon his own accommodation to that pattern, the protagonist attempts to find compensation for that lack of any cohesive or compelling faith – religious, social, or political – which defines the predicament of his culture. His private disintegration having been fed by that predicament, he seeks to mask the disintegration by conforming the personal to what he conceives of as the one available display of public unity. His assertion of war-spirit as an expression of coherence, and his associated assertion of the manliness supposedly manifested in war, display elements typical of Victorian reactions against the incertitudes of the age. The speaker of Browning's 1855 poem 'Cleon', for example, is a later classical Greek of philosophical bent whose state of mind anticipates the disabling subjectivism of the nineteenth century. Browning's Cleon thinks of the classical heroic age as a time when the content and value of manly action had not been compromised:

> We of these latter days, with greater mind
> Than our forerunners, since more composite,
> Look not so great, beside their simple way,
> To a judge who only sees one way at once . . .
> Compares the small part of a man of us
> With some whole man of the heroic age . . .
>
> (64–67, 69–70)

Tennyson's protagonist yearns for a past which he associates with integrity and an uncompromised masculinity:

> Ah God, for a man with heart, head, hand,
> Like some of the simple great ones gone . . .

> And ah for a man to arise in me,
> That the man I am may cease to be!

> > (I.389–90, 396–97)

The protagonist's understandable desire to purge himself of the pains of isolated and introverted experience does not, however, redeem the distortions inherent in the cure he proposes. I have already noted how the exacerbated tonalities and imagery of Part III point – as had comparable features in the opening section of the poem – to an infirmity in the speaker's mind and judgement. Beneath the glorification of the 'deathful-grinning mouths of the fortress' and the 'flames' of the 'blood-red blossom of war with a heart of fire' may be traced, whatever the nominal ethical justifications, the same energies of rage and violence as had been condemned by the protagonist in their private and peace-time manifestations. The difference is that these energies are rendered respectable through their identification with a publicly validated action.

In Part III the protagonist's apparent self-possession, his control of what is happening, is too crude to define what has been going on in the earlier stages of the poem. On several occasions in this third part the protagonist enters into merely automatic images of breakdown and madness and the ills of peace. Special confusions emanate from the use of a commonplace, tired language. In the following lines the allusion to pastoral activity (or sloth) constitutes an evasion of the true activity, which is commerce:

> No more shall commerce be all in all, and Peace
> Pipe on her pastoral hillock a languid note,
> And watch her harvest ripen, her herd increase,
> Nor the cannon-bullet rust on a slothful shore ...

> > (III.23–26)

Commentators have complained at the language of Part III. A.S. Byatt writes that 'the poetic tension, the *lyric* unity, is ... completely lacking ... We have blood and light but only an ersatz energy' (Armstrong 1969: 91). But ersatz energy is precisely the point. We are being told something *through* this second-hand language. The peculiar brittleness of much of the rhetoric is an essential element in the presentation of this phase of the protagonist's passion. At the centre of his desire for a public authorisation of unregenerate private energies lies a demand for the legitimisation of the darkest desire of all. As Christopher Ricks has said: 'the odds are that the hero is going to his death . . . The honourable suicide of a soldier may redeem the dishonourable suicide' (Ricks 1989: 248). The womb-oriented, regressive misconfigurations of the protagonist's death-wish have been exposed in the madhouse scenes at the end of Part II. There, an infantile language had prevailed:

> I will cry to the steps above my head
> And somebody, surely, some kind heart will come
> To bury me, bury me
> Deeper, ever so little deeper.

(II.339–42)

The self-destructive movement does not disappear in Part III, even though the language changes. Just as the suicidal impulse is channelled in Part III into a public form in the enthusiasm for war, so it moves behind the stock properties of the language ('My life has crept so long on a broken wing/Through cells of madness, haunts of horror and fear', III.1–2). The very officialness of that language enacts the attempt to render socially acceptable what is privately inadmissible.

Not all the formulations in Part III are wilfully conventional. 'Would there be sorrow for *me*?' the protagonist had asked in Part I, after he had queried whether, like his father, he too must 'creep to the hollow' and 'dash' himself 'down'. Regret of a kind is granted a place in Part III as the protagonist prepares to embrace 'the doom assigned' (III.59). The protagonist's mind recognises, at some unconscious or barely conscious level, the pointlessness of its attempt at reintegration. At a certain moment in Part III the protagonist speaks lines that, despite himself, as it were, poignantly bespeak his own unwillingness to accept, his own regret at accepting, the terms of the reintegration he has set for himself:

> And the cobweb woven across the cannon's throat
> Shall shake its threaded tears in the wind no more.

(I.27–28)

VI

If the passion of war celebrated by the speaker in Part III is dishonestly legitimate, what of the passion of love celebrated in Part I? Right through to the protagonist's first sight of Maud's 'cold and clear-cut' face (I.79) there are certain elements of the passion of love which are inextricably bound up in his psyche with the unregenerate passions he seeks to regenerate (legitimise) through a commitment to war. The important question is whether the negative possibilities evident in the earliest stages of the speaker's response to Maud are exorcised by the time of his affirmation of an achieved love for her. There is evidence to suggest they are not. In fact, an intimate connection between the two kinds of response is suggested: in the first place, by the crucial position occupied by Maud's martial song in the development of the drama.

Immediately before Maud sings her song we have heard the protagonist declaring that he will 'flee from the cruel madness of love, / The honey of poison-flowers and all the measureless ill' (I.156–57). It is immediately after he has heard Maud sing her song of war that the protagonist begins to relax his overt resistance to the idea of falling in love with her. It is clear that the singing of the ballad enables the hero to associate Maud with martial values. And it is that association which opens the way for his gradual admission that love may be a legitimate expression of passion. Progress is slow. Attempting to resist the compellingly fatal combination of love and war, the protagonist tries to separate in his mind Maud herself from her voice and the song (a separation which stresses the prime appeal of the martial note):

> Still! I will hear you no more,
> For your sweetness hardly leaves me a choice
> But to move to the meadow and fall before
> Her feet on the meadow grass, and adore,
> Not her, who is neither courtly nor kind,
> Not her, not her, but a voice.

(I.184–89)

Yet, however much the protagonist may attempt to remind himself that Maud is undesirable, her singing of war has already provoked in him an enlivened response quite different from his earlier attempt at denigration:

> Maud with her exquisite face,
> And wild voice pealing up to the sunny sky,
> And feet like sunny gems on an English green,

> Maud in the light of her youth and her grace,
> Singing of Death, and of Honour that cannot die...

(I.173–77)

In the midst of this account of Maud's 'Singing of death' there emerges a language of sanctification ('light...grace', I.176) which grows more insistent with the protagonist's growing love for Maud. The same language reappears in section vi, which follows Maud's martial ballad and describes the protagonist's first actual meeting with her. In this passage, a language of spiritual resonance is integrated with a fire imagery that anticipates at once the heats of erotic love and the fires of war at the end of the poem:

> Whom but Maud should I meet
> Last night, when the sunset burned
> On the blossomed gable-ends...
>   she touched my hand with a smile so sweet,
> She made me divine amends
> For a courtesy not returned.
>
> And thus a delicate spark
> Of glowing and growing light
> Through the livelong hours of the dark
> Kept itself warm in the heart of my dreams,
> Ready to burst in a coloured flame...

(I.196–98, 201–208)

At both narrative and imagistic levels the perception of a Maud of war is the condition of the protagonist's perception of a Maud of love. Far from being clearly distinguishable, the Maud of love is sanctioned by the Maud of war. The early evidence of interrelationship between the 'two' Mauds suggests that the spiritual regeneration through love which is claimed by the protagonist, as he speaks of Maud's will having changed his fate, is as questionable as the regeneration he claims through war. The doubtfulness of the protagonist's asserted renovation through love is evidenced, in the first place, through some of the principal image patterns of the poem.

Fire is just one element in an image complex that runs throughout *Maud.* This image complex runs alongside but is not identical with the overt narrative of the poem. Indeed, the imagery in *Maud* repeatedly subverts the narrative development that is insisted upon by the protagonist. The colour red constitutes the primary image of dangerous passion in the poem and there are numerous cognate associations with various kinds of lurid light. One of the principal identifications of redness is with blood, while there are frequent identifications of light with different manifestations of fire. The combination of redness, blood and death is first apparent in the opening lines of the poem, where the protagonist thinks of the pit in which his father's body was found:

> Its lips in the field above are dabbled with blood-red heath,
> The red-ribbed ledges drip with a silent horror of blood,
> And Echo there, whatever is asked her, answers 'Death.'

> (I.2–4)

These opening lines establish the broad context of meaning for the redness which pulses phantasmagorically throughout the lines where the speaker rails against society:

> And the vitriol madness flushes up in the ruffian's head,
> Till the filthy by-lane rings to the yell of the trampled wife ...

> While another is cheating the sick of a few last gasps, as he sits
> To pestle a poisoned poison behind his crimson lights.

> (I.37–38, 43–44)

The pernicious possibilities of the imagery of blood and redness recur throughout the poem in such lines as 'the household Fury sprinkled with blood' (I.715); or when, after the protagonist has assaulted Maud's brother, there is at once an allusion back to the opening lines of the poem and a further anticipation of the imagery of war in Part III:

> And a million horrible bellowing echoes broke
> From the red-ribbed hollow behind the wood ...
> And there rang on a sudden a passionate cry,
> A cry for a brother's blood:
> It will ring in my heart and my ears, till I die, till I die.

> (II.24–25, 33–35)

Equally, however, fire and blood motifs form part of the record of the growth and fulfilment of the protagonist's love. Not only was the speaker's heart ready to 'burst in a coloured flame' (I.208) after his first meeting with Maud, but the movement of blood in the passion of love is insisted upon when the two encounter each other again in the 'village church' (I.301). Here there is a reciprocal stimulation of the pulse:

> she lifted her eyes,
> And suddenly, sweetly, strangely blushed
> To find they were met by my own;
> And suddenly, sweetly, my heart beat stronger
> And thicker...

> (I.305–309)

With the celebration of achieved love the thickness becomes an inexorable tide of blood. Looked at one way, the passage celebrating love at the opening of section xviii of Part I is a joyous celebration of what is, in part, sexual joy. Looked at another way it is instinct with a lingeringly predatory blood-fever:

> I have led her home...
> And never yet so warmly ran my blood...
> Calming itself to the long-wished-for end,
> Full to the banks, close on the promised good.

> (I.599, 601, 603–604)

The reader is asked by the protagonist to understand the love that is achieved as signifying – at its highest level – a spiritual regeneration. But while regeneration is claimed by the protagonist it is not demonstrated in the verse. The important feature of the imagery of blood and fire in its application to love is that it is never discharged of the baleful associations which it has elsewhere in the poem. Just before the love-lyric 'I have led her home', the protagonist suggests his happiness in terms which are exaggeratedly suffused with the colour of blood:

> Go not, happy day,
>   From the shining fields,
> Go not, happy day,
>   Till the maiden yields.
> Rosy is the West,
>   Rosy is the South,
> Rosy are her cheeks,

And a rose her mouth . . .
Pass and blush the news . . .
   Blush it through the West;
Till the red man dance
   By his red cedar-tree,
And the red man's babe
   Leap, beyond the sea.
Blush from West to East,
   Blush from East to West,
Till the West is East . . .

(I.571–78, 581, 586–93)

A.S. Byatt writes that in this lyric 'blood becomes warm, glowing, positive' (Armstrong 1969: 83). But there is an element of hysteria in the fantasy of a world flushed in red. At what point do the hectic energies of a sexual love become unmanageable and spill over into frenzy? Certainly, there is an insinuation of force in the line: 'Till the maiden yields', and the dividing line between ecstasy and dementia is blurred in the overheated image of the red man dancing and his babe leaping. There is a worrying agitation, too, in the beating rhythm of the verse.

There is, apparently, no hysteria and certainly no doggerel in the lyric affirming fulfilment in love in section xviii:

I have led her home, my love, my only friend.
There is none like her, none.
And never yet so warmly ran my blood
And sweetly, on and on
Calming itself to the long-wished-for end,
Full to the banks, close on the promised good.

None like her, none.
Just now the dry-tongued laurels' pattering talk
Seemed her light foot along the garden walk,
And shook my heart to think she comes once more;
But even then I heard her close the door,
The gates of Heaven are closed, and she is gone.

(I.599–610)

Superficially, the contrast seems clear between the protagonist's condition of mind as it appears in this passage and his earlier states of mind characterised by a paradoxical tension between acute hypersensitivity and stagnation. In the self-enclosed world of the protagonist described in section v of Part I, for example, there had been only a painfully hallucinated and obsessive impinging of sounds and objects;

> Living alone in an empty house,
> Here half-hid in the gleaming wood,
> Where I hear the dead at midday moan,
> And the shrieking rush of the wainscot mouse,
> And my own sad name in corners cried,
> When the shiver of dancing leaves is thrown
> About its echoing chambers wide,
> Till a morbid-hate and horror have grown
> Of a world in which I have hardly mixt,
> And a morbid eating lichen fixt
> On a heart half-turned to stone.

(I.257–67)

Towards the end of section xviii the protagonist will assert: '*I* have climbed nearer out of lonely Hell' (I.678). But how much nearer? The 'shiver of dancing leaves...thrown / About...echoing chambers wide' (I.262–63) may be compared with 'the dry-tongued laurels' pattering talk' in 'I have led her home' (I.606). The obvious suffering of the earlier lines has withdrawn in the later. But the distinctive hypersensitivity is the same. This tense hypersensitivity exists within the supposed repletion of fulfilment. But the calm is an illusion. The steady rhythms and repetitions of 'I have led her home' define only an inward-turned world. The passage does not offer an excursive, expansive movement which embraces a person, a world, and an order beyond the self. It is, rather, a world which has been stabilised but remains self-enclosed. Painful hallucination has been displaced by gratifying fantasy. The stability is the stability of solipsistic fantasy and not of objective realisation. Connotations of an interior secretion are inherent in the metaphor used by the speaker to define Maud:

> what care I,
> Who in this stormy gulf have found a pearl
> The countercharm of space and hollow sky,
> And do accept my madness...

(I.639–42)

Love as a pearl, the protagonist's self-derived fantasy, does not grow out of or towards a universe of Love. Space and hollow sky are neither filled nor turned inside out by the speaker's projections. A highly concentrated inward point of stability – unhealthy in its concentration – should not be confused with a principle of regeneration. The morbid, introvert energies from which the fantasy is generated and on which it is poised are the same as those which had earlier generated and sustained violence and distress.

The precariousness of the fantasy is suggested in different ways throughout the section. There is, for instance, the description of the great cedar:

> O, art thou sighing for Lebanon ...
> Dark cedar ...
>   haunted by the starry head
> Of her whose gentle will has changed my fate,
> And made my life a perfumed altar-flame;
> And over whom thy darkness must have spread
> With such delight as theirs of old, thy great
> Forefathers of the thornless garden, there
> Shadowing the snow-limbed Eve from whom she came.
>
> (I.613, 616, 620–26)

The protagonist may equate his new-made life with an original inno-cence but the allusion to the lost Eden is at once ominous: it raises the shadow of the fall and the inherent potential for evil in the supposedly thornless garden of 'I have led her home'. Most important, the continuing infection of the speaker's mind by unaccommodated, unregenerate powers is presented in the swaying, darkly foreboding menace of the closing lines of section xviii:

> *I* have climbed nearer out of lonely Hell.
> Beat, happy stars, timing with things below,
> Beat with my heart more blest than heart can tell,
> Blest, *but for some dark undercurrent woe*
> *That seems to draw* – but it shall not be so:
> Let all be well, be well.
>
> (I.678–83; my italics)

The feeling of a pure and holy love is maintained by repression: 'dark undercurrent woe / That seems to draw – but it shall not be so: / Let all be well...'. There are things the protagonist cannot face. The vertiginous pull is denied, willed away. Out of mind but still there. The baleful energies that the protagonist was grappling within himself in the earlier sections of Part I have not been exorcised. Purity, here, is claimed, not demonstrated. The pressure is at once regressive, pointing back to the hellish obsessions of the past, and prophetic, pointing to the future failure of the fantasy.

The 'dark undercurrent woe' admitted at the end of section xviii gives the lie to the protagonist's claim, in section xix, to have found Truth and atonement. So, too, does the protagonist's initial – quickly corrected – classification of his fulfilment in love as a dream:

> Her brother is coming back tonight,
> Breaking up my dream of delight.
> My dream? do I dream of bliss?
> I have walked awake with Truth.
> O when did a morning shine
> So rich in atonement as this
> For my dark-dawning youth,
> Darkened watching a mother decline
> And that dead man at her heart and mine:
> For who was left to watch her but I?

> (I.684–93)

The vision of Truth, never more than a temporarily successful sublimation, 'is not', as A.S. Byatt has said, 'an atonement, after all: blood must be paid' (Armstrong 1969: 89). The idea of the dead father (and of the self that is dead at centre) returns the protagonist to his old preoccupations.

The failure of the precarious sublimation in section xviii is clearly apparent in the last section of the first Part of the poem, which is saturated with the troubling potentialities of the 'dark undercurrent woe'. In this section, 'Come into the garden, Maud', the protagonist shows himself constitutionally unable to avoid associating love with death:

> For a breeze of morning moves,
>   And the planet of Love is on high,
> Beginning to faint in the light that she loves
>   On a bed of daffodil sky,
> To faint in the light of the sun she loves,
>   To faint in his light, and to die.

> (I.856–61)

George Eliot thought 'exquisite' the manner in which 'the murmur of the verse seems to faint and die like a star' (Eliot 1963: 197). But the rhythms are not only those of fainting. Harold Nicolson's quaint sense of 'shock' at finding that the 'haunting music of *Come into the Garden, Maud*, is based on the rhythm of a mid-Victorian polka' (Nicolson 1923: 232–33) obscured for him the effect which Ruskin noticed when he said: 'The intense anxiety and agitation of the lover's mind is marked by not one of the lines being exactly similar to another in its prosody' (Cook and Wedderburn 1903–12: xxxi.339–40). Both the rose and the lily which also appear in this section – where Maud is 'Queen lily and rose in one' (I.905) – are images which recur throughout *Maud*. They are each, of course, ambivalent, as A. Dwight Culler observed:

> Death is symbolised throughout the poem by the pallor of the lily, as Love is by the ardor of the rose. But both symbols are ambiguous, for the lily also symbolises the purity and spirituality of Maud, as the rose symbolises the blood and passion that unsealed their love.
>
> (Culler 1977: 209)

When they are fused in the figure of Maud seen as 'Queen lily and rose in one', the positive and negative connotations of the images are inextricably mingled. And the figure of Maud seen as these two is complicit with the protagonist's hysteria. Tennyson's verse shows a perfectly adjusted use of form to suggest a mind teetering on the edge of the formless. Distortions of the superficial formal control in the lines betray, as Ruskin noted, the protagonist's rising mania:

> And the soul of the rose went into my blood,
>> As the music clashed in the hall . . .
>
> She is coming, my dove, my dear;
>> She is coming, my life, my fate;
> The red rose cries, 'She is near, she is near;'
>> And the white rose weeps, 'She is late;'
> The larkspur listens, 'I hear, I hear;'
>> And the lily whispers, 'I wait.'
>
> (I.882–83, 910–15)

The fusion of rose and lily in the anticipation of Maud's arrival becomes emblematic of the confusion in the protagonist's mind between love and death, purity and impurity. It is not that the protagonist cannot imagine resurrection. But when he does we are taught by the imagery that the powers of revived life are indistinguishable from the unregenerate impulses that brought about death in the first place:

> She is coming, my own, my sweet;
>   Were it ever so airy a tread,
> My heart would hear her and beat,
>   Were it earth in an earthy bed;
> My dust would hear her and beat,
>   Had I lain for a century dead;
> Would start and tremble under her feet,
>   And blossom in purple and red.

(I.916–23)

It is not surprising when the reader learns in Part II that the protagonist has assaulted Maud's brother in the garden. The old destructive forces of anger and hate – temporarily sublimated in 'I have led her home' – have been pictured resurging in 'Come into the garden, Maud.' They broke out again in the garden, as the protagonist makes clear in Part II when he describes his killing of Maud's brother and aligns the scene with the 'dreadful hollow' dripping with 'a silent horror of blood' at the very outset of the poem (I.1–3). The exploration of love as an agent of spiritual regeneration is terminated not because of some arbitrary, local act of violence by the protagonist. The exploration ceases because there has never been a purgation. It is not that the protagonist did not experience stirrings of positive feeling. It is, rather, that he was never able to achieve a real separation between the higher and the lower, the pure and the impure. The 'dark undercurrent woe' was never exorcised. The choler directed against the brother was already evident in the protagonist's fevered imagining of Maud treading on his grave at the end of 'Come into the garden'. It is the same rage as had been apparent at the opening of the poem and which continues, thinly disguised, at the very end. The protagonist's move towards a paradisal love was always fated to a further fall because it was always instinct with the energies of hell. The violence which destroyed the idyll was born of the idyll. Psychologically speaking, Tennyson's

purpose in *Maud* is to show that the fires of love and the fires of war
are kindled at the same source:

> O dawn of Eden bright over earth and sky,
> The fires of Hell brake out of thy rising sun,
> The fires of Hell and of Hate...

(II.8–10)

VII

The protagonist's claim to have isolated a higher self in his love for
Maud informs the idea of the two dream-figures or ghosts of Maud in
Parts II and III of the poem. There is, first of all, Maud as shade. Following the assault on the brother, there appears a figure of Maud that is
identified with the protagonist's own shadow:

> Then glided out of the joyous wood
> The ghastly Wraith of one that I know...
>
> Is it gone? my pulses beat –
> What was it? a lying trick of the brain?
> Yet I thought I saw her stand,
> A shadow there at my feet...

(II.31–32, 36–39)

A little later we find the protagonist

> Plagued with a flitting to and fro,
> A disease, a hard mechanic ghost...
> Why should it look like Maud?
> Am I to be overawed
> By what I cannot but know
> Is a juggle born of the brain?

(II.81–82, 87–90)

Lines 82 and 90 of this passage were adapted from 'Oh! that 'twere possible' (83–84). But the main body of material incorporated from the
1837 lyric appears in section iv of Part II of *Maud*. Here, the shadow
continues to make itself felt:

A shadow flits before me ...

It leads me forth at evening,
It lightly winds and steals
In a cold white robe before me ...

In the shuddering dawn, behold,
Without knowledge, without pity,
By the curtains of my bed
That abiding phantom cold.

Get thee hence, nor come again,
Mix not memory with doubt,
Pass, thou deathlike type of pain,
Pass and cease to move about!
'Tis the blot upon the brain
That *will* show itself without ...

It crosses here, it crosses there,
Through all that crowd confused and loud,
The shadow still the same;
And on my heavy eyelids
My anguish hangs like shame.

(II.151, 157–59, 192–201, 210–14)

This manifestation of Maud, as the speaker's own shadow, reflects the darker aspects of his personality which we have seen portrayed in the poem – including, at centre (as centrally in 'Oh! that 'twere possible'), the suicidal impulse.

There is a Maud of more positive aspect. Again, as in the lyric of 1837, this projection of being appears reluctant to manifest itself:

Would the happy spirit descend,
From the realms of light and song,
In the chamber or the street,
As she looks among the blest ...

But the broad light glares and beats,
And the shadow flits and fleets
And will not let me be ...

(II.221–24, 229–31)

In the context of the poem of 1855, however, this happy and blessed spirit, although descended from the 'Archetype that waits, / Clad in light' in 'Oh! that 'twere possible', is not simply to be equated with that archetype. Neither is it simply to be paralleled with the light aspect of Cadrilla in *The Lover's Tale*, nor with the Hallam of the shining face in *In Memoriam*. *The Lover's Tale* and 'Oh! that 'twere possible' presented a definite split between light and dark potentialities of the psyche. The split was left unresolved, but it remained real. *In Memoriam* insists finally on affirming the pre-eminence of the higher, the light. Throughout *Maud*, however, while the protagonist maintains a notion of the dualism of higher and lower, and while he pretends to a regeneration of the lower by the higher, the poem does not sustain the reality of the dualism. The real problem in *Maud* is that the happy and blessed spirit is not fundamentally separable from the abiding phantom cold. All dualistic distinctions asserted by the protagonist collapse into an undifferentiated monism. The lack of an autonomous higher potency of self is apparent in the motif of the two ghosts of Maud. The protagonist associates the 'happy spirit' of Maud with that occasion in the past when he heard her sing her martial song:

> Do I hear her sing as of old,
> My bird with the shining head,
> My own dove with the tender eye? . . .
>
> Alas for her that met me,
> That heard me softly call . . .
> In the garden by the turrets
> Of the old manorial hall.
>
> Would the happy spirit descend . . .

> (II.184–86, 215–16, 219–21)

This much appears similar to the speaker's association of the 'fair and good' phantom with the 'pleasant ditty' chanted 'of old' by the lost loved-one in 'Oh! that 'twere possible.' But there is a major difference between the recollections of the songs in the two poems. In *Maud* the song that is remembered is specifically Maud's martial ballad. The appeal of that song had been to those darker areas and impulses in the protagonist which he rationalises as a legitimate enthusiasm for war; and if the protagonist's perception of a Maud of love in Part I is conditional upon and entangled with his perception of a Maud of war, then the same entanglement is evident in the idea of the two ghosts of Maud. The identification of the 'happy spirit' of Maud with the Maud of the martial song implies no fundamental separation between the higher Maud and the 'shadow still the same'. The distinction is false and of the same order as the hero's distinction between private and public violence. Maud as shadow, a juggle of the brain, is the hero's death-wish in its private and shameful aspect. But the 'happy spirit' of Maud, at once the Maud of martial values, is the same instinct in its respectable, publicly sanctioned form. If this Maud would descend to 'the chamber or the street' from the regions of the 'blest', then the protagonist would be able to face what he cannot face when possessed by Maud as shadow; that is, the realm of social being: 'the squares and streets, / And the faces that one meets' (II.232–33). The protagonist would ask Maud in her 'higher' aspect to 'Take me, sweet, / To the regions of thy rest' (II.227–28). He would be taken to death, but under the shameless banner of the war spirit extolled in Maud's 'passionate ballad gallant and gay' (I.165). That the Maud of the shadow of death and of suicide is at root one and the same with the blessed Maud is made clear again in Part III of the poem. There it is the higher Maud which recommends officially sanctioned violence: 'She seemed to divide in a dream from a band of the blest, / And spoke of a hope for the world in the coming wars' (III.10–11). But it is, significantly, Maud as shadow who is presented as taking up the recommendation and seeking refuge in the Baltic theatre of the war with Russia: 'I saw the dreary phantom arise and fly / Far into the North, and battle, and seas of death' (III.36–37). 'I tarry for thee', the blessed spirit had said (III.13). But she waits in the same place as the 'dreary phantom'. Tennyson could hardly have been clearer about the impurity of a process in which the protagonist's darkest proclivities are assimilated to a publicly justifiable action. Cadrilla's 'fair eyes' in *The Lover's Tale* (II.162 [II.155]), the 'phantom fair' in 'Oh! that 'twere possible' (91), Hallam's 'fair face' (and, in manuscript, 'fair eyes') in *In Memoriam* (LXX.16), are echoed in the 'eyes so fair' of the blessed spirit of the lost loved-one in *Maud* (III.16); just as Cadrilla's 'empty phantom' (II.210 [II.203]), the 'phantom cold' of 'Oh! that 'twere possible' (35), the solipsistic 'phantom' of the self in *In Memoriam* (CVIII.10) are echoed in the 'dreary phantom' of Maud in *Maud* (III:36). The difference between the earlier poems and *Maud* is that in *Maud* Tennyson is no longer holding out the possibility of separating, at psychological and metaphysical levels, the higher from the lower, the light from the dark, the pure from the impure. The point is underlined in Tennyson's veiled references to the myth of Narcissus. W.E. Buckler comments that

The myth of Narcissus and Echo, with variations, is one of the subtexts of *Maud*, as the fiction suggests and as the fourth line ('And Echo there, whatever is asked her, answers "Death"') and the adoration of the 'beautiful voice' in Canto v signal.

(Buckler 1980: 226)

Buckler further speculates that 'it may have been to keep his subtext from surfacing too obviously' (Buckler 1980: 226) that Tennyson introduced the reading 'shining daffodil' (I.101, III.6) into published editions of *Maud*. Drafts of the poem in manuscripts now in the Berg Collection of the New York Public Library and in the Houghton Library, Harvard University, show Tennyson writing something else: 'sweet Narcissus' (Ricks and Day 1987–93: IV.31 and XXVIII.8). In the classical fable Echo was ruined by Narcissus' failure to reciprocate her love. She pined away until nothing was left of her but her melodious voice, which the goddess Juno had already condemned to have the status of only an echo. In the opening sections of *Maud* the universe of death which the protagonist imagines is confirmed by the way in which he receives the answer ' "Death" ' to whatever he asks. But since Echo only returns that which is in the protagonist himself, then the principle of death inherent in his own being is demonstrated. The importance of echo as a structural principle in *Maud* is considerable. It defines the detailed repetitions and recurrences of the protagonist's obsessions throughout the poem. At points, the image resurfaces explicitly to emphasise the lack of progression in the narrative of the protagonist's soul. As when, after the assault on Maud's brother, the reader is recalled to the opening of the poem by the 'million horrible bellowing echoes' which 'broke / From the red-ribbed hollow behind the wood' (II.24–25).

Along with Echo, there is Narcissus. In the myth, before Echo finally pined away to nothing, she had asked Venus to punish Narcissus by making him suffer the pangs of unrequited love. The goddess caused Narcissus to fall in love with his own face reflected in a pool. Eventually, unable to possess the object of his desire, he died worshipping his own image. In *Maud* the first allusion to the 'shining daffodil dead' occurs at the end of a passage which sets out the morbidly introverted condition of the speaker's mind and is full of intimations of the death of the self (I.96–101, quoted above p. 162). It is shortly after this passage that the hero hears Maud singing her martial song. The shining daffodil appears again in the following lines of Part III:

> My mood is changed, for it fell at a time of year
> When the face of the night is fair on the dewy downs,

And the shining daffodil dies, and the Charioteer
And starry Gemini hang like glorious crowns
Over Orion's grave low down in the west,
That like a silent lightning under the stars
She seemed to divide in a dream from a band of the blest,
And spoke of a hope for the world in the coming wars...

(III.4–11)

The passage repeats in miniature the movement that occurs in Part I from the first mention of 'The shining daffodil dead, and Orion low in his grave' (I.101) to the protagonist's hearing of Maud's martial song. In both Parts I and III, at the same time of the year, the protagonist hears the voice of the martial Maud. In Part III he asks us to accept that his mood has changed and that through his love for Maud he has discovered a healthy, outward direction of energy. But the condition of the protagonist's love for Maud is her singing of the martial ballad and that ballad strikes a chord of self-recognition in the speaker. It answers to his own enthusiasm for war as demonstrated in the opening section of the poem. The 'beautiful voice' (I.180) of the martial song is cast, as W.E. Buckler points out, as the voice of Echo. In essence, Maud's martial song stands as an echo of the protagonist's own uttered predilection for war. As an echo of the protagonist's self, Maud's martial voice gives an answer, both in Part I and in Part III, which is not fundamentally different from the answer Echo had given in the fourth line of the poem. The answer is ' "Death" ', with the difference that the martial Maud offers death in war. The importance of the echo theme is that it links the presentation of the protagonist in the opening lines of the poem with his presentation in Part III. There is an implication that the speaker's enthusiasm for war in Part III is no more than a re-presentation of the morbidly introverted, negative self we have seen at the outset of the poem. The protagonist remains self-fixated. He is still the classical Narcissus, dying out of a deluded commitment to an empty image of himself.

VIII

The emptiness of that image of a clear distinction between a higher and a lower self, a clarity which the protagonist of Maud insists upon, stands at once as the poem's image of the emptiness of traditional Western visions of reality itself. Throughout the poem the protagonist struggles to accommodate himself to received, cultural definitions of the higher and the lower, the pure and the impure; each antithesis, traditionally, having an objective, transcendental point of reference. What the protagonist repeatedly discovers in the poem – though will not admit – is the impossibility of maintaining the dualism in his experience of himself and the world. Love itself, the focal point in Western idealisation of the spirit and of the spiritual, is shown dramatically never to achieve the perfect autonomy of being that such idealisations depend upon. The protagonist asserts that he has apprehended such love. But the 'dark undercurrent woe' (I.681) running through the early sections of the poem – still apparent in the sequence of supposed fulfilment in love, re-manifest in the 'shadow' that haunts like a 'blot upon the brain' in Part II (II.151, 200), evident again in the way that foul and fair phantoms collapse into each other as both lead in the direction of war at the end of the poem – undermines the metaphysical dualism that underpins an ideal of spiritual purity. As the poem moves finally towards the 'deathful-grinning mouths of the fortress' and the 'blood-red blossom of war with a heart of fire' (III.52–53) it is only Maud as shadow, the 'ghastly Wraith' (II.32), which is granted real status in the poem. As a mere public identity, a rationalisation of negative forces within the personality, the blessed spirit of Maud defines nothing more than the 'abiding phantom cold'. The higher spirit is elided with the lower. The poem throughout shows the desperate struggles of a protagonist who is destitute of the spiritual reassurances of his cultural tradition. His insistence on having realised and, in the concluding part of the poem, of being about to pursue 'higher aims' (III.38) is an index of that destitution. He has nothing to put in place of the belief system that fails beneath his feet, and his hysterical insistence on the credibility of that value system speaks of his panic in the face of the void he confronts. The pull towards annihilation, either as suicide or as legitimised suicide in war, is symptomatic of his spiritual exhaustion in the face of the exhaustion of the spiritual.

Deep down, there is a hopelessness in *Maud*, even a nihilism, deriving from the poem's deconstruction of the narratives by which Western culture has sought to order human life. There is a despair at the Christian and the parallel Romantic narrative paradigms of despondency followed by healing and, at last, restitution of hope. The poem constitutes a parody of such narratives. Rejuvenation at the end is not what the poem, as against its protagonist, celebrates. In *Maud*, Tennyson displays an unrelenting scepticism regarding the spiritual archetype that he had finally denied in neither *The Lover's Tale* nor 'Oh! that 'twere possible'. *In Memoriam* had pursued a narrative which insisted finally on renovation.

The reader may believe in that renovation or not. But the poem, officially, endorses it. In *Maud* the poem does not support its protagonist's optimism. J.R. Lowell was right to define the contrast between the two great poems of Tennyson's maturity when he spoke of *Maud* as 'The antiphonal voice to *In Memoriam*' (Tennyson, Hallam 1897: I.393). The peculiar passion of *Maud* is a passion born of a profound scepticism. It is the passion of a fierce regret over the absence of the spiritual absolutes which the poem itself has insisted relentlessly on emptying out. In this remarkably searching poem, Tennyson returned to and vastly elaborated the kind of perception, the uncompromisingly sceptical questioning of ideas that there is a meaningful relation between the real and the ideal, which he had exhibited in early poems such as 'The Hesperides' and 'Œnone'.

In the major work of his later career, *Idylls of the King*, Tennyson again set a dream of the ideal against a deeper perception that that ideal has no verifiable, ultimate ground.

7
The Last Echo: *Idylls of the King*

Tennyson had shown one aspect of his early interest in Arthurian legends when, not long after Arthur Hallam himself had died, he wrote the 'Morte d'Arthur'. The 'Morte d'Arthur' was published in Tennyson's 1842 *Poems*, within a framing poem entitled 'The Epic' that related it to the contemporary world. But it was across twenty-six of the last thirty-three years of his life that Tennyson turned his full attention to treating Arthurian material. *Idylls of the King* came out in instalments from 1859 to 1885, with 'The Passing of Arthur', a reworked version of the 'Morte d'Arthur', constituting the final poem of the cycle.

One of Tennyson's friends, Dean Alford, described what he saw as the allegorical dimension of the treatment of the rise and fall of Arthur's order in *Idylls of the King*:

> One noble design warms and unites the whole. In Arthur's coming – his foundation of the Round table – his struggles and disappointments, and departure – we see the conflict continually maintained between the spirit and the flesh; and in the pragmatical issue, we recognise the bearing down in history and in individual man of pure and lofty Christian purpose by the lusts of the flesh, by the corruptions of superstition, by human passions and selfishness.
>
> (Tennyson, Hallam 1897: II.127–28)

Tennyson himself commented on the way in which the sequence of the *Idylls* is adjusted to the cycle of the year:

> The Coming of Arthur is on the night of the New Year; when he is wedded 'the world is white with May' [The Coming of Arthur', 481]; on a summer night the vison of the Holy Grail appears; and the 'Last

Tournament' is in the 'yellowing autumn-tide' ['The Last Tournament', 241]. Guinevere flees thro' the mists of autumn, and Arthur's death takes place at midnight in mid-winter.

(Tennyson, Hallam 1897: II.133)

The conjunction across these passages of the idea of an allegory of the spiritual life, on one hand, and the idea of the natural cycle, on the other, is germane to a reading of *Idylls of the King.*

Paul Turner has noted several nineteenth-century cultural phenomena which Tennyson had in mind when he was composing *Idylls of the King*:

> The phase of human life on which the *Idylls* comment is the history of England during Tennyson's lifetime, which he saw as a period of political and scientific progress followed by one of spiritual decline. This decline might be summarized as the outing of religion by science, of traditional morality by rationalistic, materialistic, and individualistic ethics, and of common decency by a new, permissive attitude to sex. Thus Darwin's *The Origin of Species*, which led to Thomas Huxley's Agnosticism, synchronised with J.S. Mill's *On Liberty* (1859), which argued that 'whatever crushes individuality is despotism'... Of 'the sexual insurrection' (as the *Daily Telegraph* called it in 1868) the great symptoms were the establishment of the Divorce courts (1857), in spite of Gladstone's hundred speeches against the bill; the attempts, from 1866 onwards, to legalize marriage with a deceased wife's sister; the success of Swinburne's sex-centered *Poems and Ballads* (1866); and the popularity of what was known as 'the literature of prostitution': in Tennyson's phrase, 'the troughs of Zolaism' ('Locksley Hall Sixty Years After', 145).

(Turner 1976: 152)

Tennyson's opposition to the emergence in the second half of the nineteenth century of a new way of thinking about sexuality and sexual relations, in particular, is apparent throughout *Idylls of the King.* One of the principal threats to Arthur's order comes from what is seen as a new paganism, a new naturalism, which directs sexual mores amongst some of Arthur's knights as it had begun to direct thinking and behaviour amongst avant-garde Victorians. Tennyson's anxiety, even grief, about these new attitudes called from him, in 'The Last Tournament', some of the more successful poetry in the *Idylls* cycle. In 'The Last Tournament' Tennyson captures the pathos of the 'yellowing woods' (3), the 'wet wind blowing' (137), the 'thick rain' (213), and the 'withered leaf' (247) that defines the

Autumnal decline of Arthur's civilisation. The mood demanded, at this stage in his Arthurian cycle, keys into Tennyson's genius for poetic melancholy. The fall of Arthur's enemy in this Idyll, the 'Red Knight' (440), defines less Arthur's victory than the decay of all he stands for. Because the Red Knight is not an enemy from without. He is, as Tennyson noted, Pelleas (Tennyson, Hallam 1913: 978), formerly a member of the Round Table:

> Arthur knew the voice; the face
> Wellnigh was helmet-hidden, and the name
> Went wandering somewhere darkling in his mind.
> And Arthur deigned not use of word or sword,
> But let the drunkard, as he stretched from horse
> To strike him, overbalancing his bulk,
> Down from the causeway heavily to the swamp
> Fall, as the crest of some slow-arching wave,
> Heard in dead night along that table-shore,
> Drops flat, and after the great waters break
> Whitening for half a league, and thin themselves,
> Far over sands marbled with moon and cloud,
> From less and less to nothing...

>   (454–66)

This is a figure of the dissolution of Arthur's order in the face of the enemy within. In 'The Last Tournament', the tournament itself – a set-piece occasion where Arthur's spiritually inclined knights had once chivalrically displayed their spiritual and moral superiority – is won by Tristram. But Tristram is the proponent of free love:

> Free love – free field – we love but while we may:
> The woods are hushed, their music is nor more:
> The leaf is dead, the yearning past away:
> New leaf, new life – the days of frost are o'er:
> New life, new love, to suit the newer day:
> New loves are sweet as those that went before:
> Free love – free field – we love but while we may.

>   (275–81)

Tristram, we are told, has 'grown wild beast' (632). The spiritual resolve that had inspired Arthur's order is dissipating in the face of unruly natural energies. It is this fear of reversion from what is idealised as the truly human, the highest possibility of the human, that directs Tennyson's portrayal of the purity of Arthur himself. The ideal and idealistic Arthur sometimes offers both a moral perspective and a portentously self-righteous way of articulating it that are not to much twenty-first century taste, as when, in 'Guinevere', he addresses Guinevere after having discovered her infidelity with Lancelot:

> Yet think not that I come to urge thy crimes,
> I did not come to curse thee, Guinevere,
> I, whose vast pity almost makes me die...
> Lo! I forgive thee, as Eternal God
> Forgives...
> I cannot take thy hand; that too is flesh,
> And in the flesh thou hast sinned; and mine own flesh,
> Here looking down on thine polluted, cries
> 'I loathe thee:'...O Guinevere,
> ...I was ever virgin save for thee...
> Perchance, and so thou purify thy soul,
> And so thou lean on our fair father Christ,
> Hereafter in that world where all are pure
> We two may meet before high God, and thou
> Wilt spring to me...
>   ...she grovelled at his feet...
>
>   (529–31, 541–42, 550–54, 558–62, 577)

The scene emblematises the patriarchal ideology which characterises much of the *Idylls* and which, in part though by no means exclusively, blames women for corrupting the higher values of Arthur's perfect Kingdom.

The fear of reversion from the ideal involves in *Idylls of the King* a particular view of natural process. Paul Turner points out that, in idylls published after the first four were released in 1859, Tennyson's sense of spiritual decline in his times was reinforced by a perception of the darkly disturbing implications of a specifically Darwinian idea of evolution. Darwin's 1859 *On the Origin of Species by Natural Selection* could provoke the thought that nature itself might not be redeemable. Evolution might suffer regressions which parallel, even inform, the regressions of a civilisation: allegorically, in *Idylls of the King*, British civilisation. The 'backward movement' observed by Turner in Tennyson's representation of civilisation in *Idylls of the King*

> contradicted Chambers's theory of evolution, but not Darwin's...
>   The thought that evolution has gone into reverse is expressed by an important image-pattern in the *Idylls*, based on the antithesis between

'man' and 'beast'. Arthur comes into a world 'Wherein the beast was ever more and more,/But man was less and less' ('The Coming of Arthur', 11–12). His life-work is an attempt, at first successful, to make 'men from beasts' (The Last Tournament', 358), but as he dies he realizes that his whole realm 'Reels back into the beast' ('The Passing of Arthur', 26). The pattern is emphasized by the constant attachment of beast images to characters representing threats to his humanizing programme. Edyrn begins by leading the life of a 'wolf'; Balin at first has a 'rough beast' on his shield; Vivien is associated with a snake, a rat, a worm, and a kitten; Pelleas and Gawain are both compared to dogs; Modred is 'like a subtle beast' (i.e. the snake in the Garden of Eden) and also like a 'green caterpillar'; and Tristam, 'from ever harrying wild beasts', is 'grown wild beast' himself.

(Turner 1976: 152–53)

If *Idylls of the King* comments on the internal state of British society in the second half of the nineteenth century, then it comments simultaneously on the Imperial dimension of that society. In 1982 Victor Kiernan published an essay entitled 'Tennyson, King Arthur and Imperialism'. Kiernan observes that poems by Tennyson dealing directly with Imperial issues are fairly few. 'He found it', says Kiernan, 'simpler to put all such themes into disguised, mythic form' (Kiernan 1989: 134–35); *Idylls of the King* being the most ambitious effort of this kind. The allegory of *Idylls of the King* – which Tennyson's son summarised as 'the world-wide war of Sense and Soul, typified in individuals' (Tennyson, Hallam 1897: II.130) – was, Kiernan notes, 'an elastic enough formula':

> Soul and Sense could modulate smoothly into the conflict of civilisation and barbarism, which had a powerful hold on the European and above all the British mind. Empire meant in ideal terms the bringing of order and peaceful progress to lands beyond the pale.
>
> (Kiernan 1989: 137)

In real terms, Kiernan lists what Edward Said has called 'the quite staggering range of British overseas campaigns' (Said 1994: 126) which were undertaken during the decades that Tennyson was composing *Idylls of the King*. These included, 'during 1857 and 1858, the greatest of all European colonial conflicts until after the Second World War, the outbreak and suppression of the Indian Mutiny…This was, for Tennyson as for most Englishmen and many other Europeans, a fearful display of barbarism revolting against Christian civilisation, a land only narrowly prevented from "reeling back into the beast" ["The Passing of Arthur", 26] like Arthur's Britain' (Kiernan 1989: 139). So, in the midst of the transcendentalist allegory about the conflict between the pure spirit and the depraved flesh, Kiernan reads in *Idylls of the King* an analogue of British Imperial dominion over a lower, alien 'other':

> It is by warlike prowess that Arthur convinces admirers like Gareth of his right to be king. We see him in 'Lancelot and Elaine' wading in heathen blood, crimson from plume to spur, like a true crusader. He founds his Table as a substitute for Roman law and order, as he says in 'Guinevere', and to be 'a model for the mighty world' ['Guinevere', 462] – as the British empire now was. An imperial dimension of the Arthurian story is visible throughout. Arthur's expanding kingdom is itself a small empire, subjugating or overawing less civilized areas and bringing them within the pale of Christian manners. In the same style modern Britain was carrying fire and sword, light and sweetness, into the dark places of Asia and Africa.
> (Kiernan 1989: 141)

Arthur's management of his Kingdom parallels British management of the Empire:

> In 'Geraint and Enid' he sets off to improve a neglected district, remove bad officials, break 'bandit holds', and even, less distinctly, extend agriculture, just as a commissioner in a newly annexed province of India might do. He reproaches himself with not having assumed direct control of this region sooner, instead of allowing it to become, in 'delegated hands', the 'common sewer' of the realm ['Geraint and Enid', 892, 894]; very much as, in the same year 1856 when this was written, the Governor-General of India, Lord Dalhousie, annexed the ramshackle kingdom of Oudh, on the strength of Sleeman's highly coloured report on its lamentable condition... Mark of Cornwall is refused membership of the Table, as a princely black sheep in India might be refused a coveted decoration. Like the British there, Arthur stops petty royalties from fighting among themselves, keeps the better of them as tributaries, takes their sons into his service, like those of King Lot of the Orkneys. Exalted by his vision of the grail, Galahad rides about overthrowing 'Pagan realms' and 'Pagan hordes', single-handed apparently, and 'Shattering all evil customs' ['The Holy Grail', 478–79, 477], very much like the long arm of modern Britain quelling Mad Mullahs or abolishing suttee.
> (Kiernan 1989: 142)

Likewise, Tennyson can be seen to be warning of the dangers of the abuse of British Imperial power:

> Balin has been banished from court for striking a servant, and must learn to control his hasty temper and cultivate courtesy to high and low ... There is a far graver breach of the code of chivalry in 'The Last Tournament', when moral decay has gone far. Arthur is leading in person an expeditionary force against a malefactor in his fortress. In the days of his 'Coming' he had been able to halt bloodshed as soon as the enemy turned tail, but now his men run wild, and after breaking into the enemy stronghold go on killing indiscriminately.
>
> > Till all rafters rang with woman-yells,
> > And all the pavement streamed with massacre.
> >
> > ['The Last Tournament', 475–76]
>
> Such scenes disfigured the conclusion of many sieges by British and other colonial forces, and were looked on by professional soldiers as often inevitable, if regrettable. Multan in the Punjab in 1849, Delhi and Lucknow during the Mutiny, were among the sufferers.
>
> (Kiernan 1989: 142)

In the same way that some of Arthur's Knights become tainted by the temptations of the flesh in the allegory of the wars of the spirit in the world, when the British are tainted by the same degenerate behaviour as those they rule, the Empire becomes unstable, threatened by an enemy within, unable to govern by higher spiritual and moral right. The impending fall of Britain *and* its Empire, through a collapse of spiritual resolve at home, is the nightmare and the intended warning of *Idylls of the King*.

This brings us, however, to the matter of Tennyson's perennial insecurity about the grounds of spiritual authority. The notion of Arthur as the kingly emblem of a higher, ideal truth, against which worldly values may be judged wanting, demands that his authority as King be presented as absolutely and objectively founded. But this is exactly what Tennyson refuses to do in *Idylls of the King*. There is, in the first place, the question of Arthur's origin. This is raised in 'The Coming of Arthur' when Leodogran is deciding whether or not to agree to the newly crowned Arthur's request for the hand of his daughter Guinevere. Leodogran is troubled by doubts about Arthur's legitimacy as King. He asks Bellicent, Queen of Orkney, what she knows of Arthur's parentage. 'These be secret things' (917), Bellicent says, but she proceeds to relate a tale told her, just before he died, by Bleys, the teacher of Arthur's wise counsellor Merlin. Bleys' story is of the supernatural origin of Arthur. He told Bellicent how he and Merlin, one stormy night, went out from Tintagil Castle:

> Then from the castle gateway by the chasm
> Descending through the dismal night – a night
> In which the bounds of heaven and earth were lost –
> Beheld, so high upon the dreary deeps
> It seemed in heaven, a ship, the shape thereof
> A dragon winged, and all from stem to stern
> Bright with shining people on the decks,
> And gone as soon as seen. And then the two
> Dropt to the cove, and watched the great sea fall,
> Wave after wave, each mightier than the last,
> Till last, a ninth one, gathering half the deep
> And full of voices, slowly rose and plunged
> Roaring, and all the wave was in a flame:
> And down the wave and in the flame was borne
> A naked babe, and rode to Merlin's feet,
> Who stoopt and caught the babe, and cried 'the King!' . . .
>   And this same child, he said,
> Is he who reigns; nor could I part in peace
> Till this were told.

> (369–84, 391–92)

Bellicent tells Leodogran that she asked Merlin what he thought of his old teacher's story:

>   when I met
> Merlin, and asked him if these things were truth . . .
> He laughed as is his wont, and answered me
> In riddling triplets of old time, and said:

>   'Rain, rain, and sun! a rainbow in the sky!
> A young man will be wiser by and by;
> An old man's wit may wander ere he die.
>   Rain, rain, and sun! a rainbow on the lea!
> And truth is this to me, and that to thee;
> And truth or clothed or naked let it be.
>   Rain, sun, and rain! and the free blossom blows:
> Sun, rain, and sun! and where is he who knows?
> From the great deep to the great deep he goes'

> (396–97, 400–10)

'An old man's wit may wander', 'truth is this to me, and that to thee', 'where is he who knows?' Merlin is not riddling. He is saying that old men like Bleys may be deluded, that truth is relative, and that it is an open question as to who knows anything for certain. Tennyson's supreme magician is not committing himself to magical things. Having listened to Bellicent's stories, Leodogran falls asleep and has a dream in which 'the solid earth became / As nothing, but the King stood out in heaven, / Crowned' (441–43). Accordingly, he gives Arthur permission to marry his daughter. But, even if he was not convinced by Bellicent's second-hand reporting of third-hand information, the deciding factor remains, notably, a dream, rather than any incontrovertible evidence that Arthur has spiritual legitimacy and authority.

Merlin's equivocation about the more-than-natural is a recurrent feature in *Idylls of the King*. In 'Gareth and Lynette', when Gareth and his companions approach Camelot for the first time, they are struck by the way in which the city, seen from a distance, seems a visionary, unreal place:

> Far-off they saw the silver-misty morn
> Rolling her smoke about the Royal mount,
> That rose between the forest and the field.
> At times the summit of the high city flashed;
> At times the spires and turrets half-way down
> Pricked through the mist; at times the great gate shone
> Only, that opened on the field below:
> Anon, the whole fair city had disappeared.

> (186–93)

Gareth's companions even fear that the city is the illusion of questionable 'Enchanters' (196) and that Arthur himself is 'not the King, / But only a changeling out of Fairyland' (199–200). Once they have arrived at the city gate, Gareth asks Merlin to tell them the 'truth' (247) about the nature of Camelot: 'Your city moved so weirdly in the mist' (241). Merlin responds by implicitly demythologising the magical:

> Son, I have seen the good ship sail
> Keel upward, and mast downward, in the heavens,
> And solid turrets topsy-turvy in air:
> And here is truth ...

> (249–52)

It *is* naturalistic truth. It is not magical or supernatural truth. Tennyson glossed the lines 'Refraction by mirage' (Tennyson, Hallam 1913: 965).

A. Dwight Culler has commented incisively on Tennyson's procedure in this respect:

> Merlin, in other words, is giving them a lesson in optics and physics and is simply telling them that the city is distorted by the mists in the distance so that it appears to move…it is a little disconcerting to learn that the old wizard himself does not believe in magic…Yet this technique of either providing an alternative rationalistic explanation of magic or else attributing it not to the poet but to one of the characters in the poem is Tennyson's practice throughout [*Idylls of the King*].
>
> (Culler 1977: 225)

Perhaps the most notable example of what Culler calls Tennyson's 'rationalising technique' (Culler 1977: 226) in the *Idylls* occurs in *The Holy Grail*. The medieval traditions followed by Tennyson, concerning the nature, origin and meaning of the visionary Grail, are that it is the cup which Christ used at the Last Supper and in which the blood from the wounds of his crucifixion is miraculously preserved. In an evil age the Grail cannot be seen and, hence, quest for it constitutes a quest at once for spiritual illumination in dark times and for the spiritual revival of a wasted land. The spiritual authority of the Grail is absolute. At the stage in the cycle when the quest takes place in Tennyson's 'The Holy Grail', the Arthurian order is showing clear signs of degeneration. One of the reported speakers in the idyll – 'A man wellnigh a hundred winters old' (85) – puts it thus:

> when King Arthur made
> His Table Round, and all men's hearts became
> Clean for a season, surely he had thought
> That now the Holy Grail would come again;
> But sin broke out. All, Christ, that it would come,
> And heal the world of all their wickedness!
>
> (89–94)

The problem with the presentation of the quest that Arthur's knights undertake in 'The Holy Grail' is that the truth of such visions of the Grail as are claimed is profoundly questionable. This has something to do with Tennyson's own scepticism about such visions of the supernatural. Writing to the Duke of Argyll in 1859 Tennyson observed:

> As to Macaulay's suggestion of the Sangraal I doubt whether such a subject could be handled in these days, without incurring a charge

of irreverence. It would be too much like playing with sacred things. The old writers *believed* in the Sangraal.

(Lang and Shannon 1982–90: II.244)

Tennyson's solution to the problem of his not believing in mystical visions of the cup of the Last Supper was only partly a matter of his casting the account of the quest as the account of Sir Percivale; of not giving it, in other words, his own authority. What Tennyson also did with this idyll was to write it in a manner which allows a natural explanation for all the supernatural happenings. Tennyson's wife Emily recorded in her diary that in January 1869 Tennyson

> read 'the Holy Grail' to the Bradleys, explaining the realism and sym-
> bolism, and how the natural . . . could always be made to account for
> the supernatural.
>
> (Tennyson, Hallam 1897: II.63)

When Arthur's knights first have a vision of the Holy Grail, on a summer's night in the great hall at Camelot, they do not actually *see* it. It is covered by a 'luminous cloud' (189). The quest that many of them undertake is a quest for an unmediated vision of the Grail. Sir Percivale relates the apparition in the hall as follows:

> all at once, as there we sat, we heard
> A cracking and a riving of the roofs,
> And rending, and a blast, and overhead
> Thunder, and in the thunder was a cry.
> And in the blast there smote along the hall
> A beam of light seven times more clear than day:
> And down the long beam stole the Holy Grail
> All over covered with a luminous cloud,
> And none might see who bare it, and it past . . .
> I sware a vow before them all, that I,
> Because I had not seen the Grail, would ride
> A twelvemonth and a day in quest of it,
> Until I found and saw it . . .
> and Galahad sware the vow,
> And good Sir Bors, our Lancelot's cousin, sware,
> And Lancelot sware, and many among the knights,
> And Gawain sware, and louder than the rest.

(182–90, 195–202)

The apparition in the hall falls under the terms which Tennyson described to Mrs Bradley: 'how the natural . . . could always be made to account for the supernatural'. The possibility of a natural explanation for all the apparently magical or supernatural happenings in *Idylls of the King* was articulated again by James Knowles when, in a letter to the editor of *The Spectator* in January 1870, a letter which Tennyson 'encouraged' him to compose (Tennyson, Hallam 1913: 974), he wrote:

> It is most interesting . . . to note the thread of realism which is preserved throughout [*Idylls of the King*], and which . . . serves the . . . purpose of . . . accounting naturally for all the supernatural adventures and beliefs recorded in the story itself.
>
> Thus, in 'The Holy Grail', the various apparitions of the mystic vessel are explicable by passing meteors or sudden lightening flashes seen in a season of great tempests and thunderstorms . . .
>
> (Jump 1967: 316)

Certainly, in 'The Holy Grail' itself, Arthur, who has been away during the episode of the sighting in the hall, returns to Camelot and sees from far-off nothing more than a storm of thunder and lightening over the city:

> Returning o'er the plain that then began
> To darken under Camelot . . . the King
> Looked up, calling aloud 'Lo, there! the roofs
> Of our great hall are rolled in thunder-smoke!
> Pray Heaven, they be not smitten by the bolt'.
>
> (217–21)

A different kind of naturalistic explanation of visions of the Grail applies with respect to the young nun, Percivale's sister, who was the first in 'The Holy Grail' story to have a vision of the Grail and who started off the whole obsession with the thing amongst Arthur's knights. Tennyson knowingly suggests that the nun's vision of the Grail has a very great deal to do with her being frustrated in human love. Her brother speaks of her as:

> A holy maid; though never maiden glowed,
> But that was in her earlier maidenhood,
> With such a fervent flame of human love,
> Which being rudely blunted, glanced and shot
> Only to holy things . . .
>
> (72–76)

When Percivale records his sister's own account of her vision, the colouring and rhythms she describes again imply that she was suffering more from displaced sexual feeling than from a sudden access of spiritual insight:

> then
> Streamed through my cell a cold and silver beam,
> And down the long beam stole the Holy Grail,
> Rose-red with beatings in it, as if alive,
> Till all the white walls of my cell were dyed
> With rosy colours leaping on the wall;
> And then the music faded, and the Grail
> Past, and the beam decayed, and from the walls
> The rosy quiverings died into the night.
>
> (115–23)

The nun's fervour transmits itself first to the young knight Sir Galahad. She solicits him with a confusion of romantic and spiritual rhetoric and he, susceptible in his youth, comes to believe, if not in the Grail, at least in her excitement about it:

> she, the wan sweet maiden, shore away
> Clean from her forehead, all that wealth of hair
> Which made a silken mat-work for her feet;
> And out of this she plaited broad and long
> A strong sword-belt, and wove with silver thread
> And crimson in the belt a strange device,
> A crimson grail within a silver beam;
> And saw the bright boy-knight, and bound it on him,
> Saying, 'My knight, my love, my knight of heaven,
> O thou, my love, whose love is one with mine,
> I, maiden, round thee, maiden, bind my belt.
> Go forth, for thou shalt see what I have seen,
> And break through all, till one will crown thee king
> Far in the spiritual city': and as she spake
> She sent the deathless passion in her eyes
> Through him, and made him hers, and laid her mind
> On him, and he believed in her belief.
>
> (149–65)

The obsession with the Grail spreads from here. James Knowles, commenting on the way in which the 'apparitions of the mystic vessel' (Jump 1967: 316) are explicable in terms of natural phenomena, goes on to say that these phenomena first act 'on the hysterical exaltation of an enthusiastic nun, and then, by contagion . . . upon the imaginations of a few kindred natures' (Jump 1967: 316).

The contagious hysteria which fuels the knights' quests is part of the demythologisation of the Grail vision which Tennyson undertakes at all points in the idyll. Sir Bors' glimpse, for example, of the cup –

> In colour like the fingers of a hand
> Before a burning taper, the sweet Grail
> Glided and past, and close upon it pealed
> A sharp quick thunder
>
> (690–93)

– can have a naturalistic explanation. 'It might have been a meteor', Tennyson commented drily (Tennyson, Hallam 1913: 976).

Likewise, in the same way as Galahad comes to believe in the young nun's belief, the principal narrator of 'The Holy Grail', Sir Percivale, is taken in by Galahad's belief: 'I grew / One with him, to believe as he believed' (486–87). At the end of 'The Holy Grail' Arthur, having heard the reports of his knights, will say that only 'one' of them 'hath had the vision face to face' (896). This is Galahad. But Galahad's claim, made to Percivale, that he has seen the Grail again remains subject to the principle of natural, psychological explanation. His story of what he saw remains as disturbingly coloured as the nun's inflammatory account of *her* vision:

> Never yet
> Hath what thy sister taught me first to see,
> This Holy Thing, failed from my side, nor come
> Covered, but moving with me night and day,
> Fainter by day, but always in the night
> Blood-red, and sliding down the blackened marsh
> Blood-red, and on the naked mountain top
> Blood-red, and in the sleeping mere below
> Blood-red . . .
>
> (468–76)

Galahad declares that he is about to go and be crowned king 'Far in the spiritual city' (483) and he invites Percivale to accompany him, promising Percivale that he, too, 'shalt see the vision' (484). Percivale tells how he journeyed with Galahad up a hill:

> that none but man could climb,
> Scarred with a hundred wintry water-courses –
> Storm at the top, and when we gained it, storm
> Round us and death; for every moment glanced
> His silver arms and gloomed: so quick and thick
> The lightenings here and there to left and right
> Struck, till the dry old trunks about us, dead,
> Yea, rotten with a hundred years of death,
> Sprang into fire . . .

(489–97)

Percivale reports that, having ascended this hill, he saw Galahad pursue the Grail into the 'spiritual city' (526). Once more the vision is related in terms susceptible to a natural explanation. Tennyson remarked of Galahad's assumption into the heavenly city: 'It was a time of storm when men could imagine miracles, and so storm is emphasised' (Tennyson, Hallam 1913: 976).

Arthur was always doubtful about the quest for a vision of the Holy Grail. At the end of the idyll he makes it clear that he saw the quest as a questionable distraction from the practical business of the Round Table. He uses the very word 'vision' to define emptiness as he affirms his own intuitive sense of the reality of God. He has 'moments', he says, when he 'feels he cannot die, / And knows himself no vision to himself, / Nor the high God a vision' (912–14). This is like the speaker of *In Memoriam*, who at one point asserts that if he

> heard an ever-breaking shore
> That tumbled in the Godless deep;
>
> A warmth within the breast would melt
> The freezing reason's colder part,
> And like a man in wrath the heart
> Stood up and answered 'I have felt'.

(CXXIV.11–16)

But a question about the authority of pure feeling is recorded at the heart of this assertion: 'like a man in *wrath*'. The violence renders the feeling unstable and unreliable. Comparably, Arthur's assertion of feeling as the ground of conviction and hope carries no more than a subjective authority. The rationalisable experiences of the knights in their quests, together with Arthur's scepticism about visionary experience, leave the question of the ultimate spiritual ground of Arthur's authority and order unanswered and unproven.

It is the same thing at the closing of the *Idylls* cycle. The last idyll is called 'The passing of Arthur', though the euphemism 'passing' was substituted in the 1869 published version to alter the title as it had stood in the 1868 trial edition: 'The Death of Arthur' (Wise 1908: II.197–209). 'The Passing of Arthur' tells of the 'last, dim, weird battle of the west' (94) and of how Arthur, wounded and dying, comes to his end. The idyll does not retract the rational perspective within which *Idylls of the King* as a whole is held, though Tennyson necessarily follows the details of the myth of King Arthur and has the story recounting the way in which Sir Bedivere last saw the King as he was received into a death-barge that was to carry him to Avalon:

> all the decks were dense with stately forms,
> Black-stoled, black-hooded, like a dream – by these
> Three Queens with crowns of gold: and from them rose
> A cry that shivered to the tingling stars,
> And, as it were one voice, an agony
> Of lamentation, like a wind that shrills
> All night in a waste land, where no one comes,
> Or hath come, since the making of the world.
>
> (364–71)

There remains, however, a question as to the destination of the barge. The story has Bedivere recalling that he 'saw, / . . . Or *thought* he saw' (my italics) the 'speck that bare the King' (463–65):

> Down that long water opening on the deep
> Somewhere far off, pass on and on, and go
> From less to less and vanish into light.
>
> (466–68)

But even if Bedivere *did* see the speck so vanish, the realm into which it vanishes remains uncertain. We hear that

> from the dawn it seemed there came, but faint
> As from beyond the limit of the world,
> Like the last echo born of a great cry,

> Sounds, as if some fair city were one voice
> Around a king returning from his wars.
>
> (457–61)

This is, of course, Bedivere's account, told 'when the man was no more than a voice / In the white winter of his age' and reported via 'those' to whom he told it, the first generation of myth-makers, as it were: 'those / With whom he dwelt, new faces, other minds' (3–5). The attenuated authority of the source of the tale is endorsed by the qualifiers in the passage: 'it *seemed* there came', '*As* from', '*Like* the', '*as if* some fair city'. Nothing true is being claimed here. Even an echo is hollow. And echoes may, in any case, be duplicitous things. They reverberate in unpredictable ways. The echo here might take its point of origin in this world, repeating no more than humanity's cry that a higher world *should* exist. Tennyson is careful to conceive 'The Passing of Arthur' in such a way that the only certain thing is *this* world and its measurable realities. The very last line of the poem, 'And the new sun rose bringing the new year' (469), returns us to this world. The dolor of the renewal of the natural cycle is that it is bereft of the spiritual renewal that Arthur and his order had insisted upon. The understanding of renewal in the line is an entirely temporal one.

In *In Memoriam*, Tennyson sought at points to sustain a vision of evolutionary and spiritual progress:

> Arise and fly
> The reeling Faun, the sensual feast;
> Move upward, working out the beast,
> And let the ape and tiger die.
>
> (CXVIII.25–28)

Idylls of the King is about an attempt to move upward. But the poem itself does not mimic this attempt. The natural and naturalistic cycle overwhelms Arthur's spiritual ideal. Arthur's idealistic order 'Reels', as Arthur himself puts it, 'back into the beast' (26) and there is no validation of the ultimate reality of the spiritual authority that had been claimed for that order. The natural cycle is envisaged through a secular lens. Arthur's spiritual ideal is a temporary aberration in the cycle. Nature, in the last resort, is neither redeemed nor redeemable. *Idylls of the King* is a bleak poem. A. Dwight Culler, speaking of the relocation of Tennyson's 'Morte d'Arthur' in *Idylls of the King*, notes that:

it is remarkable how different is the meaning it takes on in its new context at the end of *Idylls of the King*. In 1842, when it was set in the framework of 'The Epic', it was a much less dark and pessimistic poem. There was relatively more emphasis upon the rebirth of Arthur, and this was intensified by being repeated in modern dress in the framework of the poem. But in the *Idylls* the passing comes at the end of a long process of disintegration and decay, and there is no frame, set in the future, to suggest that life will go on. The structure, in other words, is apocalyptic rather than elegiac…What was originally written as an elegy for Arthur Hallam has been transformed, simply by its setting, into a prophecy of doom for Victorian society.

(Culler 1977: 216–17)

In the same breath it is a prophecy of doom for the Victorian Empire. In a lecture to students on 'How to Study Natural History', published in 1885, the year that *Idylls of the King* was completed, Charles Kingsley gave voice to the nineteenth-century British imperial imagination when he observed that it has 'pleased God' that Englishmen

> should improve [the] precious heirloom of science, inventing, pro-ducing, exporting, importing, till it seems as if the whole human race, and every land from the equator to the pole must henceforth bear the indelible impress and sign manual of English science…
>
>   Do you not see, then, that by following these studies…you are training in yourselves that habit of mind which God has approved as the one which He has ordained for Englishmen, and are doing what in you lies toward carrying out, in after life, the glorious work which God seems to have laid on the English race, to replenish the earth and subdue it?

(Kingsley 1885: 308)

'With God on our Side'. British Imperialism, like Arthur's order, claimed to be spiritually ordained. Tennyson's scepticism in *Idylls of the King* about the divine authority of Arthur's empire is a scepticism about the authority of the British imperial state and at once a scepticism about the ultimate sanction of human life itself.

Afterword

In his essay, 'Tennyson and the Cultural Politics of Prophesy', referred to in the Introduction to this book, Alan Sinfield sets the visionary against the sceptical in stark dichotomy. If the 'visionary' has a politically and culturally conservative, even reactionary, dimension, then there is an implication that the 'sceptical' carries an inherently progressive agenda. Tennyson's work does not sustain such a straightforward contrast. The condition of thought and feeling explored in his poetry is more subtle. It is certainly open to criticise Tennyson for his inadequacy as, say, a sympathiser with imperial values, and the like. These kinds of feature are obvious enough on the surface of his poetry, though it remains useful that they have been commented upon. There is, however, a more telling insufficiency that does not lie with Tennyson. Many may nowadays take for granted that neither life nor such things as imperial attitude have God on their side. Tennyson, by contrast, yearned for there to be a spiritual meaning to existence. Some of his minor poems, like 'The Ancient Sage', express this yearning, albeit often in dramatic form. Tennyson could feel visceral dread at the thought of an alien universe. But close attention shows that many of his most important poems examine, with a powerful, almost pathological intensity, the ways in which his desire for a higher meaning to life was constantly contradicted and sometimes blocked by a profound scepticism that there is any such meaning. We may nowadays be less used than the Victorians to this kind of tension, where scepticism connects not so much with a secular, materialist view of the world than with vibrant spiritual inclination. It is, however, this conflict which generates the intricate texture of Tennyson's verse. It is a contemporary view, historically and culturally *in*sensitive, which is inadequate to reading the perturbed condition of mind that is at play in his work when it sees an aching for the spiritual necessarily excluding the possibility of a profound scepticism. It is an inadequacy based, paradoxically, on a commitment to purity. What is lost in attempts to found value on some purity of ideological perspective is the capacity to comprehend a multivalence of thought and emotion. In the Introduction to her collection of critical essays on Tennyson, Rebecca Stott observed that:

> Just as the DNA of dinosaurs can be reconstructed from the fossilised remains of a single mosquito in [Steven Spielberg's 1993 film] *Jurassic Park*, so it seems the Victorian Age can be reconstructed from the exquisite and delicately detailed poetry of Tennyson.
>
> (Stott 1996: 1)

This is a quaint analogy. The Victorian Age emerges as prehistoric. Notwithstanding the compliments of 'exquisite' and 'delicately detailed', Tennyson himself takes the form of an antiquated mosquito, as dead as the dinosaurs. The comparison of Tennyson and the Victorians with the age of the dinosaurs is particularly misconceived because it was, of course, in the nineteenth century that dinosaurs were 'discovered' and the significance of the discovery first *understood*. It was that understanding, and a host of others like it, which helped to establish the terms of the secular and sceptical modernity that now enables what is sometimes easy criticism of Victorian thought. Tennyson's poetry, with its abiding scepticism, partakes in the complex generation of the modern that was taking place in his era and it is inadequate to misrepresent its nuances through the formulaic imposition of one-dimensional ideological perspectives.

Appendix: The Harvard Notebook 8 Draft of *The Lover's Tale*

Two major pre-*1832* manuscript drafts of *The Lover's Tale* survive: in Harvard Notebook 8 at the Houghton Library, Harvard University (Ricks and Day 1987–93: II.91–154) and in Trinity Notebook 18, Trinity College, Cambridge (Ricks and Day 1987–93: XII.1–73). Internal evidence (dated inscriptions, the particular poems drafted, watermarks, etc.) indicates that both these notebooks were principally in use from 1828 to 1830. Trinity Notebook 18 is dated by Tennyson 'Jan[uary] 10 1828' (Ricks and Day 1987–93: XII.3). Inside the front cover (according to the present foliation) of Harvard Notebook 8, which is watermarked 1825, Tennyson wrote 'Thursday/19th June' (Ricks and Day 1987–93: II.92). June 19 fell on a Thursday in 1828 (see also p. 74; and Ricks 1987: I.73, 327). But the draft material relating to *The Lover's Tale* in Harvard Notebook 8 very clearly represents an earlier stage in the textual development of the poem than the material in Trinity Notebook 18. While the material in Trinity Notebook 18 is fragmentary, the drafts for what was to become Part I in *1832* (865 lines) amount to some 665 lines (including repetitions and deletions). Of the thirty-two intact leaves in Harvard Notebook 8 only two pages (ff. 31^r and 30^v) present drafts of lines from what was to become Part I of *1832* (the sequence of the draft poem runs in reverse direction to the present foliation of the MS). However, there is draft material relating to *The Lover's Tale* on several stubs near ff. 31^r and 30^v. A significant number of the half lines that are discernible on these stubs can be completed from the draft version of Part I of *1832* which appears on ff. 20^v–32^v of Trinity Notebook 18. Using Trinity Notebook 18 it is, indeed, possible to reconstruct from Harvard Notebook 8 a complete early version, comprising 111 lines (including repetitions and deletions), of what was to become 1832 Part I. The draft lines of *The Lover's Tale* on f. 30^v of Harvard Notebook 8 represent the concluding lines of this notebook's version of Part I of the poem (the last line on f. 30^v is identical to the last line of Part I in both *1832* and *1879*). At no stage in this notebook is *The Lover's Tale* draft material divided into numbered sections. The most that happens is that certain passages are followed or preceded by a short rule.

There is also less complete, but important, evidence in Harvard Notebook 8 of what may be Tennyson's attempt to continue the poem beyond the point at which Part I of *1832* concludes. After the conclusion of the Harvard Notebook 8 version of Part I of *1832* there follows, on f. 30^r, a passage of 18 lines, preceded by a short rule, beginning 'Fair face! fair form'. As I suggest on pp. 95–98, the central theme of the 'Fair face! fair form' passage on f.30^r can be related to the theme of Part II of *1832*. Following 30^r there are a number of leaves missing from the notebook before the appearance of further stubs inscribed with half-lines apparently drafted for *The Lover's Tale*. There are 59 such half-lines. Two of them (right hand stub, Ricks and Day 1987–93: II.136) were to become *1832*, I.58–59 [*1879*, I.54–70]. The remaining half-lines on these stubs cannot be completed from any known version of *The Lover's Tale*.

What follows is a transcription of the 111-line Harvard Notebook 8 version of *1832* Part I, together with the 'Fair Face! fair form' passage which immediately follows in the notebook. The half-lines on stubs, which represent the first 70 lines of this 111-line version of Part I of the poem, are completed from lines in the Trinity Notebook 18 draft. In respect of these lines, the Harvard Notebook 8 material is presented on the left and the lines from Trinity Notebook 18 on the right. I have included only such lines from Trinity Notebook 18 as correspond to lines in Harvard Notebook 8 (omission of lines from the Trinity Notebook 18 draft is indicated by a row of asterisks). Identification of stubs and leaves in both the Harvard and the Trinity Notebooks is keyed in with the volume and page numbers on which facsimiles of the MSS appear in *The Tennyson Archive*, ed. Christopher Ricks and Aidan Day, 31 vols, 1987–93. Line numbers immediately to the left of each transcription refer to the line numbering (including repetitions and deletions) of the manuscript. Arabic line numbers enclosed in round brackets in the left-hand margin of the Trinity Notebook 18 transcription key to the line numbers in the Harvard Notebook 8 draft. Section and line numbers in the left-hand margin of the Harvard Notebook 8 transcription refer to the text of *The Lover's Tale* in *1832* and *1879* (the *1879* references enclosed in square brackets). I have retained neither Tennyson's use of the long 'f' nor the apostrophe which he used in writing 'its' as 'it's'.

Key

[?won] = conjectural reading

Rain
~~Speak~~ = word deleted with interlineated substitute

[?]   = illegible word

[-?-]   = illegible word deleted

[-----] = short rule

208 *Appendix*

Tennyson Archive Vol. II.128
H.Nbk. 8, *Lover's Tale* stub
Unadopted[†]

 1 A casement brac'd...
 2 (Thorough whose wrea...
 3 The fretted noonlig...
 4 Though well-nigh s...
 5 Half-clasp'd let i...
 6 The measur'd moan...
 7 W[h] slept in mur...
 8 Rising & falling...
 9 Of some hush'd...
10 Pales on his unvex...
11 To all his littl...
12 From gleaning of f...
13 And even breathing...
14 Fall on the wakef...
15 The stillest night...
      [-----]
16 It was a rust...
17 And nested on...
18 W[h] straightway...

[†] *The Lover's Tale* opens in both H.Nbk. 8 and T.Nbk. 18 with a 15-line description of the casement of a summerhouse, followed by 20 lines on the summerhouse. The lines describing the summerhouse were reduced as *1832* I.41–43 [*1879* I.39–41]. The first five lines of the poem in *1832* and *1879* do not appear in the H.Nbk 8 draft.

Tennyson Archive Vol. XII.40
T.Nbk.18, f. 20^v, *Lover's Tale*
Unadopted

	1	A casement braced & traversed with lithe herbs
	2	(Thorough whose woven spice of flower & leaf
	3	The fretted noonlight won its ambushed way
	4	Though wellnigh softened to its pale decline†
(5)	5	Halfclasped, let inward from the lower air
	6	The measured moan of summer-swelling seas
	7	W^h slept in murmur & in motion
	8	Rising & falling like the placid breast
	9	Of some hushed infant, when ye pendant lamp
(10)	10	Pales on his unvexed features deeply lost
	11	To all his little learnt & sweetly stayed
	12	From gleaning of fresh thought when his suppressed
	13	And even moanings from an inner room
	14	Fall on ye wakeful mother's ear, what time
(15)	15	The stillest night is rung out from ye clocks.
		[-----]
	16	It was a rustic summerhouse perched high
	17	And nested on the manypeaked cliff
	18	W^h straightway from the slumbrous Element

---

† The parenthesis is not closed.

Tennyson Archive Vol. II.129
H.Nbk. 8, *Lover's Tale* left hand stub
Unadopted

Pine

19   . . . undecaying ~~Pine~~ [-?-]

where highest plac'd

20   . . . ose odorous deeps ~~upsprung~~
21   . . . f ~~the~~ a cone
22   . . . the vast unstirr'd
23   . . . ~~unseen~~

the sea
~~nor far~~

24   . . . mountain bloom: [-?-]

blasts

25   . . . 'd ~~winds~~ so rudely here

slender stems & pale

26   . . . their ~~vivid~~
27   . . . :but if ever voice
28   . . . gh them it was light & clear
29   . . . f rich perfume
30   . . . land vallies: yellow bees

31   . . . polish'd boles &
31   . . . the hours

32   . . . ible & merry birds
33   . . . ter of their lavish plumes
34   . . . nce of exceeding joy
35   . . . such a goodly dwelling-place

Tennyson Archive Vol. XII.40
T.Nbk.18, f. 20ᵛ (cont.), *Lover's Tale*
Unadopted

       19 Rose cinctured with yᵉ undecaying Pine
(20) 20 From out whose odorous deeps where highest placed
       21 Started the sloping lustre of a cone
       22 Its lower bedded in the vast unstirred
       23 Of leaves & secret intercourse of boughs
       24 Wʰ shrouded many a mountainbloom: yᵉ Sea
(25) 25 Rolled not his gathered blasts so rudely here
       26 With power to snap their slender stems or pale
       27 Their bright expression: but if ever voice
       28 Of wind sung thro' them it was light & clear

Tennyson Archive Vol. XII.41
T.Nbk.18, f. 21ʳ, *Lover's Tale*
Unadopted

       29 And shrill & warm & full of rich perfume
(30) 30 Rapt from the inland valleys: yellow bees
       31 Stole by the polished boles & wore the hours

                 merry
       32 In musings audible & ~~little~~ birds
       33 With thrilling flutter of their lavish plumes
       34 And rapid utterance of exceeding joy
(35) 35 Praised God for such a goodly dwelling place

Tennyson Archive Vol. II.129
H.Nbk. 8, *Lover's Tale* right hand stub

[-----]

I.6 [I.6]	36	Oh! pleasant brea...
	37	(Where the chafed...
	38	Sank powerless,...
		And withers on the
I.10 [I.10]	39	Upon
	40	Even now the s...
	41	Her well-remem...
I.22 [I.22]	42	I come, great M...
	43	~~Borrow thy~~ [-?-]...
		Oh
	44	~~To~~ [-?-] Lead me...
		Rain
	45	~~Speak~~ thro' mine...
		~~Mine~~
	46	~~The~~ utterance with...
	47	Have hollow'd o...
	48	Betwixt the s...
	49	A little momen...
	50	Shall waft me o...

Tennyson Archive Vol. XII.41
T.Nbk.18, f. 21ʳ (cont.), *Lover's Tale*

* *†

(36)	41	Oh pleasant breast of waters quiet bay
	42	(Where the chafed billow of the outer sea
	43	Sank powerless even as anger falls aside
	44	And withers on the breast of quiet love)
(40)	45	Even now the subtil Memory hath unrolled
	46	Her wellremembered chart of wave & hill
	47	I come great Mistress of the ear & eye
	48	Oh lead me delicately lest yᵉ mind
(45)	49	Rain thro' mine eyes & strangling sorrow weigh
	50	Mine utterance with lameness: the long years
	51	Have hollowed out a valley & a gulf
	52	Betwixt the Springtide of my Love & me
	53	A little moment & thy faery sail
(50)	54	Shall waft me onward & the Alchemy

† What were to become *1832* I.1–5 and *1879* I.1–5 are drafted in T.Nbk 18, f. 21ʳ, ll.36–40.

Tennyson Archive Vol. II.130
H.Nbk. 8, *Lover's Tale* left hand stub

		erve
	51	...[?] & fashion my worn frame
	52	...& love –
	52	Permit me, prithee
I.32 [I.30]	53	...hand across mine eyes & muse
	54	...s w^h never more shall meet
	55	...& aches beneath my touch
	56	...t a heart in either eye

[-?-]
lights

	57	...are darken'd thus
I.37 [I.35]	58	...ision hath a keener edge

the semicircle
narrow fringe [-?-] of

	59	...ow – the ~~curving beach~~

dripping

	60	...[-?-] wreathes of green
	61	...the pleasure-boat w^h rock'd
	62	...keel to keel, ~~light green~~
	63	...of the dappled wave

its

	64	...~~his~~ side –
I.46 [I.44]	64	Oh Love! oh Hope
	65	...the darkness of my brain
	66	...the moon-lit nights
	67	...aks & the amber Eves
I.54 [I.51]	68	...drilla, thou & I
	69	...nd the little bay, or moor'd
	70	...brow'd cavern, where the tide

57–58   These lines are not in T.Nbk.18 but reappeared as *1832* I.36–37 and then as *1879* I.34–35: 'For when the outer lights are darkened thus, / The memory's vision hath a keener edge'.

Tennyson Archive Vol. XII.41
T.Nbk.18, f. 21ʳ (cont.), *Lover's Tale*

(51) 55 Of thought shall nerve & fashion my worn frame
      56 To strength & youth & love.
                                    Permit me prythee

Tennyson Archive Vol. XII.42
T.Nbk.18, f. 21ᵛ, *Lover's Tale*

      57 To pass my hand across my eyes & muse
      58 On those dear hills wʰ never more shall meet
(55) 59 The sight that throbs & aches beneath my touch
(56) 60 As tho' there beat a heart in either eye
(59) 61 It grows upon me now – the semicircle
(59) 62 Of darkblue waters & the narrow fringe
(60) 63 Of curving beach – its wreaths of dripping green
      64 Its pale pink shells – the pleasureboat wʰ rocked
      65 Lightgreen with its own shadow keel to keel
      66 Upon the crispings of the dappled wave
      67 Which blanched upon its side.
                                    Oh Love oh Hope
      68 They flash athwart the darkness of my brain
      69 The many pleasant days, the moonlit nights
      70 The gorgeous daybreaks & the amber Evens
      71 When thou & I Cadrilla, thou & I
      72 Borne round & round the little bay or moored
(70) 73 Beneath some lowbrowed cavern where yᵉ wave

       ✻✻

Tennyson Archive Vol. II.131
H.Nbk. 8, *Lover's Tale* f. 31^r

I.57 [I.54]	71	~~Plash'd~~, sapping its worn ribs, spoke pleasantly
	72	As youth might speak with fearless interchange
	73	Of words, nor words alone, for every thought

was woven
74   Embrac'd its brother, ~~thought &~~ every hope

own   back
75   ~~Was woven~~ with its likeness & gave ∧ itself
76   Unalter'd ~~thro'~~ in the mirror of our speech
77   Ah! turn the telescope, one hope, one wish
78   Was thrown to utter distance, brotherless
79   Unanswered, like a stranger in a land
80   Of enemies, a weary bird on wing
81   Curs'd never to alight; no resting-place
82   No stay – no shrouding of the weary head
83   Beneath the weary plume, but onward still
84   Sustaining with no pleasant balm of thought
85   That inner fire w^h eats into the soul
86   But will not [?wear] the framework –
86   – Some light hearts
87   Held by strong cables of unbroken Hope
I.846 [I.793]   88   ~~Even~~ On the sharp ridge of utmost doom, ride highly
89   Above the perilous seas of Chance & Change

Nay, more
90   ~~And even~~ hold out to others far away
91   Bright lights of [? solace] unto safety

Tennyson Archive Vol. II.133
H.Nbk. 8, *Lover's Tale* f. 30ᵛ

[-----]

the
I.849 [I.796]   92   As ~~some~~ tall ship thro' many a varied year
                 93   Knit to some dreary sandbank far at sea

                                        ~~buoyancy~~
                 94   ~~Secure in its own lightness~~
                 95   All thro' the livelong hours of utter dark
                 96   Showers slanting light upon the dolorous wave
                 97   For me, all other hope did sway from that
                 98   Wʰ hung the frailest: falling, they fell too
                 99   Crush'd, link on link, into the beaten Earth
                100   She [-?-] ~~And Love & Hope smil'd farewell~~

                                   did walk
                101   And Love ~~relaxed~~ with banish'd Hope no more
I.857 [I.802]   102   It was ill done to part ye, sisters fair

                      ~~For Love~~   [-?-] [-?-]
                103   ~~For ye were~~ [-?-] [-?-] ~~the breath~~
                104   Love's arms were wreath'd about yᵉ neck of Hope
                105   And Hope kissed Love & Love drew in her breath

                                   drank
I.860 [I.805]   106   In that close kiss & ~~turn'd her~~ her whisper'd tales
                107   They said that Love wᵈ die when Hope was gone
                108   And Love mourn'd long & sorrow'd after Hope

                      At last she sought
                109   ~~But love did search~~ out Memory & they trod
                110   The same old paths where Love had walk'd with Hope
I.865 [I.810]   111   And Memory fed the soul of Love with tears

---

108   This line was inserted by interlineation. It forms part of the revision of l.109 which at first followed directly from l. 107.

Tennyson Archive Vol. II.134
H.Nbk. 8, 'Fair face! fair form' f. 30^{r}

[-----]

Fair face! fair form [?sole ?sad] tenant of a brain

griefs

Peopled with ~~thoughts~~ whose blackness cannot mar
Your lustre, when fatigued with things less fair

e

Th~~is~~e eyes roll~~s~~ inward, gazing as they gazed
5   Upon the archetype in happier hours
Beautiful permanence! indwelling light
Unvanishing! w^{h} never transient thought
Supplants or shades, for thou dost glow thro' all
Intense~~ly~~ Idea; ~~like~~ though I close the lids
10   Of mental vision on thee thou dost burn
As sunlight, thro' them: Slumber is no veil
For thou art up & broad awake in dreams
O deeply lov'd: yet like a cruel foe
Fast-centr'd in the heart thou hast undone

~~must exist for ever~~

15   ~~W^{h} cannot~~ [?pass] ~~Can it lose~~
~~Thy presence when this~~ head is low in dust?
And [?won] unto thyself & sendest thence
Sharp arrows, from the fort w^{h} was mine own

---

4   This eye rolls *1st reading*
15   cannot [?pass] *altered to* must exist for ever *followed by cancellation of entire line*

Notes

4 The archetype: *The Lover's Tale* (1832)

1. In his *1879* headnote Tennyson commented that *1832* was 'marred by the many misprints of the compositor'. In quoting from *1832* I have silently included the substantive corrections (not the revisions) marked up by Tennyson in the British Library copy. Occasionally, the *1879* revisions were so thoroughgoing as to make the identification of a parallel between lines in *1832* and in *1879* no more than very approximate. Where this occurs, an asterisk before a line-reference means 'corresponding to' the lines of the final text.
2. Further information on Harvard Notebook 8 is in the Appendix, which includes a transcription of the draft of Part I, together with other lines in the Notebook probably related to *The Lover's Tale*, since this material has a bearing on my critical discussion of the poem.
3. Ford comments on the *1879* text of *The Lover's Tale* but what he has to say of the tone of *1879*, as well as of some of the specific Keatsian echoes, applies equally to the 1832 state of the poem.
4. The concluding line 59 of Part III in *1879* ('There, there, my latest vision – then the event') does not appear in the Harvard Notebook 12 draft of this Part. It first appears in *1868* to link with the newly composed material that was to form Part IV in *1879*.
5. The form in which Mrs Bradley read *The Lover's Tale* is not certain. Several passages from Part I of the poem are transcribed by Mrs Bradley in the Diary immediately preceding her entry for 24 January 1868. These passages are prefaced: 'Extracts from an unpublished Poem of A. Tennyson's lent by him – Jan 24. 1868 – called The Lover's Tale'. The passages in the Diary do not incorporate any of the new readings which were to appear in *1868*. At the same time, substantive variants in the passages transcribed by Mrs Bradley show that she was not copying from *1832*. The variant readings in her transcriptions conform to readings in the passages copied in the Heath Commonplace Book at the Fitzwilliam Museum, Cambridge (Ricks and Day 1987–93: XXIX.8–9, 27). It appears that Tennyson lent her either the actual manuscript copied by Heath or a MS. version of the poem closely related to that seen by him.

Bibliography

Allen, Peter (1978) *The Cambridge Apostles: The Early Years*, Cambridge.

Allingham, William (1967) *William Allingham's Diary*, introduced by Geoffrey Grigson, Fontwell, Sussex.

Armstrong, Isobel (ed.) (1969) *The Major Victorian Poets: Reconsiderations*, London.

——(1993) *Victorian Poetry: Poetry, Poetics and Politics*, London and New York.

Auden, W.H. (ed.) (1944) Introduction, *A Selection from the Poems of Tennyson*, New York.

Baker, Carlos (1948) *Shelley's Major Poetry: The Fabric of a Vision*, Princeton.

Basler, Roy P. (1944) 'Tennyson the Psychologist', *South Atlantic Quarterly*, 43.

Bayley, John (1957) *The Romantic Survival: A Study in Poetic Evolution*, London.

Bloom, Harold (1969) *Shelley's Mythmaking*, 1st published 1959, Ithaca, N.Y.

Bradley, A.C. (1909) *Oxford Lectures on Poetry*, Oxford.

——(1915) *A Commentary on Tennyson's 'In Memoriam'*, 1st published 1901, London.

Brooke, Stopford (1894) *Tennyson: His Art and Relation to Modern Life*, London.

Buckler, W.E. (1980) *The Victorian Imagination: Essays in Aesthetic Exploration*, Brighton, Sussex.

Bush, Douglas (1969) *Mythology and the Romantic Tradition in English Poetry*, 1st published 1937, New York.

Campbell, Nancie (1971–73) *Tennyson in Lincoln: A Catalogue of the Collections in the Research Centre*, 2 vols, Lincoln.

Carey, John (ed.) (1971) *Milton: Complete Shorter Poems*, London.

Carlyle, Thomas (1869–72) '*Collected Works of Thomas Carlyle*', Library Edition, 34 vols, London.

Carr, Arthur J. (1960) 'Tennyson as a Modern Poet', 1st published 1950, reprinted in John Killham, ed., *Critical Essays on the Poetry of Tennyson*, London.

Chambers, Robert (1969) *Vestiges of the Natural History of Creation*, 1st published 1844, introduced by Gavin de Beer, Leicester.

Collins, Churton (ed.) (1902) '*In Memoriam', 'The Princess', 'Maud', by Alfred, Lord Tennyson*, London.

Cook, E.T. and Wedderburn, Alexander (eds) (1903–1912) *The Works of John Ruskin*, Library Edition, 39 vols, London.

Cowling, Maurice (ed.) (1968) *Selected Writings of John Stuart Mill*, New York, Toronto, London.

Culler, A. Dwight (1977) *The Poetry of Tennyson*, New Haven and London.

Dodsworth, Martin (1969) 'Patterns of Morbidity: Repetition in Tennyson's Poetry' in Armstrong, Isobel, ed., *The Major Victorian Poets: Reconsiderations*, London.

Eliot, George (1963) 'Tennyson's *Maud*', 1st published 1855, reprinted in Thomas Pinney, ed., *Essays of George Eliot*, London.

Eliot, T.S. (1953) 'Tennyson's *In Memoriam*', 1st published 1936, reprinted in John Hayward, ed., *T.S. Eliot: Selected Prose*, London, Melbourne, Baltimore.

Ford, G.H. (1944) *Keats and the Victorians*, New Haven.

Fowler, Alastair (ed.) (1971) *Milton: Paradise Lost*, London.

Fricke, Donna (1970) 'Tennyson's "The Hesperides": East of Eden and Variations on the Theme', *Tennyson Research Bulletin*, I.4.

Froude, J.A. (1897) *Thomas Carlyle: A History of his Life in London, 1834–1881*, 1st published 1884, reprinted, 2 vols, London.

Gaskell, J.M. (1883) *Records of an Eton Schoolboy*, ed. Charles Milnes Gaskell, London.

Green, Joyce (1951) 'Tennyson's Development During the "Ten Year's Silence" (1832–42)', *PMLA*, LXVI.

Griffiths, Eric (1989) *The Printed Voice of Victorian Poetry*, Oxford.

Houghton, Walter E. (1973) *The Victorian Frame of Mind, 1830–1870*, 1st published 1957, New Haven and London.

Hulme, T.E. (1936) *Speculations*, 2nd edn, London.

Ingpen, Roger and Peck, Walter E. (eds) (1926–30) *The Complete Works of Percy Bysshe Shelley*, 10 vols, Julian Edition, London and New York.

Jacobs, Joseph (1892) *Tennyson and 'In Memoriam': An Appreciation and a Study*, London.

Jordan, Elaine (1968) 'Tennyson's "In Memoriam": An Echo of Goethe', *Notes and Queries*, 15.

——(1988) *Alfred Tennyson*, Cambridge.

Jump, John D. (ed.) (1967) *Tennyson: The Critical Heritage*, London and New York.

Kiernan, V.G. (1989) 'Tennyson, King Arthur and Imperialism', 1st published 1982, reprinted in Harvey J. Kaye, ed., *Poets, Politics and the People*, London.

Killham, John (1958) *Tennyson and 'The Princess': Reflections of an Age*, London.

Kingsley, Charles (1885) *Scientific Lectures and Essays*, Vol. 19 of *Works*, 1880–85, 28 vols, London.

Kolb, Jack (ed.) (1981) *The Letters of Arthur Henry Hallam*, Columbus, Ohio.

Lang, Cecil Y. and Shannon Jr, Edgar F. (eds) (1982–90), *The Letters of Alfred Lord Tennyson*, 3 vols, Oxford.

Leishman, J.B. (1969) *Milton's Minor Poems*, London.

Lourie, Margaret (1979) 'Below the Thunders of the Upper Deep: Tennyson as Romantic Revisionist', *Studies in Romanticism*, 18.

Lyell, Charles (1997) *Principles of Geology*, 1st published 1830–33, edited by James A. Secord, Harmondsworth, Middlesex.

Lyotard, Jean François (1986) *The Postmodern Condition*, 1st published 1979, Manchester.

Lytton, Edward Bulwer (1874) *England and the English*, 1st published 1833, London and New York.

Makdisi, Saree (1998) *Romantic Imperialism: Universal Empire and the Culture of Modernity*, Cambridge.

Marshall, G.O. (1963) 'Tennyson's "Oh! that 'twere possible": A link between *In Memoriam* and *Maud*', *PMLA*, LXXVIII.

Martin, Robert Bernard (1980) *Tennyson: The Unquiet Heart*, Oxford.

Motter, T.H. Vail (ed.) (1943) *The Writings of Arthur Hallam*, New York and London.

Nicolson, Harold (1923) *Tennyson: Aspects of his Life, Character, and Poetry*, London.

Paden, W.D. (1942) *Tennyson in Egypt: A Study of the Imagery in his Earlier Work*, Lawrence, Kansas.

——(1965) 'Tennyson's *The Lover's Tale*, R.H. Shepherd, and T.J. Wise', *Studies in Bibliography*, 18.

Page, Norman (ed.) (1983) *Tennyson: Interviews and Recollections*, London.

Priestley, F.E.L. (1973) *Language and Structure in Tennyson's Poetry*, London.

Ray, Gordon N. (1968) *Tennyson Reads 'Maud'*, Vancouver.

Ricks, Christopher (ed.) (1987) *The Poems of Tennyson*, 2nd edn, 3 vols, Harlow, Essex.

Ricks, Christopher (1989) *Tennyson*, 2nd edition, Basingstoke and London.

Ricks, Christopher and Day, Aidan (eds) (1987–93) *The Tennyson Archive*, 31 vols, New York and London.

Rose, H.J. (1928) *A Handbook to Greek Mythology, Including Its Extension to Rome*, London.

Said, Edward (1994) Culture and Imperialism, 1st published 1993; Great Britain, London.

Schweik, Robert C. (1960) 'The "Peace or War" Passages in Tennyson's *Maud*', *Notes and Queries*, 7.

Shatto, Susan (ed.) (1986) *Tennyson's 'Maud': A Definitive Edition*, London.

Short, Clarice (1967) 'Tennyson and *The Lover's Tale*', *PMLA*, LXXXII.

Sinfield, Alan (1976) ' "That Which is": The Platonic Indicative in *In Memoriam* XCV', *Victorian Poetry*, 14.

Sinfield, Alan (1996) 'Tennyson and the Cultural Politics of Prophesy', 1st published 1990, reprinted in Rebecca Stott, ed., *Tennyson*, London and New York.

Stange, G. Robert (1960) 'Tennyson's Garden of Art: A Study of "The Hesperides" ', 1st published 1952, reprinted in John Killham, ed., *Critical Essays on the Poetry of Tennyson*, London.

Stott, Rebecca (ed.) (1996) *Tennyson, Longman Critical Readers*, London and New York.

Super, R.H. (ed.) (1960–77) *The Complete Prose Works of Matthew Arnold*, 11 vols, Ann Arbor.

Tennyson, Charles (1954) *Six Tennyson Essays*, London.

——(1968) *Alfred Tennyson*, 1st published 1949, reissued (with alterations), London, Melbourne, Toronto.

Tennyson, G.B. (ed.) (1984) *A Carlyle Reader: Selections from the Writings of Thomas Carlyle*, 1st published 1969, Cambridge.

Tennyson, Hallam (1897) *Alfred Lord Tennyson: A Memoir by His Son*, 2 vols, London.

——(ed.) (1913) *The Works of Tennyson: With notes by the Author*, London.

Tucker, Herbert F. (1988) *Tennyson and the Doom of Romanticism*, Cambridge, Mass. and London.

Turner, Paul (1962) 'Some Ancient Light on Tennyson's "Œnone" ', *Journal of English and Germanic Philology*, LXI.

——(1976) *Tennyson*, London, Henley and Boston.

Van Dyke, Henry (1920) *Studies in Tennyson*, New York.

Warner, Marina (1987) *Monuments and Maidens. The Allegory of the Female Form*, 1st published 1985, London.

Wise, Thomas (1908) *A Bibliography of the Writings of Alfred, Lord Tennyson*, 2 vols, London.

Index